The World of Samuel Beckett

Ann Ferguson

Psychiatry and the Humanities, Volume 12

Assistant Editor
Gloria H. Parloff

Published under the auspices of the
Forum on Psychiatry and the Humanities,
The Washington School of Psychiatry

Samuel Beckett, Stuttgart, 1979. Courtesy of Rick Cluchey.
Photograph, Hugo Jehle.

The World of Samuel Beckett

Joseph H. Smith, *Editor*

The Johns Hopkins University Press
Baltimore and London

The Johns Hopkins University Press, 701 West 40th Street,
Baltimore, Maryland 21211
The Johns Hopkins Press Ltd., London

∞
The paper used in this book meets the minimum requirements of American National Standard for Information Sciences—Permanence of Paper for Printed Library Materials, ANSI Z39.48–1984.

Library of Congress Cataloging-in-Publication Data

The World of Samuel Beckett / Joseph H. Smith, editor.
    p.   cm. —(Psychiatry and the humanities ; v. 12)
  Includes bibliographical references and index.
  ISBN 0-8018-4079-1 (alk. paper). —ISBN 0-8018-4135-
6 (pbk.)
    1. Beckett, Samuel, 1906–   —Criticism and interpre-
tation—Congresses.   2. Psychoanalysis and literature—
Congresses.
I. Smith, Joseph H., 1927–   .   II. Series.
PR6003.E282Z96   1990
848′.91409—dc20   90-40273
                                                                CIP

In memoriam
Samuel Beckett
1906–1989

Contributors

Stephen Barker
School of Fine Arts—Drama, University of California—Irvine; Director, Program in Interdisciplinary Studies

Herbert Blau
Distinguished Professor of English, Center for Twentieth Century Studies, The University of Wisconsin—Milwaukee

Mary F. Catanzaro
Lecturer, Department of English, Marquette University

Jon Erickson
Assistant Professor (Drama), Department of English, Ohio State University

Martin Esslin
Professor Emeritus of Drama, Stanford University

Anthony Kubiak
Assistant Professor, Department of English, Harvard University

John H. Lutterbie
Assistant Professor, Department of Theatre Arts, State University of New York at Stony Brook

Angela Moorjani
Associate Professor of French, Department of Modern Languages and Linguistics, University of Maryland, Baltimore County Campus, Baltimore

Bennett Simon
Department of Psychiatry, Cambridge Hospital, Harvard Medical School; Boston Psychoanalytic Society and Institute

Joseph H. Smith
Chairman, Forum on Psychiatry and the Humanities, Washington School of Psychiatry; Supervising and Training Analyst, Washington Psychoanalytic Institute; Clinical Professor, Uniformed Services University of the Health Sciences

Robert Winer
Chair, Psychoanalytic Family Therapy Training Program, Washington School of Psychiatry; Board, Forum for the Psychoanalytic Study of Film

Nicholas Zurbrugg
Senior Lecturer, Comparative Literature Division of Humanities, Griffith University, Brisbane, Australia

Contents

Acknowledgments

On 3–5 March 1989, a Smithsonian Institution Symposium, "The World of Samuel Beckett," heard presentations by Herbert Blau, Martin Esslin, Bennett Simon, Robert Winer, and Joseph Smith, all of which are included in this volume. Panel discussants and other participants included Rick Cluchey, Gene Gordon, Alan Mandell, and Bruce Sklarew. The program was introduced by Stephanie Mondzac and Edmund Worthy, both of whom had major roles in organizing and coordinating the symposium.

Cosponsored by the Resident Associate Program, Smithsonian Institution; the Forum on Psychiatry and the Humanities, Washington School of Psychiatry; The Forum for the Psychoanalytic Study of Film; and the Visual Press, University of Maryland, the symposium was the occasion for the premiere screening of the video productions of *Waiting for Godot* and *Krapp's Last Tape,* taped in Paris during the months preceding, with Beckett's involvement. The productions were part of the "Beckett Directs Beckett" project coproduced by John Fuegi and Mitchell Lifton of the Visual Press with European partners. Lifton introduced the screening of *Krapp* and Fuegi that of *Godot.* In addition to the video premieres, informal live performances were given by Rick Cluchey of *Eh Joe* and by Alan Mandell of excerpts from *Company.* Both appeared in *Ohio Impromptu.*

The liveliness and depth of engagement among audience, actors, and speakers in wrestling with Beckett's thought and art was remarkable, and I was convinced that the presentations should be included in a special edition of *Psychiatry and the Humanities.* With the support and assistance of Herbert Blau, the project was made easy by the eager participation of the contributors, both those at the conference and the others who were subsequently invited.

Introduction

Joseph H. Smith

The world of Samuel Beckett that is introduced and displayed in the articles in this book is not really only Beckett's world. It is ours as much as his. Beckett's words—"austere, hermetic, and constrained," Herbert Blau says, "like a vow of poverty"—refer to aspects of ourselves and our world that we perpetually cover, and to an inner and surrounding real that is not even a part of our linguistically constituted selves and world. Like Freud, Beckett usurps defense.

The analysand who can tolerate the analyst's waiting comes to discover that what he most urgently covers and flees from, what he fears will most drastically threaten love and work and play, and what he dimly experiences as most uniquely wrong is the point of access to what is universal in the human situation. It is at the point of alienation that we separate ourselves off and discover that difference is the essential property we have in common. And beyond difference from others that we all share, there is difference, dividedness, and decenteredness within—the self never identical with itself.

Harry Stack Sullivan, whose major work was with schizophrenic patients, believed, without an iota of sentimentality, that people are "much more simply human than otherwise" (1953, 16). According to Esslin in this volume, Beckett similarly regarded "the schizophrenic mind merely as an extreme example of how the human mind in general works." The "oddities" of Beckettian characters always also portray the particular embodiment of universal issues. The issues are usually splitting, fragmentation, isolation, nothingness, and death, presented in a fashion that appalls, while, at the same time, posing the question of how moments of laughter, liveliness, love, grace, and con-

solation occur. More precisely, he doesn't pose the question. He just
shows that such moments do occur.

Esslin writes that Beckett's works are dialogues between parts of
the self, translated into dramatic form. In *That Time* (1981) "moments
of one and the same voice A B C relay one another without solution
of continuity." C in *That Time* would not be one of those legendary
tramps of the thirties, with their freedom/fate to travel, beg, wear torn
clothes, be dirty, and tell stories. Maybe *Godot*'s Gogo and Didi would
come close, but not C. He (along with him of *How It Is* and her of *Not
I* [whom I here designate and distance as "not I"]) would be, instead,
a street person of the current era from whom, off stage, in real life,
almost everyone turns away. Street person ("always winter then always raining always slipping in somewhere when no one would be
looking in off the street out of the cold and rain" [34]) and figure of
death ("not a sound only the old breath and the leaves turning and
then suddenly ... dust ... something like that come and gone come
and gone no one come and gone in no time gone in no time" [37]), C
would not be the kind to whom, in the thirties, my brothers and I
would steal away with food to trade for stories.

As for her of *Not I,* on the tracks of the Illinois Central, there were
no women. *They,* in the days before the terror of deinstitutionaliza-
tion, were in insane asylums, or secluded in the homes of their em-
barrassed loved ones, or, sometimes, in the Vermillion County old
folk's home. But, to focus the question, if tramps, street persons, bag
ladies, and psychotics don't usually have the same thoughts as A B C
or the wayfaring couple of "Enough" or him of *How It Is* (presumably
not many would list the need to shit and vomit as among "my great
categories of being"), are they not, no matter how dimly, living out
(like the rest of us) the same situation? I'm certain that some *do* have
the same thoughts as "not I." And surely many, like him of *How It Is,*
lying in the mud or on a grate or on a seclusion room floor ready to
conclude "that no one will ever come again and shine his light on me
and nothing ever again of other days other nights no," are subject to

> next another image yet another so soon again the third perhaps they'll
> soon cease it's me all of me and my mother's face I see it from below
> it's like nothing I ever saw
>
> we are on a veranda smothered in verbena the scented sun dapples the
> red tiles yes I assure you
>
> the huge head hatted with birds and flowers is bowed down over my
> curls the eyes burn with severe love I offer her mine pale upcast to the

sky whence cometh our help and which I know perhaps even then with time shall pass away

in a word bolt upright on a cushion on my knees whelmed in a night-shirt I pray according to her instructions

that's not all she closes her eyes and drones a snatch of the so-called Apostles' Creed I steal a look at her lips

she stops her eyes burn down on me again I cast up mine in haste and repeat awry

the air thrills with the hum of insects

that's all it goes out like a lamp blown out   [*How It Is,* 1964, 15–16]

But not "not I." She was spared all that.

so no love...spared that...no love such as normally vented on the... speechless infant...in the home...no...nor indeed for that matter any of any kind...no love of any kind...at any subsequent stage.   [*Not I,* 1984, 216][1]

Beckettian characters can't help but remind therapists of their clients and, often enough, evoke thoughts of cure, not only of Beckettian characters but also of their author. It is an issue I address in my article, which emphasizes that Beckett, like Freud and Lacan, challenges any notions of cure as the easy achievement of happiness. Cure is not getting around, over, or away from all the darkness of which Beckett writes; it is the product of a turn toward darkness and nothingness within.

In working with Mitchell Lifton, John Fuegi, Rick Cluchey, and Alan Mandell on the video productions to be premiered, and also through a visit by Herbert Blau, Beckett was aware of the Smithsonian Symposium from which this volume arose. The opening and closing articles, presented at the conference, are by his longtime associates and colleagues Herbert Blau and Martin Esslin. Beckett's death on 22 December 1989 occurred just as the manuscript was being completed, prompting our dedication and the epilogue by Blau.

In his opening article, Blau plunges us immediately into Beckett's world in terms of "an unmooring aspect of language itself" wherein we are confronted with a balance of terror ("despair not, one of the thieves was saved; presume not, one of the thieves was damned"), the "insidious proposition of a double sentence: the sentence in *grammar* and the sentence in *punishment,*" and the "*pensum* of *The Unnam-able.*" It is an apt introduction in that it recounts the history of Blau's own encounter with Beckett but in a style that is more an enactment than a telling. "There may be a sense," Blau writes, "in which what is . . . beguiling in Beckett has desensitized us to what he shows." But "it's still an appalling vision . . . and not even the wan and lyrical stasis that, at certain ineffable moments, seems to envelop the wounds makes them any easier to endure."

Blau sees the subtlety of Beckett's idea of theater as arising from the conjunction of language and the look. His closing discussion is a multiallusional treatment of that topic.

Mary Catanzaro documents the seeming impossibility of coupling and partnership in Beckett. In a reading of "Enough" Catanzaro explores the full range of broken promise in the separateness and otherness that undermine agreement and accord. She explores how Beckett shows these complexities by way of the narrative voice and the inner voice speaking to itself. Catanzaro maintains that while Beckett's thought about the voice can appear forbiddingly abstract, careful reading can find his expositions of that topic to be intensely emotional as well. Accordingly, in "Enough," "Beckett never loses sight entirely of a quite traditional, humanistic view of the couple in terms of loss and sorrow."

Nicholas Zurbrugg redefines postmodernism in terms of seven modes and discusses the evolution of Beckett's work, and postmodern culture in general, by considering their respective phases, one in terms of the other. Zurbrugg, expressing conclusions similar to those of Catanzaro and Winer, believes that in his final writings, Beckett "seems to have abandoned his early images of partially resigned, partially grotesque, and partially impassioned anguish for carefully crafted images of affection, grace, and harmony." He speaks of Beckett's "antithetical power to becalm and to console. Here is Zurbrugg commenting on and quoting from *Ill seen ill said:*

> At its most elegiac, this text evokes occasions when "the eye closes in the dark and sees" the calm carefully balanced vista of a mysterious "she," who, "in a twin movement full of grace," drinks from a bowl which "she slowly raises . . . toward her lips while at the same time with equal slowness bowing her head to join it."

Angela Moorjani sees Beckett's writing as the product of his listening to a cryptic text inscribed within. (See in Esslin's essay Beckett's account to Esslin of how he wrote.) This duality of the artistic imaginary—"the self divided from self, contemplating its otherness and harmonizing or synthesizing the conscious and the unconscious"—has an extensive history in aesthetic theory that Moorjani traces from Schelling and his mystic predecessors (including the gnostics) to Hegel, Schopenhauer, Nietzsche, and Heidegger. She believes that the ideas in that tradition echo particularly in the topology of mourning as elaborated in the work of Freud, Klein, Torok, Abraham, and Derrida. Clearly, Freud's method of analysis in *The Interpretation of Dreams* was in response to his assumption of a conscious/unconscious textual duality. He proceeded, furthermore, not as a "decoder" who already knows the language, but in the manner of a "cryptanalyst" who must first break the code in order to decipher the message. Moorjani's account of the tradition within which Beckett writes sets the stage for her own intricate and interesting analysis of *Molloy.*

Robert Winer sees Beckett's characters as profoundly fractured and takes the fracturing to be a way of avoiding pain—the pain of shame, grief, love, or recognition of one's own destructiveness. He focuses on *Eh Joe* and *Ohio Impromptu* and argues that in them Beckett is suggesting that the opening up of desire and the acceptance of mourning are the remedies that heal fractured narrative. Much of psychoanalytic work with patients, Winer believes, "involves the unsilencing of passion: reversing Freud, where ego was, id once again shall be." He highlights aspects of Beckett's own history pertaining to the plays and includes a reading of *Ohio Impromptu* as an analysis.

In *Eh Joe,* Winer finds a moment of tenderness in Joe's remembrance of the suicide of a woman who had loved him, a woman that Winer associates with the green-eyed Peggy Sinclair who loved Beckett. Under a viaduct, still alive after her failure to drown herself or to kill herself by cutting her wrists, she took tablets and scooped out a place for her face in the wet stones, where she finally died. In the voice Joe hears, we hear:

> Scoops a little cup for her face in the stones...The green one...The narrow one...Always pale...The pale eyes...The look they shed before...The way they opened after...Spirit made light."

Not *With I* as text, John Lutterbie confronts the distance that defines the differences between the conscious subject and the subject of the unconscious and finds "no center in which I can locate myself." But the situation is more complicated than merely the difference between what Lacan would call the ego and the subject. As Lutterbie writes, the ever-increasing number of signs used to define one's self fragments that self. "Far from a stable term through which I can claim identity, this 'I' is nothing but an illusory anchor to which I cling while

'I' sense my disappearance in the interstices of an ever-fragmenting, ever-disseminating articulation of subjectivity."

Lutterbie goes on to discuss subjectivity, subjection, and the systems of power and representation within a patriarchal society. But here, between Winer and Lutterbie, the question of fragmentation as defense, fragmentation as failure of defense, and fragmentation as the inevitable product of language is joined. It is a question that pervades the entire volume. When or how is fragmentation contingent and when or how universal?

Beginning with a consideration of *Breath,* Anthony Kubiak notes theories of mind or unconscious as *mise-en-scène* developed by Blau, Lyotard, Foucault, Deleuze, and Derrida and asserts that Beckett also pushes us to ponder the dissolution of boundaries between mind and stage. For Kubiak the world we enter and share "is, quite literally, theater."

Kubiak sees this theater/world as the locus for the production of a false history, history as "fiction that comforts and paralyzes us." It is the site, he writes, illustrating his points by quoting from *Not I,* "of a specific coercion, a particular and subtle ideological production ('brought up as she had been to believe...in a merciful [*Brief laugh.*] ...God')." Such constructions of "history" and "memory" are "at once unconscious and theatrical: [again quoting from *Not I*] 'notion of punishment...for some sin or other...or for the lot...or no particular reason ...for its own sake.'"

Kubiak concludes with a convincing discussion of history and theater as representing the trauma that is unrecoverable. Both Kubiak and Lutterbie touch on guilt, ideology, and religion, issues to be briefly discussed in my conclusion.

Stephen Barker's topic is recovering the *néant* (the nothing), and his text, for that reason, is Beckett's *The Unnamable.* How to think about what cannot be thought? With Blau, Barker takes Beckett's versions of the postmodern to be always subversions; Beckett explores "the nature of human action as it does and does not constitute meaning and value." Beckett's "nothing to say," "nothing, nothing to discover, nothing to recover, nothing that can lessen what remains to say," is here engaged with the thought of Nietzsche, Freud, Heidegger, Lacan, and Derrida.

Bennett Simon is, to my knowledge, the only American psychoanalyst who has studied and written extensively on Beckett. Simon examines the self ("disintegrated, deconstructed, shadowed, fragmented, submerged, unstable") in current art and psychoanalysis and explores what he takes to be a related modern concern and anxiety about personal and sexual intercourse, conception, contraception, and procreation. The "chicken-and-egg" question he poses is: "Does a faulty self lead to a lack of will for and lack of faith in procreation and in progeny, or do disturbances in the will for, capacity for, and faith in procreation and in progeny 'beget' disturbances of the self?"

Jon Erickson writes on Beckettian, Kierkegaardian, and Proustian modes of repetition. His categories of ritual, routine, habit, and addiction lead to a view that Krapp's actions change him from a subject of ritual to an object or effect of an addiction. "Ritual is the self-conscious maintenance of an integrated relation of self to reality. It is the expression of internalized beliefs that provides a sense of coherence for the self and its community. The attempt to free oneself completely from this internalized structure of belief (in part the heritage of the Enlightenment ideal of individualism) only binds one more completely to the caprices of external change, disintegrating the internal coherence."

My own notes on *Krapp* and *Endgame* set the stage for a discussion of the current status of "applied" psychoanalysis.

The well-known expression "theater of the absurd" was coined by Martin Esslin and was the title of his 1961 book. In the concluding article here, Esslin challenges the impression that Beckett is a difficult and depressing author. While granting some truth to that idea, Esslin contends that once one has grasped what Beckett is concerned with, "he is not difficult or elitist. On the contrary, he deals with the basic problems of human existence on the most down-to-earth level. . . . In fact, Beckett regarded himself as—and was—basically a comic writer, a humorist, even though his humor is black humor, gallows humor."

Why not? If we take those with the keenest readiness to laugh as also having the keenest sense of fragmentation, loss, and mourning and perhaps also the sharpest suspicion of words as a means of dissimulating, Beckett was bound to have been a consummate humorist.

For Beckett, words neither hide nor tell but are. Esslin demonstrates this by citing Beckett writing of Joyce:

> You complain that this stuff is not written in English. It is not written at all. It is not to be read. It is to be looked at and listened to. His writing is not *about* something; *it is that something itself*. . . . When the sense is sleep, the words go to sleep. . . . When the sense is dancing, the words dance. . . . This writing that you find so obscure is a quintessential extraction of language and painting and gesture, with all the inevitable clarity of the old articulation. Here is the savage economy of hiero-

glyphics. Here words are not the polite contortions of 20th century printer's ink. They are alive. [Beckett 1929, in *Disjecta,* 1983, 27; emphasis in original]

In conclusion I shall briefly discuss the issues of guilt, ideology, and religion touched on by Lutterbie and Kubiak. Lutterbie writes that the complicity of "not I" with "the ideological system that marks her oppression is affirmed by the significant investment she makes in religion" and notes that "the connection between faith in God and the return of love was made at the same time, and in the same circumstances, that cathexes with other people as positive objects of desire were repressed." Like Lutterbie, Kubiak, with Nietzsche, Marx, Freud (the three "masters of suspicion" according to Ricoeur [1970, 33]), and perhaps Beckett as allies, conflates at least one meaning of theater (which does not "teach us what to think [but] keeps us from thinking") with religion. I don't doubt there is some truth to such criticism, but I don't doubt that it also tends to teach us to think in a suspicious way.

Of course, Ricoeur is by no means unilaterally suspicious of suspicion and reminds us of Heidegger's thought in *Being and Time* that destruction "is a moment of every new foundation, including the destruction of religion, insofar as religion is, in Nietzsche's phrase, a 'Platonism for the people'" (1970, 33). Ricoeur, I take it, assumes that religious participation and belief (or for that matter disbelief), like the response to any enduring feature of a cultural order, can be undertaken for either defensive or nondefensive reasons and, in fact, regularly involve a mixture of both (Smith 1989, 1990, 1991). A stance that passes a blanket negative judgment in advance denies this variousness of meaning and in so doing denies its own ambivalence—its own nostalgia and desire. To take such a position could be to resist belief in *any* benevolence or wisdom handed down from forebears. But it is one thing to issue a manifesto against coercive ideologies and quite another for a Beckett to create a work of art out of being moved by a distraught woman pacing to and fro outside a cafe, awaiting God knows whom or what.

None of this is to say that Beckett, like Freud, wouldn't have wanted religion, or at least the infantile and defensive uses of religion, to pass away. Nor is it to contradict Blau's reading of "the appalling vision" that was, finally, Beckett's bequest. But Beckett didn't *blame* religion or theater for the original sin of being born. That has to do, as Lutterbie and Kubiak would agree, with separation, loss, fragmentation, death, and being an animal with speech. Whatever history one has or is obviously combines elements of comforting illusion with elements of facing or making one's truth. Primitive guilt I take to be a universal. I have attempted to show its relationship with the primitive lack of differentiation between being wronged and being wrong, with primal splitting, primal repression, and language acquisition (1986). These structural determinants are such that only a very powerful ideology could lull us into believing that primitive guilt, rather than being a part of the human lot, is only the product of or is only perpetuated by an ideology.

Beckett, to my knowledge, never had a good thing to say about either religion or his mother. But, as in the passage from *How It Is* cited previously, his irony is not always vicious, and, often enough, nostalgia is embedded within it.

As for his mother, correlatives like Krapp's black ball, funereal perambulator and dark nurse, and the ashbins to which parents are assigned in *Endgame* are objects that both defend against and say what can hardly be directly said about ashes as the universal destiny. At every level Beckett deals with the paradox of how to say that there is nothing to be said—how to say nothing.

To glimpse, through his way of saying there is nothing to be said, his capacity to know his mother's silence, mourning, and life, walk into the rocky meadow of *Ill seen ill said.* Grieving and defending against loss are continuous in everyone. Grief as such is always too much. Grief is a matter of one's mode of defending against grief, of dealing with it, of doing it in one's own way. In *Ill seen ill said* the stones themselves bear mute witness to the constancy of grief and also to a beyond of grief, a detachment achieved in recognizing grief's constancy. Like stones everywhere, they are, he would have agreed, Beckettian stones.

Nostalgia, Nietzsche notwithstanding, is not per se a bad thing. It *can* be the mourning of everyday life, the ordinary, ongoing grief pertaining to the daily encounter with past, present, and anticipated loss. And according to Zurbrugg, Winer, and, as I read her, Catanzaro, Beckett was turning more toward that kind of expression in his final years.

Note

1. In this quotation and elsewhere in the book, Beckett's serial periods are shown closed up in order to distinguish them from more widely spaced ellipsis points, used to indicate omitted text.

References

Beckett, Samuel. *How It Is.* New York: Grove Press, 1964.

―――. *That Time.* In *Ends and Odds: Nine Dramatic Pieces.* New York: Grove Press, 1981.

―――. *Disjecta: Miscellaneous Writings and a Dramatic Fragment.* Edited by Ruby Cohn. London: John Calder, 1983.

―――. *The Collected Shorter Plays of Samuel Beckett.* New York: Grove Press, 1984.

Ricoeur, Paul. *Freud and Philosophy.* New Haven: Yale University Press, 1970.

Smith, Joseph. "Primitive Guilt." In *Pragmatism's Freud: The Moral Disposition of Psychoanalysis,* edited by Joseph Smith and William Kerrigan. Psychiatry and the Humanities, vol. 9. Baltimore: Johns Hopkins University Press, 1986.

―――. "Evening the Score." *Modern Language Notes* 104 (December 1989): 1050–65.

―――. "On the Question of Nondefensive Religion." In *Psychoanalysis and Religion,* edited by Joseph Smith and Susan Handelman. Psychiatry and the Humanities, vol. 11. Baltimore: Johns Hopkins University Press, 1990.

―――. Review of *In the Beginning Was Love: Psychoanalysis and Faith,* by Julia Kristeva. *Journal of the American Psychoanalytic Association* 39, no. 3 (1991): in press.

Sullivan, Harry Stack. *Conceptions of Modern Psychiatry.* New York: W. W. Norton, 1953.

The World of Samuel Beckett

1   Quaquaquaqua: The Babel of Beckett

Herbert Blau

This may get more theoretical later, somewhat roundabout, but I want to begin with a sort of historicizing preface to what I had intended to say, for I came here directly from Paris, where I saw Beckett last week. He is in his eighties now and, as some of you know, has not been well. But while "the circulation," as he said, "leaves something to be desired," there were two neatly ready glasses on a small writing table, and we toasted each other with a shot of Irish whiskey (Bushmill's, to be precise)—the particular occasion being, rehearsed as afterthought, that we had met almost exactly thirty years ago, winter it was, that time, was there ever any other time? as he might say, even if the circulation should happen to return. That time was the time I first went to Paris, the day after we opened in San Francisco, at the old Actor's Workshop there, one of the earliest stagings of *Endgame,* which I had directed.

I had known of Beckett's work, though it was hard to come by then, shortly after the war—I mean the last of those Great Wars, of course, World War II, after which for a while, that time, we didn't have any wars, but rather "bandit raids" and "police actions," like that in Korea, whose landscape apparently resembled for those who had been there (San Francisco was a port of debarkation, and some of them showed up at our plays) the bleak denuded landscape of *Waiting for Godot,* with the same purposeless sense of a missing action or the repetitive expectation of an encounter yet to come. As for that other "preventive measure," not at first a war but an undeclared facsimile of a war, that

This talk, given at the Smithsonian Institution Symposium, *The World of Samuel Beckett,* Washington, D.C., 3 March 1989, is reproduced here without change.

eventually vain and demoralizing enterprise against insurgency in a jungle, *that* might have been a real war or a winnable war if, as General Curtis Le May wanted us to (or was that in Korea? that other time, I forget), we could have leveled them.

But in this case the preventive measure was a lingering mechanism of the Cold War, the Balance of Terror. If that was to become for Henry Kissinger the basis of détente and, within a huge global theater, the Doctrine of Credibility, it was also for Beckett the basis of his dramaturgy, where the issue of credibility, so germane to conventional theater, seemed to be utterly and hopelessly displaced in the dissolution of character and the dispersion of plot that became the disjunct paratactical strategies that we call postmodern today. What seemed to me evident then was that, at the psychic level at least, the nerve ends of perception itself, it was the Balance of Terror that Beckett was writing about (of course it was funny, always funny, the *risus purus,* laughing up the sleeve, the laugh, as he said, laughing at the laugh), along with the Energy Crisis, paralysis, *debility,* the exhaustion of Western culture, before the idea of an energy crisis was materialized as economic fact in the geopolitics of a postindustrial world, with what seemed inevitable in *due* time, the debility of a debit, in the distressing modulations of the microphysics of power and the ominous emergence of OPEC.

It was not quite price-fixing, however, that Beckett had in mind, though we shall come back in a moment to the matter of price. When he thought of a balanced terror, it was in one respect Augustinian, as in his fondness for that nicely proportioned sentence of which Didi vaguely recalls a dubious fragment, before he moves into his little hermeneutic study of the Gospels, the story of the two thieves, whereupon Gogo concludes on the basis of conflicting accounts by the apostles, all of which are variously believed, that people are really bloody ignorant apes. Here's the sentence, though in the faultiness of memory, from which I'm quoting, the balance may be faulty too: "Despair not, one of the thieves was saved; presume not, one of the thieves was damned." As you try to think of what would happen to the fineness of its balance if you tried to say it the other way around, let me move on a critical nuance to what else, relative to the generic terror, Beckett had in mind.

That might be described as an unmooring aspect of language itself, what Roland Barthes would later call the accumulative "terror of uncertain signs," though among those signs for Beckett is a certain certainty, the *pensum* of *The Unnamable,* the long sinuous if not insidious proposition of a double sentence: the sentence in *grammar* and the sentence in *punishment,* pronounced by a judge in a court of law. It is a strange court, however, and an even stranger law, for if it seems eternally written it still needs *writing,* as it appears to do in Kafka, where it escapes interpretation. It's as if the writing itself were its mode of operation. And if the judges themselves are dubious, confused, reluctant, or absent, what does that matter to the law? which is indelibly if invisibly, and entirely arbitrary, always already and watchfully there. *Every look is the law,* according to Kafka, and the subtlety of Beckett's idea of theater arises from the conjunction of language and the look, as in the stabbing and judgmental light of *Play.* Or when, with a sense of the air full of our cries, Didi is gazing at the sleeping Gogo—who is always disturbed by his dreams, the *specularity* of his dreams—while we are gazing at the gazing Didi.

I shall say more in a while about the look and the gaze—and if time permits, this time, may even examine the function of the gaze, its cross-eyed uncertainties at the beginning of *Endgame,* and their relation to language, the elemental structure of the sentence, its subject and object, and the quiet but quite frightening balance of terror, if you think about it, in their disjuncture, subject and object: "Me—to play," says Hamm, with a great big yawn, as big as the Cartesian abyss, between the objective case in which he identifies himself, not *I,* and the infinitive that marks the drama. It is a sentence for which in another time one (not-I) might have been punished—the ungrammaticality of it, or is it ungrammatical? In any case, Hamm *is* punished, or *acts out* a punishment, for Hamm may be a pretender, an Imaginary Invalid; indeed, we know he is, since he is only and always an actor in what, however, by Beckett's own testimony is his most "clawing" or punishing play, all the more severe from thinking too much.

As you can see already, I trust, the terms of the double sentence, the grammar and the punishment, are by no means unconnected, even at this moment, in the vicissitudes of thought. And as I've tried to suggest briefly so far, they are also connected to the look and the gaze, as Nietzsche also knew, who said that God is in the grammar, an all-seeing God that . . . *which* (should it be *that* or *which?* and should it, whichever, be capitalized for God?) *Who* (?) watches over our mistakes, as they still do with the *pensum,* which (that? without the comma of course) is also the name for those little Cartesian books with cross-hatched lines in which children learn to write and do mathematics in French schools—as my little six-year-old daughter, back in Paris, is doing now. What Nietzsche, Beckett, and that stern taskmaster Hamm (a pedagogue if there ever was one) also understand is that God is in the grammar—and the look of the law—even when words slip slide decay, the syntax sprawls, the modifiers squint, and the structure of the grammar appears to disintegrate, everything falling apart, all the rules! nothing logical but aleatory, as it is in Lucky's speech, where we are nevertheless given a quite ordered history of the devolution of Western metaphysics since the Middle Ages, quaquaquaqua, beginning with the uttering forth of the existence of "a personal God," *this* time "outside time without extension who from the heights of divine apathia divine athambia divine aphasia," with the sublime indifference of an active forgetfulness, "loves us dearly but time will tell. . . ."

(I am particularly conscious of my grammar today because, on the plane from Paris to Washington, I was—when not rewriting this—reading the copy-edited text of a new book of mine, in which the copy editor had fastidiously checked all restrictive and nonrestrictive modifiers, changing *which* to *that* even where, knowing the rule, I'd rather not have that, which I tried to make respectfully clear in no uncertain terms by changing everything back.)

Be that as it may (in this Beckettian/grammatical context, is that a subjunctive or merely cliché?), be that as it *was* (?), it continues (reference? time? God?) *what* continues?—"let us resume," as Lucky says—*it* continues to exact the *pensum,* which also means, as Beckett dolefully writes, "a task to be performed," the egregious task of talking about oneself, "before one can be at rest." Strange compulsive paranoid self-reflexive task, and speaking of the look and the gaze, overseen by *whom?* and should *that* be capitalized? *can* it be capitalized, realizing as Marx did that capitalization, *capital,* has to do with *money,* as Beckett did when he didn't have any—and as we did in San Francisco when we first started to do his plays and very few showed up and some of those walked out because God was also in the dramaturgy saying it was incoherent and whoever gave you the idea that *this* was a play? sometimes punctuating the question by asking for their money back.

Those were the days—ah, the "old style," Winnie says—when people asked without embarrassment: *Who is Godot?* expecting to get a better answer than Beckett's own if I knew who Godot was I'd say so, which we, among others, repeated over and over, like T. S. Eliot's line about it being impossible, in words slipping sliding decaying with imprecision, to say what I mean, I mean him, saying what *he* means, until now both of them are somewhat clichés, habitually repeated ("Habit is the great deadener") to justify not the dark obscure of modernist language that/which deranges words into meaning, the meaning which like thought itself always escapes, but to certify instead, in those of little mind, the brain-damaged substance of words that—even if God *is* in the grammar, a merciful God—don't mean very much at all. And not because of the terror of uncertain signs or—to use the language of the Law—any consciousness thereof quaquaquaqua which is the repetitive burden of the *pensum* in Beckett, a virtual disease of consciousness, curled up worm of encyclical thought suddenly unwinding in the labyrinth of the ear like the "mortal coil" of *Hamlet* running down the hill of heaven as low as to the fiends, words words words, the *intractability* of the Unnamable, repeating itself in its traces while searching the origin of the word, which is the *trace,* the origin of the memory from which it appears, as Derrida tells us today as he defines the fatal *différance,* which I won't try to define, words words words, which if they have any virtue at all, like what I'm saying now, only serve to keep the discourse from coming to an end because its subject is somewhat lost or the lesson has been forgotten, the brain pursuing them like mad, as out of the Mouth of *Not I,* the words which never cease, which may have been a punishment for the misfortune of being born.

In this respect, of course, Beckett is quite classical. Erudite as he is, and given to certain unexpected and surprising, even exotic locutions, like the *fontanelles* (in *Endgame*), his vocabulary is, not unsurprisingly, austere, hermetic, and constrained, like a vow of poverty. It resembles the language of no other dramatist so much as Racine, whose drama also proceeds, so to speak, from an exhausted *donnée,* as if it were all used up before it began. As for the punishment of being born, the burden is invariably that birth is the death of him—"ghastly grinning ever since. Up at the lid to come. In cradle and crib. At such first fiasco"—as we remember the ancients saying, in play after play, in similar punishments, so repetitively painful they're finally funny, siphoning the comedy out for another festival. (Beckett is also performed now in international festivals, but for his grievous hilarity there is only the recourse, as with Pozzo's watch, of a "deadbeat escapement.") "Better never to have been born," the ancient choruses would say, after the madness of interrogation had subsided and there was nothing more to say.

"Nothing will come of nothing," said the father who was mad to the daughter who was dumb, until in the fugitive deadend of desperation there is the harrowing image of the gouged-out eyes, and "the worst returns to laughter." I am now speaking of *King Lear* (though the blindness of Oedipus still resonates in Hamm) and Beckett seems also to have taken the (dis)articulated wisdom of its ravings to heart. Over the last generation, however, the *pensum* seems to have been reversed

in the productions of *Lear*—Peter Brook's, my own, those more recently in Eastern Europe and the Far East—that seem derived from
Beckett: "Nothing will come of nothing" but there's still "Nothing to
be *done*" (emphasis mine). Which is the evacuated datum from which
the play, the waiting in *Godot,* the play within the play, proceeds: "I'm
beginning to come round to that opinion." And that's where they
came, *round,* as if the repetitions dismantled habit and wore away the
clichés. Or came through exhaustion to a virulent energy, like the dog
that came into the kitchen, in Didi's loud song that opens the second
act, "And stole a crust of bread. / Then cook up with a ladle / And beat
him till he was dead / Then all the dogs came running / And dug the
dog a tomb / And wrote upon the tombstone"—is that not in a sense
what Beckett was doing?—"For the eyes of dogs to come:" etc. etc., in
the resuming round:

I resume: what we have, then, in the *pensum* is a verbal hallucination, a mutilated sentence, "as a result of the labors left unfinished," by
whom? who can say? Fartov and Belcher? Puncher and Wattman?, one
long almost unendurable sentence, like that which ends/rounds *The
Unnamable* or, for that matter, Lucky's speech, quaquaquaqua, a sort
of penitential insistence of runaway thought turning upon itself, for
which they beat him up, then—in the words of the Gospel—"Raise
him up!" He thinks and they think, thinking of course to no apparent
conclusion, as a result of the labors left unfinished, for who is ever
finished with the apparency of thought? "Think! Think! Think!" the
hapless figures say, squeezing their brains to a standstill even with the
bowlers off. "You can think, you two?" says Pozzo, aghast at the possibility of thought, though "the trouble is," as Didi warned, "to have
thought," leaving us with the ambiguity of tense and possession: to
have thought, incredible!, when thought is always escaping, to think
and have it too.

As for Beckett himself, the more he thinks the more he apparently
feels—as if the *pensum* were intersected by the price of OPEC oil—
that for the *fact* of living itself (he would hardly say the *privilege*) we
are always paying a price. William Carlos Williams wrote once of "the
poetry of the movement of costs," and however mutilated the sentence the one inarguable apparency is that Beckett is a poet, whether
he works in theater, prose, video, or film. He seems to understand,
almost ontologically, the *economy* of each of these forms, its nuclear
power. Speaking of which, and the poetry of the movement of costs,
remember J. Robert Oppenheimer's poetic and Buddhist response to

the dazzling white light of the Bomb bursting in air—from which, I suppose, as a result of the labors left unfinished, came in a splintered reverberation George Bush's "thousand points of light," which seems a far (disingenuously callow) cry from the dread of nuclear power and the historical point from which I started, assaying the cost, for Beckett, of World War II. It was not, I think, merely the era of existentialism nor its principle of the Absurd that caused him to echo the question that Winston Churchill, one of the great affirmative spirits of the age, had also asked, a question I remember quoting at the first rehearsal of our production of *Waiting for Godot,* when Beckett, as I've suggested, was hardly a household word in this country and barely known in the academy, which went through the customary stages of disdain and resistance before he entered the canon.

Anyhow, the question: "On this soil of Europe, yes or no, is man dead?" I must admit to thinking at the time—the rehearsal was in my house in San Francisco, just above the Haight-Ashbury district, where the counterculture was presently to assemble—that it was a somewhat un-American question. What would the House Un-American Activities Committee, which soon turned up in San Francisco (it was high tide of the McCarthy era), think of this bleak, encrypted, and morbid play? Never mind them, what would Walt Whitman think? or William Carlos Williams, who detested T. S. Eliot all his life for being too European? Not to mention, *this* time, the actors who were there, not one of whom, before we announced we would do the play (they thought I was mad) had *ever* heard of Beckett.

As for Europe, I can report from recent observation that, despite fallout from Chernobyl, which contaminated its soil, it appears to be quite alive and stirring. On the threshold, in the nineties, of the European Economic Community, that great corporate merger of the national states that gave us Western culture, capital is moving in a hyperexcited economy of exchange, crossing barriers, channels, customs, languages in a kind of recombinant DNA or redemptive mortagaging of Babel. But the question was, on this soil of Europe, is *man* dead? And they are still talking, at least in *theory* (what came to us as *deconstruction*), of the long-awaited end of man (corresponding to the repeatedly proclaimed end of ideology), that is, the tradition of bourgeois humanism (which even tainted Marx), with its logocentrism, phallic domination, Oedipus and his Viennese complex, and the old Freudian family romance, with its hermetic and suffocating nuclear family, at the center of which is the "fatal couple" and the structure of reproduction and representation—all of which is condensed by Beckett, in dessicated memory, into the video image of "the familiar cham-

ber" of *Ghost Trio,* the door, the floor, the wall, its solipsistic emptiness, that *kind* of door, that *kind* of floor, that *kind* of wall which,
having seen, "you have seen it all," repeated over and over, in theater,
in narrative, in film, and TV, where the soaps, *Dynasty, Dallas, Days
of Our Lives,* bring the eternal chamber drama, magnified and ex-
truded, extended, deferred, delayed, paratactically restructured into
the concurrence of popular culture and postmodern forms, like a
demonstration of *différance.*

  "Will you never have done? (*Pause.*) Will you never have done...
revolving it all?"—the one tired, attenuated, interminable tale, however splintered or disjunct, as Beckett revolves it in *Footfalls:*
"(*Pause.*) It?"—there we go with the grammar again, faulty reference,
wouldn't they say? who? *they?* the indefinite plural, we all know
them—"(*Pause.*) It? (*Pause.*) It all. (*Pause.*) In your poor mind.
(*Pause.*) It all. (*Pause.*) It all"—including the fiction that there is any
reference at all, anything like a reliable subject and object, or even
predicate for that matter, the worst of all possible words, perhaps,
being not that feeble effort at the objectification of subjectivity in *It,*
but the personal pronoun *I,* with which I started this talk today, a word
that Lévi-Strauss, referring to the special complications of the French
first person, called the most contemptible in the language, whereas in
English we have what is maybe a more disturbing if telltale complica-
tion, the perfect assonance of *I* and *eye,* identity and sight, which
Shakespeare explores with terrifying subtlety in his plays and sonnets,
all of it summed up in the notorious pun, "when first your eye I eyed,"
which begins a sonnet that also contains one of his most remarkable
quatrains, pivoting on the relation of the word, identity, subject and
object, the look and the gaze:

> Ah, yet doth beauty, like a dial hand,
> Steal from his figure, and no pace perceived;
> So your sweet hue, which methinks still doth stand,
> Hath motion, and mine eye may be deceived.

If, then, that pronoun *I* and all it represents is either contemptible
or deceitful, one can understand (notice that shifty *one*) why it
seemed important to break up the whole signifying system of reproduction. For if traced through the sinister traces of its economy of
exchange, whose principle is specularity, it turns out to be—with illusions looking like nature—a structure of domination and power. If
it has extended its hegemony over the face of the earth, as phallocracy
or imperialism, it has also colonized the space of the unconscious, the
terrain that Beckett works, it all, it all, the familiar chamber, where no

one sees the motion but the motion, the rudimentary construct of a repressive psychology, that which goes with the I (both eyes), the autonomous self or imperious ego, neither of which can quite break up because they never really existed, occulted as they were in the libidinal economy of the West, mythic and untenable as the Federal Reserve—or at least, in the world of leverage buyouts and arbitrage, an independent and rational monetary system.

Now, if Gogo—pressed by Didi to remember what happened a moment ago—says, "I'm not a historian," Beckett obviously makes no claims to being an economist, nor—despite *What Where,* the play he recently dedicated to the dissident Czech playwright Václav Havel— does he have a specific interest in politics. Although he was active during the war in the French Resistance (while playing chess at Rousillon), I remember his saying years ago that political solutions to the world's problems are like going from one insane asylum to another. Yet that doesn't prevent him from reading, daily, the socialist paper *Libération.* Nor did it prevent *Waiting for Godot*—that plaintive elegy of catatonia in which nothing happens, twice—from becoming the greatest political drama of the fifties, a virtual preface as an exemplary model or paradigm of *waiting* to the passive resistance of the early sixties that was waiting in the wings, along with the strategies of indeterminacy and activated forgetfulness that characterized the Movement, before it lost its patience, and its historical memory, in the Days of Rage. (Postscript: when I visited him recently, on returning to Paris, the front page of *Libération* was spread out on the writing table, with the picture of the unknown Chinese student, waiting, confronting the tanks alone.)

What all of this suggests is not merely another image of the poet as prophet, but the degree to which, perhaps, my own thought—long intimate with the plays, and the prose, which seemed from the beginning to be intimate with what, much younger then, I didn't quite know I thought—remains inhabited by Beckettian ideas and images. I should add, however, that as with any intimacy (and this seems Beckettian too) I have also found myself resisting this tendency of my own mind that, over the years, seems inseparable from his thought, so that I'm no longer sure when reading his work, or seeing it staged, that what I see is really there or, like Lévi-Strauss with the Bororo Indians, merely a projection of my own mind. No matter, Beckett might say, for in any case we are dealing with what, in his precocious essay on Proust, he described as dyssynchronous systems of perception and, no matter whose thought it is, it's what in the process of being thought fails us anyhow.

Which brings me back through these rather expanded and circuitous prefatory remarks (questions are remarks, said Wallace Stevens, but remarks are questions too) to the collage of Beckettian thought with which I thought I'd start, but which has, I think, already started, delaying the start, Beckett, after all, *not* I, and "the brain still...still sufficiently...oh very much so!...at this stage...in control...under control ...to question even this..." Meanwhile, in the circuitry of what follows—or circulation, leaving much to be desired—I will, as I said, be moving theoretically to aspects of Beckett I haven't questioned yet, as a result of the labors left unfinished, as this talk may be, perhaps, "finished, it must be nearly finished," what seems to come back, it all, it all...or "the semblance. Faint though by no means invisible in a certain light. (*Pause.*)," from the Enlightenment to deconstruction, "the light the light the light of the labors lost," as Lucky says in his torrential disquisition, the monstrous enunciation in a remotely remembered logic of the dissolution of Western metaphysics from the (im)personal, aphasic divinity uttered forth by Aquinas to the waste land of T. S. Eliot. "It has a structure," Beckett said, over our Bushmill's, "empty heavens, diminished man, abortive stones"—that's what I heard, abortive stones, and who can doubt it, though Lucky says *abode,* "abode of stones who can doubt it I resume but not so fast I resume. . . ."

It was very strange when it first came on the scene, the babble of Beckett, neither a bang nor a whimper, but a whisper a rustle, making a noise like leaves like ashes like leaves (pause) the heap the little heap, finished, it's nearly finished, yet arising from the silence in Babylonian proportions, they whisper they rustle they all speak at once, and what do they say? "Where now? Who now? When now? Unquestioning. I, say I. Unbelieving." But you better believe it, and you better question it, the forlorn pronoun of a delinquent identity, I, say I, the signifier slipping in a world of becoming, the metonymic erosions and macerations "up to the mouth" and the grievously exquisite shift into a visible language, funny then no longer funny because "something is taking its course" that only makes it worse: the running sores, the wounds, the mutilations, the abortive stones and slimy abortions, the stumps the stanchers I resume the skulls and, when it seems to be subsiding, no need for the painkiller, the leak in the fontanelles, "never but the first and last time curled up worm in slime when they lugged you out and wiped you off," that time, the cruelly extorted *pensum* of a minimal quantum of being. Or even less, as in the purgatorial mathematics of *The Lost Ones,* the combinatory sets of annihilation, "in cold darkness motionless flesh," if not exactly insentient, still, the annals of rigor mortis.

"What I'd like now," said the narrator of the book that Beckett's wife brought to forty-seven publishers before it was accepted, "What I'd like now is to speak the things that are left, say my good-byes, finish dying. They don't want that." But after years of exile, silence, and relative anonymity in the shadow of Joyce, Beckett has become, with the Nobel Prize, the one indisputable venerable figure amongst us, and as he syncopates the dying through the excruciating successions of lessness they always seem to want more. I remember that time, however, when his plays were first performed and people who now swear by Beckett—including actors in my company in San Francisco who refused to be in *Godot*—were not only taken aback or confounded but revolted by his vision. It is a curious thing, however, that sometimes the know-nothings are on to something, in their unrepressed resistance to what most of us disguise. Were they right to begin with? "Nothing to be done"? Really, when you think about it, who wants to live with that? Yet just before I left Paris there opened at Beaubourg, the Centre Pompidou, a retrospective exhibit of the Situationist Internationale, the ecological movement of politicized anarchism which anticipated the sixties, and which, by the way, was never intended to end up in a museum, no more than Beckett was expected to be performed, as he is now being performed, at the Comédie Française, which has always been execrated in the French avant-garde and would be, if the Situationists had had their way, a heap, blown up, a little heap. While they rejected virtually the whole tradition of Western culture, and all its artists with few exceptions, Beckett was one of them, exemplary and exempt.

Nothing to be done: it hardly seems like a prescription for radical change. Yet today, wherever you go, Beckett is almost universally admired, as if he were beyond all partisanship or ideology, for the integrity of the babble, the inexhaustible documentation at the level of the drives of what, by any other measure, is an encyclopedic mess. A miniaturist of impeccable patience, he has endowed us with the monstrous elegy of the sadomasochistic facts of life in a doomsday book of humiliation. There may be a sense in which what is also beguiling in Beckett has desensitized us to what he shows, which accounts for various productions, say, in which—when it's not mere brainless response or selective inattention—they're eager to laugh him off. But through all the hilarious figurations of the comic geometry of behavior it's still an appalling vision, as Didi says, "AP-PALLED"—and not even the wan and lyrical stasis that, at certain ineffable moments, seems to envelope the wounds makes them any easier to endure.

Endurance is the elemental issue in Beckett which could exhaust this entire session, but lest that get too painful, let us turn, in the evasive way of theory, to what I deferred before, the omnipresent subject and surreptitious operations of the look and the gaze:

The look and the gaze—the distinction between them, and their relations with the unseen visibility of desire—are among the more mystifying concepts in recent theory. But they are no more mystifying than that seeing body on the theatrical scene, the specular accretion called the audience, which materializes in the space between the look and the gaze. The look in its dispossession seems to be, if not a renegade, an avatar of the Law. For it is out to make distinctions and, like the Furies of classical drama, on the hunting path of truth, which circles back upon us—as in Beckett's dead imagining or the recurring dream of Freud's Wolf Man—as "the eye of prey," that cross-eyed subjectivity where the look becomes the gaze.

"Why shouldn't I go hunting, too?" says Hilda Wangel, in Ibsen's *The Master Builder,* when the haunted Solness "*looks deep into her eyes.*" "Get the prey I want? If only I can get my claws into it!" In the hunting pack as conceived by Elias Canetti (in his startling book on *Crowds and Power*) the one who sights the game may be honored in its distribution as much as or more than the one who made the kill. "But even those who were only distant witnesses of the kill may have claim to part of the prey. When this is the case, spectators are counted as accomplices of the deed. . . . Whatever the way in which distribution is regulated, the two decisive factors are the *sighting* and the *killing* of the prey."

The case of the Wolf Man offers a paradigm, however, of that inverted voyeurism where, at some primordial level of desire, the child's dream of being silently stared at (by wolves in a tree) is a cover-up for his own staring presence at the primal scene, the decisive sighting of the prey in which the kill is yet to come. It is part of the self-conscious tradition of theater that its hypnotic power is derived from the transposition of the primal scene, a reversal which also seems to remember that, when we came into the world, we occupied the center of the stage. Jonas Barish is invoking this tradition when he asks these questions in *The Anti-Theatrical Prejudice:* "Does the greediness of our gaze point to a buried memory of the earlier thirst to be gazed at, and our satisfaction when that thirst was slaked? Is our desire to sit as beholders merely the other side of the coin of our wish to be beheld, our unacknowledged exhibitionism? If so, perhaps the antitheatrical prejudice reflects a form of self-disgust brought on by our conflicted longing to occupy the center of the stage once more." As Beckett suggests, more likely than not.

In a theatricalized society, the prejudice—residual puritanism or insistent Platonism—may itself be repressed. For we may see the conflicted longing in the manifest content of the theater, through the evolution of its drama and the devolution of its heroes. Storing up alms for oblivion, the economy of the theater seems based upon the conversion of overinflated characters into objects of self-liquidating perception: from Agamemnon to Richard II to Flamineo and Danton, Ibsen's Borkman and Pirandello's Henry IV, and never more intensely than in the liminal figures and corroded heroes of Beckett's anti-plays: above all, Hamm, who sits with supreme disgust in the center of the stage, eminently conscious in his "blindness" of seeing and being seen; or, with all the grandiloquence of an easily punctured vanity, the tyrant Pozzo, out-Heroding Herod, who asks as he performs whether everybody is looking at him; or, in the blind relay of the diminishing look, the unslaked babble of the Mouth of *Not I,* with its silent Auditor; or, as the buried memory bottoms out: "No eye. No mind"—the talking heads in the funereal urns, stabbed by light and repeating themselves in *Play.* "Am I as much as...being seen?"

The line is designated by Beckett to be repeated at the closing of the repetition of the play, which implicates the observers in the plaintively cunning question, if we want to check it out. But in order to do that we have to repeat ourselves—an impossible proposition at the repetitive heart of theater which, for all the repetition, is never what it *was.* Yet if we engage in the repetition, we are deeper in collusion with the obtrusive and imperious light, giving sanction to its inquisition, whose partial objects we've become. In whatever ontological or economic ways the I is *as much as* being seen, we have to be there to see it, if it is to be even the vaguest approximation to what was seen before. (Not to mention, as they do in *That Time,* that it was "never the same, but the same as what for God's sake did you ever say I to yourself in your life come on now [*Eyes close.*] could you ever say I to yourself in your life....") In this respect, we are trapped by the repetition, like the disarticulated creatures in the (im)memorial urns. Thus, we find ourselves, uncannily, in an archaic and familiar part, as audience, forced to play it again, but not quite knowing how to do it, and still very much in the dark—"all dark, all still, all over"—about the dispersed and vanishing subject of the incapacitated I: "I mean... not merely over, but as if...never been—"

If the light forces the issue in *Play,* the blind but specular Hamm does the forcing in *Endgame*—though he attributes the necessity of the repetition, when Clov makes an issue of that, to the *dialogue.* Himself a figure of speech, Hamm sees through every thought like the preying eye of a camera obscura, observing the nuances of each word as if it were an object. If there's something dripping in his head that requires a painkiller, it seems—at the very quick of perception—as if the dripping were a brain scan. Narcissistic as he is, he also seems to perceive at the level of primary process, with an ear for the pun in prey, as we may see in his mordant pieties. "Let us pray," he says, archly cloying, and all the more clawing for that. Hamm materializes to our attention like a ruined totem, in black specs, doubly veiled, the hand-kerchief under the cloth like a Veronica on his face. The *I* which en-counters the gaze encounters the gaze as object: "Me—(*he yawns*)—to play." The grammar specifically articulates, over the yawning iden-tity, the estranged contingency of the subject. We are at the very onset at the depleted limit of the scopic field (gray, zero), as if the world were exhausted by being seen and the theater by too much sight.

In his staged blindness, Hamm is a kind of sadomasochistic mock-ery of the entirely hidden gaze:

> HAMM: Did you ever see my eyes?
> CLOV: No.
> HAMM: Did you never have the curiosity, while I was sleeping, to take off my glasses and look at my eyes?
> CLOV: Pulling back the lids?
> (*Pause.*)
> No.
> HAMM: One of these days I'll show them to you.

In the S/M business, Clov is no slouch either, as we can plainly see, who stare in fascination at the pregnant pause. What he seems to be remembering in case we have forgotten is that if the eye is seen we do not see the gaze. If the voyeur—the viewing subject as pervert—is looking for some shadow of presence behind lid or curtain, a fantasy to admire, what is encountered here is a stalemate, not the phallus but a fetish.

Now, as we know from Freud, the power of the fetish is that it both reveals and blocks the discovery of a fundamental wound or loss; which is to say, castration. And what we have in the conception of Hamm is a sort of insidious reification of the castrated subject. For he is not only the thing on display but the teasing *voyeur* as well, for whom—as Lacan says of the *exhibitionist*—"what is intended by the subject is what is realized in the other." But how can he be the voyeur if he is really blind? (Of course he is not really blind, since he is only an actor, pretending to be blind. Which raises the problem, if we pursue the riddle of acting further, of whether it is a true pretense or a false pretense. But this is an enigma over which for the moment—as it might be escalated to the point of vertigo by Genet—we shall mercifully pass:) If we take Hamm on faith, then the voyeurism is displaced. It moves into the ear, spiral to the eye's sphere. He watches by listening, with the seductive intimations of the acutest vigilance. If he has been somehow victimized, he is "the victim as referred to some other who is looking at him." As to the condition for which he requires the painkiller, it comes in the sadomasochistic drive when, as Lacan speculates, "the loop is closed, . . . and the other has come into play, when the subject has taken himself as the end, the terminus of the drive. At this moment, pain comes into play in so far as the subject experiences it from the other."

There are times in *Endgame* when it appears that Hamm, with his stethoscopic ear, is monitoring feedback from the audience, as in the cryptic sufferance of the last rites when, the circuit of pain restored, he seems to acknowledge another presence abjected onto himself. "You...remain," he says, as he recovers himself with the handkerchief in the brief tableau before the curtain. In the concept of *aphanisis*—the term used by Ernest Jones for the disappearance of sexual desire—the movement of disappearance is, most radically, the manifestation of the subject. (As the abolition of sexuality is not identical with castration, so aphanisis is the object of a fear even more profound than castration.) If the veil itself, "Old stancher!," does double duty, that's because, in this unabating, relentless, corrosive play, not even finished when it's finished, the vanishing of the subject seems more lethal than before. Meanwhile, who/what it is that remains remains an open question, which partially depends—as it certainly did, prior to Beckett's canonization—on whether *you* are still there in the audience.

Samuel Beckett, Paris, 1974. Courtesy of Rick Cluchey.
Photograph, Ian Dryden.

Bert Lahr and E. G. Marshall in 1956 production of Waiting for Godot, *John Golden Theater. Courtesy of Billy Rose Theater Collection, Dorothy Swerdlove, Curator, Lincoln Center Library. Photo Pix, New York.*

Alan Mandell and Rick Cluchey in the Smithsonian Beckett Symposium per-formance of Ohio Impromptu, *March 1989. Courtesy of Smithsonian Insti-tution. Photograph, Jeffery Crespi.*

Rick Cluchey in the Smithsonian Beckett Symposium performance of Eh Joe, *March 1989. Courtesy of Smithsonian Institution. Photograph, Jeffery Crespi.*

2 Enough or Too Little? Voicings of Desire and Discontent in Beckett's "Enough"

Mary F. Catanzaro

Coupling and partnership—and their seeming impossibility—have always been central to Beckett. That was already apparent in his critical study of Proust in 1931, where one sees the full range of broken promise in the separateness and otherness that undermine agreement and accord. By 1946 he had coined the self-defining term *pseudocouple* in *Mercier and Camier.* In the physical impediments and emotional ruptures of the pseudocouple there is a virtual metaphysics of discord.

During the middle 1960s, the character of Beckett's style changed drastically and gave way to a new mode of expression whose structure was based on the transformation of language densities and texture. In "Enough" (1966), Beckett reduces sentence length, sets in motion patterns of repetition, and utilizes poetic and often ambiguous vocabulary. This style, while sometimes perplexing, serves to define a new narrative function and, moreover, to visualize the plight of the couple, and woman's place in it. The paradox of woman's position with a loved one or partner is that her place, or role, is defined in this work in the constructs of the voice in the text rather than in the testament of the body.

The central significance of couples for Beckett is that they shift among interpersonal, psychological, grammatical, and conceptual variants. Beckett grounds his notion of the couple in an increasingly theoretical foundation of the voice. This voice does not communicate or inform as we would ordinarily expect, but is governed entirely by its relationship with the subject speaking. The voice points out what is before the scene of the narrator's inner gaze rather than what is visible to the senses. In other words, the voice relates to what is inside the subject all the while. The most productive approach here will be to look at how Beckett reevaluates the couple through the narrative voice and the inner voice speaking to itself. In each case it is necessary to forget the usual meaning of the word *voice*, which in this work is defined as *external* to the self. Much of Beckett's exposition of the voice can appear forbiddingly abstract on a superficial reading, but those who devote some effort to penetrating his language often find this work to be intensely emotional as well. Accordingly, Beckett never loses sight entirely of a quite traditional, humanistic view of the couple in terms of loss and sorrow. Both approaches are indeed at work in "Enough," hence the greater emphasis on just how and where they intersect and evolve.

In "Enough," the couple is articulated through the narrative voice that speaks in cyclical and repeated structures. One device that the narrator employs is the utterance of a noun or noun phrase used as a sentence. "Our meeting" (1974, 54); "Night" (59); "Attitude at rest" (59) are a few examples. The rest of the paragraph then provides a fuller description of the word or phrase. In this manner, the narrator's language seems to mirror her memories. The narrator also repeatedly refers to their partnership not in terms of specific time but in vague references to three circumstances: her age ("I cannot have been more than six when he took me by the hand" [54]); their mileage covered ("we must have covered several times the equivalent of the terrestrial equator. At an average speed of roughly three miles per day and night" [55]); and the weather ("eternally mild," "sudden pelting downpours," "this endless equinox" [59]). Three times the narrator says, "I never asked myself the question." The couple, then, emerges from within the subject through a voice that is released from present time, for its obsession is with past, future, future anterior, and subjunctive cases. In a peculiarly frequent avoidance of the present tense, the narrator seems to continue to connect herself with her mentor by speaking in a past tense that is juxtaposed with the future anterior. Perhaps her unstraightforward use of verb forms bespeaks an ambiguous desire for him that that will not die: "The future proved him right. That part of it at least we were to make past of together" (56). Out of all the textual hindrances, the couple is paradoxically rescued, even refined, in the complexities of that language itself. Thus, through language manipulation Beckett develops a resistance to the couple's defeat and thwarts its annihilation. Such friction against failure appears to lie in illusion, where dream, imagination, memory, and even humiliation *maintain* coupling rather than destroy it.

This illusion is found specifically in the voice. The internal voice speaking of itself evolves into a subject that relates to a "created" object, and its recurrent presence is one of Beckett's most clever narrative machinations. What is its substance, its deep structure? It is at once complex and polysemous, spreading its liquid inner dialogue everywhere into the text. There are deeply rooted sources in the inner voice, whose history is that of living memory and whose nature is quirky and elusively adaptable. The voice is not easy to dissect, and it is strongly attached to traditions and, more important, to the body's interrogations and denunciations of past experiences and memories. The example of "Enough" is valuable here, for it is not of a subject inspired by intellectual themes; quite the contrary, it is intent on voicing what the subject has seen and felt in ordinary experiences.

In placing the troubles of partnerships in the realm of the speaking voice, Beckett shows that communication as we commonly know it is an inadequate bonding device to preserve togetherness. This idea must be understood in terms of Beckett's seeming lack of faith in ordinary language to convey even the most minimal personal feeling. This is a fetish on Beckett's part; he realizes, of course, that couples still talk. What he does want to make plain is his faith in the will to overcome the problems intrinsic to coupling, in order to make apparent other avenues that subjects might take, whether they have been thrown together or have chosen each other.

But there are probably no clear limits as to what actually constitutes the couple. The task I set myself here, rather, is to reflect on the circularity that makes one very comprehensible couple pass over into an abstract one. Since *Waiting for Godot,* Beckett had been obsessed with mingling and separation between subject and object. The displacement of the couple into forms of absence, negativity, silence, or emptiness does not essentially matter, so long as one can determine the leap that Beckett takes in both its sound and its form and gather the meaning there.

After all his wordy outbursts in *How It Is* and *The Unnamable,* what else was left except linguistic shrinkage and devastation? Even where there is no longer an intact couple, friction, irritability, and a seeming inability to cope with loss is manifested between entities. Saint Augustine's famous motto, first used in *Waiting for Godot:* "Do not despair, one of the thieves was saved; do not presume, one of the thieves was damned," is the dialectic upon which "Enough" is built. It preserves the symmetry of hope and despair that is at the very foundation of the couple.

Briefly, "Enough" is about a first-person narrator who speaks of walking adventures in the past with a male partner. The story focuses on a couple, but the narrator's actual gender is not at all clear. This figure relives her activities with her mentor, whose considerations are primarily sexual, aesthetic, scientific, and religious. At the time of the narration, however, the speaker is alone and much older—"entering night" (53). Her "life" is thus bound by two specific events: the day her mentor alluded to his infirmity and the day he told her to leave him. By day they walk on flowers, and at night they sleep "Wedged together bent in three" (59). Her style is simple, spare, and punctuated by repetitions, particularly the words "desire" and "old." What is particularly problematic is the suppression of questions, for they are raised in the *reader:* Who are these figures? Are they permanently separated? What are the limits of suffering? How much sufferance, or the power to survive one's suffering, can one endure? What does anyone know of the universe? Is it possible to forget one's past?

So begins Beckett's bittersweet tale of the narrator in "Enough," who, cast off and abandoned, rises up to assert herself in her voice and, with great drama, is ultimately reunited to her loved one in her memory. Caught between her mentor's domination of her will and the sophistication of his knowledge, between the instincts of her faith in him and her self-skepticism, the narrator serves Beckett as an ideal figure with which to explore the tension that characterizes the strife inherent in every couple.

But, of course, the technical choices Beckett makes render his subjects more or less devoid of personality. They are, rather, vehicles, pure expressions of his own thematic concerns—with the temporary, illusory nature of human relationships; with the problems of expressive structure and communication; with the fragile boundaries between fantasy and reality, life and death, desire and aversion, passivity and violence. Beckett is particularly concerned with the dissolution of the boundary that separates *enough* from *too little.* Thus his subjects function as representations of *ideas* of coupling that implode and explode. When lovers are betrayed or abandoned, when thoughts wind down tortured roads ending in futility, Beckett seems to say life takes you one way, takes you another. You have no control over it. Just when you think you have something, you don't. Just when you think you've caught onto something and can hold it (like a long-standing relationship), it is gone.

Although "Enough" presents a clear-cut couple, the themes of loss and banishment are present from the start. Although the language appears orderly and conventionally constructed, it is marked by turns of phrase that indicate revolt, rebellion, frustration, resignation; all these turn on double meanings. Is the word *enough,* for example, a simple statement that the couple's partnership was truly sufficient? Or might it indicate that the mentor or mentee has had "enough" and desires no more companionship? Or again, because the word is mentioned in the last line, does this suggest that the story is over—that we as readers have been given "enough" information to know what Beckett wants to say? The striking symptom of "Enough" is that a couple was once able to manage in spite of their differences, with only the threat (lurking about for years) that their differences might create violence or an abrupt change in their partnership.

In "Enough" the couple is overtly present, and nothing unusual happens except that they meet and part. A voice discourses on her life with him, and the couple's basic position is of one figure's yielding to the needs of the other. That the speaker's gender is not entirely clear at the outset should concern us, for the capacity of the subject to represent or to recognize herself in apparently impersonal generalities is a crucial narrative motivation. The reader finally figures out that it is the feminine voice that speaks. Bisexuality thus figures powerfully in this work and suggests that coupling by nature is an odd notion, forever undone. We learn that she feels uncomfortably out of place in this unassimilated environment with him as her mentor. What she seems to detest most of all is being dragged under by all that submission symbolizes, that it might be replicating itself insidiously in her own life into a *syndrome,* a cluster of telltale "wifely" behaviors. She even comments on her own conduct. Because her mentor's spinal bones ("his sacral ruins" [57]) were bent, she says, "I bowed down as usual to save him having to repeat himself"; or as to whether his poor vision was a delusion, "I never asked myself the question" (56).

Part of the narrator's struggle is to distance herself from the kind of helpless obedience that she recognizes is traditional in wives or female companions but that she fears has manifested itself in passivity in her own life. She was taught to desire nothing, to swallow other people's misery, to eat her own bitterness. With a weary fatalism, she confesses to surrendering everything to her mentor without caring what she got in return:

> I did all he desired. I desired it too. For him. Whenever he desired something so did I. He only had to say what thing. When he didn't desire anything neither did I. In this way I didn't live without desires. . . . I only had the desires he manifested. But he must have manifested them all. All his desires and needs. [53]

We hear nothing of how the mentor served the pupil, other than to impart knowledge about the universe and the terrain they covered. Ruby Cohn has argued vigorously that their relationship was harmonious; and their travels over beds of flowers would seem to support the notion that theirs was an eternal spring, a paradise—while it lasted (1973, 244). But I would argue rather that it is common even among couples who have been together for a long time (and they have been together "Ten years at the very least" [57]) that partnership inevitably suffers from the wear and tear of differences. Their differently shaped hands symbolize and confirm this in particular:

> If the question were put to me I would say that odd hands are ill-fitted for intimacy. Mine never felt at home in his. Sometimes they let each other go. The clasp loosened and they fell apart. Whole minutes often passed before they clasped again. Before his clasped mine again.   [54]

And when she says, "The same needs and the same satisfactions" (53), I am inclined to think that this suggests bitterness and rebelliousness on her part; for later, when she speaks of his murmurs, she says, "Nine times out of ten they did not concern me" (55). That is not to say that two people, if they are honest, must not face differences every day. But no mention is made of the narrator's bodily needs or desires. The second paragraph, for example, describes the mentor's every need being met. It appears, then, that she taught herself to desire only what he desired.

The third paragraph opens with the sentence, "One day he told me to leave him" (53). When she remarks later of their life together, "We turn over as one man," this phrase of seeming unity is immediately followed by "when *he* manifests the desire" (59; emphasis mine). It seems to me that everything in the text (and even in her memory) is going on at the level of phallic power and authority. The implication is that the very idea of the feminine is derived from the (masculine) *voice speaking,* as the following line suggests, "When he told me to lick his penis I hastened to do so" (53). If there is any kind of resentment directed toward him at all, it lies in the verbal authority that he holds over her. What Beckett appears to be saying is that there seems to be no way out of logocentrism and phallic power. Despite all the complexity of its manifold structures, the *voice speaking* is emblematic of the deep conflict and disharmony between two apparently united people. "Enough" therefore suggests the question: Is coupling in the long run impossible, or, if it is to be sustained, must there be sufficient distance between subject and object?

It follows, then, that if they indeed had the same needs and same satisfactions, one must question, or at least take note of, their other physical differences. The mentor walks bent, but the pupil is upright; he likes the mountains, but she prefers the flats; she mentions the need for words, but the mentor speaks less and less frequently. The pupil says, "my voice [is] too weak at times" (53), but his appears to be strong—at least it seems to her to be assertive. The dialectical tension manifested between these two interacting forces is unequivocally manifested in their bodies: "He gave me his hand like a tired old ape with the elbow lifted as high as it would go. I had only to straighten up to be head and shoulders above him" (55). Yet there seems to be even here a nostalgia for the romantic, for a return to the Primordial One ("we turn over as one man"). But there is also a confusion of verb tenses, the description of events is not organized, and contraries abound in the text, even as they do between the two figures. At first she says her banishment took place just short of a crest. Later, however, she comments, "On the contrary it was on the flat in a great calm" (58).

Ambiguity between the couple here serves to emphasize Fredric Jameson's remark that "all human relations are bound to have something vaguely ominous about them; and the more heightened moments of scandal or violence prove to be nothing but the convulsive effort to free one's self from one's interlocutor" (1979, 38). Thus, when she is told to leave him and she says, "Gone from reach of his voice I was gone from his life" (53), there is apparently something about the mentor's voice that disturbs, even angers, the pupil. It resembles what Barthes has called the domestic "scene." Scenes, for Barthes (and perhaps for the pupil as well), "lay bare the cancer of language. Language is impotent to close language" (1977, 159). But even more important, it is the violence of the most civilized scenes that Barthes finds terrifying: "violence always organized itself into a *scene:* the most transitive of behavior (to eliminate, to kill, to wound, to humble) was also the most theatrical. . . . [In] all violence, he could not keep from discerning, strangely, a literary kernel: how many conjugal scenes must be classified under the label of some great genre painting: *the wife cast out,* or, again, *the repudiation!*" (160). In "Enough," the pupil also refers to her verbal ejection as the "scene of my disgrace" (58).

From that vantage point, is "Enough" simply a revolt against the demands placed on domestic partnership, or is it a discourse of desire? The mentor is indeed imperious, demanding, and intelligent, and she meets his every need. Her tone, however, is not one of joy in fulfilling those demands; they are stated simply and factually, even dryly. She is clearly the servant, for she claims ignorance, "What do I know of man's destiny?" (60). As far as bodily contact went, since "*He* did not like to feel against his skin the skin of another" (54; emphasis mine), they shared a pair of gloves. But for her part, she says the "notion of calm [came] from him. Without him I would not have had it" (60).

One crucial question stands at the forefront of the narrator's remarks: how much importance ought to be placed on the gender of the subjects when one of Beckett's principal strategies is to erase boundaries between subject and object? The question of gender, including that of the voice speaking, seems to be a central issue in this work. In other words, power is implicated via the body, and its prominent existence in the text reveals how one person can exercise power over another, by eliciting or communicating messages against the other person's will. And further, power enters into the constitution of the signifying system itself, not simply into that of its application. For the language of the body is a powerful one, in which, for example, a single signifier—the hand—does duty for more than one signified, and power penetrates at such gaps in the system, through the process of adjudging between interpretations. Here is but one example: "With his upper hand he held and touched me where he wished. Up to a certain point. The other was twined in my hair" (59–60). Another concerns the gloves and skin contact: "Mucous membrane is a different matter. Yet he sometimes took off his glove. Then I had to take off mine" (54). In the passages just quoted, the narrator's interpretation of a single sign—the hand—is set against the mentor's, and it is his that prevails: he speaks and acts from a position of knowledge and authority—the authority that, within the social relations represented in the text, a husband or lover enjoys over a wife or mistress.

Traditionally, the subject/object categories of body and mind are understood in opposition to each other. And although sexual difference is formulated via textual frameworks, theorists wishing to demonstrate it are faced nevertheless with the very problem that has haunted, and occasioned, much of Western thought: that of the antagonism between the body and the mind. If the narrator's body—desire—speaks in "Enough," it never speaks unquestionably about itself but always of its relation to the other, a relation that can only be lived in the narrative voice; and it is the narrative voice—fragmented, multiple, contradictory—that absorbs and refracts her *body's* voice. Beckett's deployment of the feminine body, accordingly, as well as his discussion of its position within the wider context of a concern for human destiny, must not be understood to be grounded on an entirely masculine perspective.

Granted, the binary division between matter and form, body and mind, subject and object, or sex and text has functioned as the bedrock of Western patriarchal thinking, and the assumption of such a dualism has allowed sexist theories and practices to continue. For whenever and wherever the mind is thought to function without recourse to the body (and vice versa), there is at work an unspoken logic or cultural thinking that, by aligning bodies with women and minds with men, asserts the superiority of the mental to the corporal and in so doing elevates masculinity (and the mind) over femininity (and the body). Beckett, however, reverses this trend and attempts to theorize a possible feminine specificity in the voice of language. The feminine is heard in the subject, who plays the servant or who expresses feelings, emotions, or pain that go against the grain of the manifest didacticisms of the partner. In "Enough," coupling is registered in the oscillation of memory and voice. Although the work focuses on them as a couple, the lack of boundaries between them needs questioning, for the coupling actually takes place in the intangible space of their exchanges, as, for example, "When I bowed down to receive his communications I felt on my eye a glint of blue bloodshot apparently affected" (56). This space—that hymeneal tissue—is necessary for *self*-reflection, not to desensitize, but to show a willingness to admit pain. Beckett confronts pain openly in this work, for he seems to agree with Freud that the admission—or emission—of pain is the very ground of self-reflection, and this exemplifies the notion that there are times when suffering produces a softening effect.

It seems that out of the drive for contact comes the drive to produce matter analytically, as this work does with the narrator's recollections. The world of the couple is here a recuperative medium not because any insufficiency might be at its center but rather because love cannot endure direct relations; it can exist only in the alternation of realization and latency. A relationship is passive and active at once; if the whole self acts an action it must sooner or later approach passivity, for partnership does away with intercessory actions. "Enough" sums up this position, and Beckett argues it with considerable thoroughness. Yet the idea of a subject and an object whose borders collapse, exchange, and blend may seem a bit tenuous. It depends on whether one is willing to accept this distinction of coupling.

In such a passage as, "That was enough for him" (54), are we witnessing contempt for the other or self-loathing? If it *is* enough, then in spite of the mentor's deteriorating physical condition, why the banishment? why the imposition of suffering? Cohn observes that "too much" is mentioned four times in the opening paragraph, but notes also that the last sentence begins with "enough." She reads this optimistically as deriving from an old Latin proverb that says *Satis est quod sufficit:* "enough is what satisfies" (1973, 244).

But Knowlson and Pilling argue from a slightly different standpoint, noting that the I–he contrasts require us to see them as aspects of the same personality, even though they are separate—as a younger self and an older self. Thus, the older figure can endure, but the younger self must talk herself into calmness (1979, 151). This reading accordingly places more strength of character on the older (masculine) figure. Might Beckett in fact be uncovering the corruptibility of phallic power? For though the mentor is sure of matters, especially scientific ones, the narrator is more given to hypotheses. And feeling. Again, the feeling arises that despite the differences between the two, her memories at any rate are passionate, and the feeling of loss is very real.

There is, then, a double effect between the voice and the text. On the one hand, it is a simple description of a couple. On the other hand, this narration imposes a sort of blank imprint of the *concept* of the couple. It forms the idea of the couple without changing anything in the usual connotation. For example, one could speak, in a certain sense, of a fiction of the couple, here seen in the recollection of the pupil about her mentor, and what it is like in her imagination. The whole analysis of this short work seems to shift between these two modes of coupling.

The couple, therefore, can never be summarily described or pinpointed quite simply, for Beckett's pairs, even when unified, constantly pose the threat of dispersal. And the random threat of the other's disappearance is not simply a "notion" on Beckett's part. It serves rather to define even ordinary couples. This situation, of course, leaves open the possibility of instability at all times. In "Enough," Beckett has worked the tension in through the voice to point to the insufficiency of language to bond and harness the couple. The device is unsettling because the voice is not merely a device. This and the banishment and humiliation of the narrator make the couple's separation and falling apart evident.

At the same time, whatever or whoever the subjects become as singular identities is not as important as the fact that their relationship to each other seems to remain and provide a stable system of coordinates to which common values and the *idea* of permanence may possibly be cemented. But part of what causes the fragmentation of the couple is the combative stance of the subjects, in collision with each other in their consciousnesses and in their language, for both, almost without exception, have built into them a polarity, a veer toward subject-centeredness.

The couple is thus always vanishing, for in the urge to identify the suffering, we find that the couple's troubles are rooted in the assumption that, as Buber has said, "You has no borders" (1930, 55). That is to say, every couple is doomed to become entangled in events that are dual. "Enough" executes on various levels separation and togetherness, passivity and assertion, as the following passage demonstrates:

> There are questions you see and don't ask yourself. He must have been on his last legs. I on the contrary was far from my last legs. I belonged to an entirely different generation. It didn't last. Now that I'm entering night I have kinds of gleams in my skull. Stony ground but not entirely. Given three or four lives I might have accomplished something.
>
> I cannot have been more than six when he took me by the hand. . . . But it didn't take me long to emerge altogether. It was the left hand. To be on the right was more than he could bear. We advanced side by side hand in hand.   [53–54]

In one sense, all of Beckett's works have been based on a series of developments about sound and new ways of voicing. "Enough" is marked by the voice that controls its own fluctuating masses, color, densities, and intensities of sound. In "Enough," the subject's narrative is surrounded by her own "commentaries," and it is the model for the basic pattern and mode of language and inner voicing that become dominant in Beckett's later works. This technique is used not to project a faithful or distorted image against "live" sound but to extend and project the subject's relatively fixed and discrete actions and events onto a broader continuum, which comments indirectly on the couple's inability to communicate simply and honestly to each other.

Beckett's gestures of effacing the couple and yet keeping it in and out of focus are obviously his own idiosyncratic means of articulating it. The perceived self, as well as the couple perceiving itself, is shaped by absence, by what is *not*-there; for condensation, concealment, and displacement—like the dream—constitute the couple. The couple is therefore discovered through the reader's location of the movement in the text that latches subjects together, if only fleetingly. To discern this moment is perhaps the most frustrating task that Beckett asks of his readers. His subjects are most often half-seen presences roaming country roads or stalking their spaces, dwelling in a limbo of imposed (and self-imposed) defeat. Yet—as proof of some irrepressible life force that flows through them—they can never quite resist the impulse to continue in the throes of a hapless, hopeless love. If the subjects' hearts are more often than not betrayed, crushed by seeming failure, they are still clearly impelled, to the bitter end, by love and need. Thus the narrator ends her tale: "Now I'll wipe out everything but the flowers. No more rain. No more mounds. Nothing but the two of us dragging through the flowers. Enough my old breasts feel his old hand" (60).

The need for pathos and drama and the concern with verbal and language possibilities—voice as language, language as voice, the coupling of meaning to voice, of content to voice, even of linguistic to musical structure—are illustrated in all Beckett's works but are strikingly evident in "Enough." Here language is driven out of the concrete world of the subject's experiences into her memory and imagination, into a kind of self-analysis. Psychoanalysis indeed has become literally the study of a subject's rhetoric, an explication of defensive tropes and schemes. Truth liberates, we are told, and if a speaker's words foster growth in the listener or in the self, then the language or rhetoric used to describe differs little from language used to heal. In this sense, the narrator's rhetoric mirrors psychology, each mapping the effect of *logos* upon *psyche.* The narrator soothes herself, indeed lives most fully, in her brief recitation; for language, as Kristeva and recent Freudians observe, becomes an instrument of desire, out of which the ego is born. The way in which Beckett uses the voice, then, becomes a healing device and unmasks what we ordinarily do not dwell on. Domestic tensions or violence are not studied as tokens of repression in general. But Beckett wants to show that the dualistic fury and insufficiency of language are intrinsic, even *necessary,* features of partnership and coupling.

What does all this mean? Through the veil of its tender pathos, "Enough" unfolds a gradual process of degradation, a kind of stunted violence of the soul. We realize that the narrator's situation is one of isolation. For her, the locus of all that is other and sinister can only function within a phallic economy, and Beckett is sensitive to this fact. She realizes perfectly well that her mentor's law is one whose respect is socially learned and therefore mandates obedience, for she readily obeys the calls of his body—his failing blue eyes, his ruined bones, his penis. But most of all, she knows that it is the hand that chooses to touch or not to touch her that is *the* signifying accident of his tenderness or disaffection toward her. Her gender thus shapes our reading of the work. In a special and remarkable way, "Enough" has a very particular appeal. Rather than imposing a *total* vision of the couple, it seeks to rationalize the relationship of a subject to her experience of what Beckett sees is, more often that not, a painful world to live in.

And yet, the mechanisms of separation between the narrator and her mentor are the very devices that Beckett employs to bring the two together as a couple—the cotton gloves, his dependence on her to lead him because of his failing vision, the calculated and measured touches.

Why does Beckett persist in saving the couple? A strange task indeed, for while "Enough" addresses the couple at the impasse of the impossible, Beckett stubbornly refuses to let go of the couple. It exists obstinately, sustained by what brought them together in the first place—love and necessity. In "Enough," the couple seems to work out a sort of penance for their "sin of having been born," for their unresolved differences, for their unspoken violence toward each other, in the almost superstitious hope that small gestures will help salvage the relationship. Like a hairshirt or a bed of nails, the more they hate the relationship, the more they feel united to each other. They need each other to be with, hounded by the suspicion that theirs is the only life they are likely to enjoy. So speaks the narrator, "If the question were put to me suitably framed I would say yes indeed the end of this long outing was my life" (56).

But as exhilaration sometimes sweeps through the narrator, there is also a lurking tension, a fear that flits in the corners of her mind but takes no obvious shape: "He murmured of things that for him were no more and for me could not have been" (60). Thus, it is the detritus of life that we see in "Enough." The work is a two-track voicing, in which the consciousness of the speaker sifts through her younger, fragmented consciousness even as she is still trying to reconstruct her memories *here and now.* Her body is displaced because there seems to be no place, or space for it, for she has filled the textual space with her imagination and memories of time past, which have now hypertrophied through time. Time stops and starts, advances and retreats, splits and merges.

But one needn't worry that the couple will vanish. What one does worry about, as always, is one's own relationship to the silence of an indifferent universe. Beckett's couples, united and divided at once, lack autonomy and are ultimately forced to turn to each other to achieve psychic unity.

One might say, then, that the ordinary frustrations and the depressiveness of day-to-day living with the same partner stem from the burden or image that a change imposes, which challenges a person's ability to adapt. The peg of identification of all of Beckett's couples lies in the fact that many people are more comfortable in a familiar but unhappy situation than in a potentially better but unpredictable one.

Hence the old Spanish saying that it is better to sit at dinner with a known devil than to court a strange angel. Who knows this better than the pupil in "Enough"?

References

Barthes, Roland. *Roland Barthes*. Translated by Richard Howard. New York: Hill and Wang, 1977.

Beckett, Samuel. "Enough." In *First Love and Other Shorts*. New York: Grove Press, 1974.

Buber, Martin. *I and Thou*. Translated by Walter Kaufmann. New York: Scribner's, 1930.

Cohn, Ruby. *Back to Beckett*. Princeton: Princeton University Press, 1973.

Jameson, Fredric. "Agons of the Pseudo-couple." In *Fables of Aggression: Wyndham Lewis, the Modernist as Fascist*. Berkeley and Los Angeles: University of California Press, 1979.

Knowlson, James, and Pilling, John. *Frescoes of the Skull: The Later Prose and Drama of Samuel Beckett*. New York: Grove Press, 1979.

3   Seven Types of Postmodernity: Several Types of Samuel Beckett

Nicholas Zurbrugg

To what extent may the work of Samuel Beckett be equated with postmodernism? There is obviously no easy answer to this question. Over the last half-century both Beckett's writing and the postmodern sensibility have undergone a series of shifts in emphasis and impact. It is the intention of this essay to clarify the evolution of Beckett's work, and postmodern culture in general, by considering their respective phases, one in terms of the other.

As will become evident, Beckett's achievement—and the multifaceted range of postmodern creativity as a whole—requires far more comprehensive definition than the now fashionable tendency to dismiss the postmodern as a "depthless, styleless, dehistoricized [culture of] surfaces," in which "there is no longer any subject to be alienated and nothing to be alienated from, 'authenticity' having been less rejected than merely forgotten" (Eagleton 1985, 61). According to critics such as Terry Eagleton and Fredric Jameson, the postmodern sensibility is "no longer subjective in the older sense [of] knowing the limits of the individual subject and the human ego [but is] a kind of non-humanist experience of limits beyond which you get dissolved" (Jameson 1986, 69).

Accordingly, Jameson argues that we no longer inhabit modes of deep time but enter a zone of hyperspace (1986, 70), characterized by neutral "intensities of highs and lows, [which] have nothing to do with 'feelings' that offer clues to meaning in the way anxiety did" (69). In Jean Baudrillard's terms, the postmodern condition introduces a new form of schizophrenia, in which there is "no more hysteria, no more projective paranoia ... but this state of terror proper to

30

the schizophrenic: too great a proximity of everything" (1983b, 132). For Baudrillard, the postmodern sensibility is characterized not so much by "the loss of the real [as by] the total instantaneity of things . . . the overexposure and transparence of the world" (133).

As this essay will attempt to indicate, the cutting edge of recent postmodern debate hinges upon two antithetical responses to this sense of exposure to new perceptual limits and new intensities of perceptual instantaneity. On the one hand, apocalyptic pessimists such as Eagleton, Jameson, and Baudrillard annunciate the dissolution of all values. On the other hand, postmodern creators such as Beckett, Cage, and Burroughs suggest that the contemporary sensibility is perfectly commensurate with the accelerated tempo of postmodern existence, and may still find "clues to meanings" in terms of the positive or negative feelings that Jameson rather curiously believes to be a thing of the past.

Looking back on present times, cultural historians may well reiterate the famous first lines of Dickens's *A Tale of Two Cities* (1859) and conclude:

> It was the best of times, it was the worst of times, it was the age of wisdom, it was the age of foolishness, it was the epoch of belief, it was the epoch of incredulity, it was the season of Light, it was the season of Darkness, it was the spring of hope, it was the winter of despair.

According to such prophets of incredulity and Darkness as Baudrillard, the "mediatory diffusion" of postmodern information accelerates our sense of reality beyond "the referential orbit of things" (Baudrillard 1988b, 36), negating and neutralizing all distinctions between the true and the false, the real and the unreal. Baudrillard's essay "The Year 2000 Has Already Happened" (1985) characteristically announces: "Each fact, each trait, political, historical, or cultural, is endowed . . . with a kinetic energy which breaks itself from its own space, for always, and propels itself into a hyperspace where it loses all meaning, since it will never return" (Baudrillard 1988a, 36).

Such allusions to hyperspace and the loss of all meaning typify the way in which Baudrillardian theory generates a kind of worst-possible-scenario science fiction, as it tracks down ever more extravagant examples of mediatory incongruity. Attempting to demonstrate that "the body no longer exists" or, at least, that "like Baudrillard's emancipated sign before it, health has lost its representational capacity," Arthur and Marilouise Kroker cite a *New York Times* story—about plans to show pilots strategic information on screens within helmets that block out normal occular vision—as "perfect" evidence of the "obsolescence of the body" in "the new universe of virtual technology" and "the new world of panic science" (Kroker and Kroker 1988, 21, 30, 32, 31).

At the other extreme of postmodern theory, the writings of John Cage assert that the kinds of kinetic energies that Baudrillard associates with the implosion or explosion of meaning, and that the Krokers equate with panic culture, are perfectly acceptable and accessible, insofar as "our souls are conveniently electronic (omniattentive)" (Kostelanetz 1974, 167). Rather than subscribing to the myth of postmodern culture's irredeemable confusion, Cage proposes that certain forms of chance-based creativity permit one to synthesize different levels of experience. Outlining this best-possible-scenario hypothesis, Cage's address "Experimental Music" (1957) specifies that "this . . . is an affirmation of life—not an attempt to bring order out of chaos nor to suggest improvements in creation, but simply a way of waking up to the very life we're living, which is so excellent once one gets one's mind and one's desires out of its way and lets it act of its own accord" (in Cage 1983, 12).

According to this argument, experiments with metaphorically electronic sensitivity, and with technologically electronic media, permit one to make maximum sense of an unprecedented era of "reflection, collage, transparency [in which] we see several things at once" (Cage 1987, 6).

Samuel Beckett's position in the cosmos of postmodern theory is extremely ambiguous. On the one hand, the characters in his plays and prose seem extremely impatient to reduce their experience to the kind of meaningless hyperreality discussed by Baudrillard. But on the other hand, they find it impossible to achieve this ambition. As the following lines from Beckett's *Worstward Ho* (1983a) intimate, Beckett's characters cannot permanently dim such profound anxieties as the stare of self-awareness, or their memories of past shades. At best, disturbing realities drift away temporarily, only to undim and leave the mind exposed once again to "the hell of all" (Beckett 1983a, 44). The narrating consciousness of this text morosely muses: "Stare by words dimmed. Shades dimmed. Void dimmed. Dim dimmed...Then all undimmed. Stare undimmed. That words had dimmed" (39).

Confronted by such texts, it is tempting to discuss both Beckett's work, and postmodernism in general, as the negation of modernism's more euphoric visions. Indeed, as I have previously argued, there is considerable evidence to suggest that postmodern fiction is marked by disjunction and a sense of *métaphore manquée* (Zurbrugg 1986, 68–90), as opposed to modernism's elaboration of harmonious metaphorical revelations. The latest writings of Beckett and other post-modern veterans, such as Cage and Burroughs, suggest that there are substantial grounds for modifying this judgment. Although much post-modern writing appears fragmentary and nihilistic, the final phases of postmodernism appear to evince surprisingly harmonious alternatives to the panic sensibility.

As critics such as Fredric Jameson and Charles Jencks indicate, the temptation to dismiss postmodernism as a failed version or a dwarf version of modernism is virtually irresistible. Despite his claim to offer postmodernism "a positive description . . . as a new cultural logic in its own right," Jameson repeatedly insists that postmodernism cannot possibly better modernism; that postmodern literature lacks modern-ism's "complexity of language, irony [and] symbolic system" (1986, 69); that postmodernism's new collective subject (70) does not "rein-vent style in the old sense" (71); and that even postmodernism's new modes of multimedia "space [are] not original in the world historical sense of the great modernist creator" (72). Pondering upon postmod-ern art and architecture, Jencks similarly insists that the postmodern avant-garde cannot better its precursors, since this possibility "might mean a strange, even paradoxical thing; becoming more modern than Modern, more avant-garde" (Jencks 1987, 12).

For all their good intentions, most critics dismiss postmodern crea-tivity far too rapidly, just as earlier generations of critics impatiently typecast dadaism as the black sheep of modernism—arguing, for ex-ample, that the nihilist impulse constituted dada's "primary, even sol-itary, psychic condition" (Poggioli 1968, 62). As the dadaist artist Mar-cel Janco advises, dada makes best sense when it is considered in terms of two speeds (rather than one psychic condition): an initial negative speed and a subsequent positive attitude (1971, 36–37). Beckett's successive works, and the successive phases of postmodern-ism, similarly necessitate analysis in terms of the pluralistic context of what one might think of as their different speeds and the different ways in which they neutralize, realize, synthesize, and, at best, better the creative aspirations of modernism. As the title of my essay sug-gests, Beckett's work lends itself to analysis in terms of seven main types of postmodernity.

The most prevalent early accounts of postmodern culture empha-sized its negation of modernist values. Interviewed by Israel Shenker in 1956, Beckett himself remarked that whereas Joyce was a superb manipulator of material, he was "working with impotence, ignorance" (1956, 3); and as early as 1938, in a book review discussing the poems of Denis Devlin, Beckett enthusiastically rejected the optimism of the modernist masters, remarking: "art has nothing to do with clarity, does not dabble in the clear and does not make clear" (1983b, 94). His *Dialogues* with Georges Duthuit, of 1949, similarly annunciate "an art . . . weary of pretending to be able, of being able, of doing a little better the same old thing" (1965, 103). Relating this kind of self-conscious pessimism to the temper of postmodern literature as a whole, Raymond Federman's 1977 article, "Fiction Today or The Pursuit of Non-Knowledge," contended that most postmodern novelists were "more concerned with the problems of writing their books, of letting the difficulty of writing fiction transpire in the fiction itself . . . than . . . with the problems of man" (1977, 10). Reading novels such as Beckett's *Malone Dies* (1958), in which Malone despairingly erupts with such asides as "What tedium" and "What half-truths" (1975, 15, 10), it is easy to sympathize with Federman's conclusion.

A second reading of postmodernism's early identity centered around the existential anxiety that Federman refers to as the problems of man. In this respect, Beckett's famous aspiration to find a form that accommodates "the mess" (1961, 23) typifies the way in which early postmodern writings often seem obsessed both with the impossibility of writing and with the more general impossibility of either explaining or enduring the "absurd."

Something of this dilemma emerges quite rapidly in Beckett's play *Waiting for Godot* (1956), in which the two main characters, Estragon and Vladimir, "daren't even laugh any more" (Beckett 1968, 11). As Estragon intimates, this is also a postpoetic condition. When Vladimir comments: "You should have been a poet," Estragon promptly replies: "I was" (12). A few pages later, allusions to the intolerable and unspeakable quality of existence converge when Vladimir wakens the sleeping Estragon, restoring him to "the horror of his condition" (15), as he attempts to articulate "private nightmares," which Vladimir insists "remain private" (16). Beckett's *Watt* (1953) rather similarly examines the same questions:

> who may tell the tale
> of the old man?
> weigh absence in a scale?
> mete want with a span?
> the sum assess
> of the world's woes?   [Beckett 1963, 247]

Although the English critic George Steiner never discusses postmodernism as such, his *Language and Silence* (1967) traces much the same fears dramatized by Beckett. Defining his central theme as

dismay before the way in which "the established media of civilization—the universities, the arts, the book world—failed to offer adequate resistance to political bestiality" (Steiner 1969, 15), Steiner
ponders upon the way in which "poetry is tempted by silence" (25)
insofar as there can be "No poetry after Auschwitz" (75). Steiner's
essay "Silence and the Poet" tellingly concludes: "When the words in
the city are full of savagery and lies, nothing speaks louder than the
unwritten poem" (76).

Placing his argument within a more personal context, Steiner ad-
ditionally confides, "the black mystery of what happened in Europe is
to me indivisible from my own identity ... because I was not there,
because an accident of good fortune struck my name from the roll"
(1969, 119). The autobiographical and geographical register of these
remarks overlaps with a third early type of postmodern writing: those
texts preoccupied with predominantly national or collective modes of
anxiety, such as the poems of Allen Ginsberg and the plays of Heiner
Müller.

As becomes evident, this third, collective postmodern sensibility
is usually characterized by highly detailed confessional narrative.
Whereas Beckett's *Godot* refers to "A country road. A tree" (1968, 7),
Ginsberg's *Howl* (1956) elaborately chronicles the misadventures of
the "the best minds of my generation ... who passed through universities ... who were expelled from the academies ... who got busted
... who talked continuously seventy hours" (Ginsberg 1960, 182–
83). As William Burroughs suggests, certain writers virtually give birth
to "a generation waiting to be written" (1985b, 176). *Howl* seems to
be postmodern in the twofold sense that it invents the unprecedent-
edly intense colloquialisms of its "long saxophone-like chorus lines"
(415) and at the same time writes a new generational identity across
America, across Western Europe, and across Eastern Europe, where
Ginsberg was crowned King of May in Prague in 1965.

Living in what he calls "a schizophrenic position [with] one leg on
each side of the wall" (Müller 1982, 51), the East German playwright
Heiner Müller appears to be making a similarly transatlantic impact
on contemporary audiences. Many of Müller's plays, such as *Hamletmachine* (1977), dwell upon the dilemma of the defeated Marxist
revolutionary, or what he calls "the man between the ages who knows
that the old age is obsolete [yet feels that] the new age has barbarian
features he simply cannot stomach" (Weber 1980, 137). Like Ginsberg, Müller employs complex collaged narratives and violent, partially surreal, partially expressionist imagery. Somewhat like Ginsberg's circle, who tend to walk all night "with their shoes full of blood

on the snow-bank docks waiting for . . . opium" (Ginsberg 1960, 186), Müller's Ophelia introduces herself as "the woman with her arteries cut open. . . . The woman with her head in the gas stove" (Müller 1984, 54). In both cases autobiographical reminiscence transmutes into more general, mythological allusion. But whereas Ginsberg's vision tends to elaborate relatively frivolous reference to "Dreams! adorations! illuminations! religions! the whole boatload of sensitive bullshit!" (1960, 190), Müller's play emphasizes "The petrification of . . . hope," and closes with reference to Charles Manson's threat of "butcher knives [carrying] the truth" (1984, 56, 58).

At his most optimistic, Müller argues that "literature is an affair of the people [and] illiterates are the hope of literature," in the sense that popular utterance necessitates "the disappearance of the author," and permits "the universal discourse which omits nothing and excludes no one" (1979a, 57). Somewhat as Müller associates this universal discourse with "the proletarian art of the subway" (56), Umberto Eco and Jean Baudrillard detect similarly primitive energy in the breakdancer's movements (Eco 1987, 76; Baudrillard 1988b, 19). Other European intellectuals turn to still more exotic models, such as the "self-legitimating anecdotes of the Cashinahua Indians" (Lyotard and Thébaud 1985, 194) discussed by Jean-François Lyotard. At their most basic, these evocations culminate in the sentimentality of the final scene of Günter Grass's *Headbirths,* in which "more and more children, all foreign . . . all cheerful" counterpoint the alienation of the novel's central characters, a childless yuppie couple, who sit dumbstruck, "not knowing what to say in German" (1984, 128).

As Grass explains, his disquietude focuses upon contemporary Europe's incapacity to appreciate third-world values; at best, German tourists display "the new arrogance: We've come to learn" (15). In their turn Müller and Baudrillard point to the "time wall" (Müller 1982, 37) that Müller perceives between different cultures, and the "chasm of modernity [and] unbridgeable rift" between Europe and America (Baudrillard 1988b, 73). Baudrillard also proposes that European culture is equally inaccessible to America's "nostalgic eye," and will not really cross the ocean (79), while Müller describes America as a void that, "like a vampire, needs to suck in foreign material in order to survive" (Müller 1979b, 83). By contrast, Ginsberg asserts that his generation may easily enjoy assorted modes of "ancient heavenly connection" (1960, 182), be this by retreating to "Rocky Mount to tender Buddha" (187), or by blissing out in Kansas, where "the Cosmos instinctively vibrated at their feet" (184).

Predictably, Beckett's writings evince little trace of such "instinc-tive" spiritual revelation. On the contrary, Beckett's portrayals of spir-itual crisis usually evoke the anguish of the "dud mystic" (Beckett 1933, 165–66), rather than Ginsbergian illuminations. And when Beckett places a listening figure in a "loose black djellaba" in *Not I* (1973), he does so in order to emphasize the figure's anonymity, leav-ing it "enveloped from head to foot, . . . sex undeterminable" (Beckett 1984, 216). As this play's title suggests, it concerns rejection rather than celebration of identity. Watched with "helpless compassion" (215) by the figure in the djellaba, Mouth repeatedly denies her iden-tity, refusing to utter the word "I," protesting: "what?...who?...no!...she!" (221), as she involuntarily awakens from "the dark" (217) to find her "lips moving" (219) and her brain "flickering away like mad" (222).

Beckett's anonymous visions of personal anxiety, and the more na-tional, collective anxiety evoked by Ginsberg, Müller, Grass, and Baud-rillard, all appear short-circuited by a fourth, predominantly American mode of postmodernity: the playful, Zen-based, chance compositional strategies associated with the composer John Cage. Whereas Beckett's writing seems to start with the conviction that existence is "unutter-able or ineffable, so that any attempt to utter or eff it is doomed to fail, doomed, doomed to fail" (Beckett 1963, 61), Cage assumes that it is unproductive and unnecessary to aspire to say "I." As his notes accompanying the record of *Indeterminacy* (1959) indicate, Cage is more interested in random configurations than any personal idea of relationship. Introducing his aesthetic in terms of the question, "What, then is your final goal?" Cage recounts:

> I said that I did not see that we were going to a goal, but that we were living in process, and that process is eternal. My intention . . . is to sug-gest that all things, sounds, stories (and, by extension, beings), *are* re-lated, and that this complexity is more evident when it is not over-simplified by an idea of relationship in one person's mind.

Cage's concept of art as "purposeful purposelessness or . . . pur-poseless play" (1983, 12) elegantly sidesteps the twofold dilemma implicit in Beckett's attempt to find a form to accommodate the mess. First, it rejects conventional definitions of form and mess by asserting that apparent disorder may well constitute unfamiliar modes of order. "Disharmony," Cage claims, is perhaps "a harmony to which many are unaccustomed" (12). Second, Cage proposes that materials that might usually appear worthless, or a mess, may well seem far more valuable if contemplated attentively. "In Zen they say: If something is boring after two minutes, try it for four. If still boring, try it for eight, sixteen, thirty-two, and so on. Eventually one discovers that it's not boring at all but very interesting" (93).

Taken to extremes, Cage's considerations could well provoke a society worthy of Swiftian satire. But considered more generally, Cage's philosophy emerges as an appeal for tolerance and flexibility, and as a timely antidote to the perils of the "increasingly total system or logic" (Jameson 1984, 57) that Jameson associates with much contemporary theory. Jameson explains: "Insofar as the theorist wins . . . by constructing an increasingly closed and terrifying machine, to that degree he loses, since the critical capacity of his work is thereby paralysed, and the impulses of negation and revolt . . . are increasingly perceived as vain and trivial in the face of the model itself" (57).

Paradoxically, perhaps, Cage's reluctance to pass immediate judgment upon experimental art appears to allow him to respond more judiciously to unfamiliar creativity. Asked by the critic Richard Kostelanetz whether certain recent experimental theater pieces were better than others (Kostelanetz 1980, 27), Cage memorably replied: "Why do you waste your time and mine by trying to get value judgements? Don't you see that when you get a value judgement, that's all you have? . . . They are destructive to our proper business which is curiosity and awareness. . . . We must exercise our time positively" (27–28).

This is not to imply that Cage abandons *all* value judgments. Rather, he encourages the judicious suspension of judgment. Comparison of Beckett's texts with those of Cage suggests that despite his emphasis upon the word *perhaps* (Beckett 1961, 23), his fictional and dramatic visions frequently approximate to what Jameson would call "an increasingly closed and terrifying machine." For example, while Beckett's dialogues with Duthuit complain: "there is nothing to express, nothing with which to express, nothing from which to express, no power to express, no desire to express, together with the obligation to express" (Beckett 1965, 103), Cage's "Lecture on Nothing" (1959) reverses this hypothesis, announcing: "I have nothing to say, and I am saying it and that is poetry as I need it" (Cage 1983, 109). Likewise, whereas Beckett's essay on Proust regrets that there are "no vehicles of communication [for] valid expressions of the personality" (1965, 64), Cage dismisses this whole issue, arguing that "Personality is a flimsy thing on which to build an art" (1983, 90).

Of course, Cage's art never literally extricates *all* traces of his personality. Rather, it delegates such traces to what one might think of as secondary rather than primary dimensions of performance. For example, *Indeterminacy* requires Cage to read a series of stories of vary-ing lengths, one per minute, at differing speeds, in combination with an independently prerecorded sound track prepared by David Tudor from Cage's earlier works. Accordingly, the pace of Cage's narration, and its relation to Tudor's sound track, are indeterminate, rather than "over-simplified by an idea of relationship in one person's mind" (Cage 1959).

However, even though *Indeterminacy* is devised to eliminate the presence of personal choice and emphasis, its subject matter contin-ually evokes autobiographical anecdote, and its performance is inim-itably Cageian, in terms of both its eccentric, partially accelerated, and partially decelerated delivery and Cage's unmistakable intonation. Re-ferring to his special sense of what he had to do in *Indeterminacy,* Cage tells how a recording engineer asked him to speak naturally, prompting the riposte: "But this is what I have to do. I tell one story a minute, and when it's a short one, I have to spread it out. Later on, when I come to a long one, I have to speak as rapidly as I can" (1959).

Like his compatriot the novelist William Burroughs, Cage accepts the confusions between impersonality and personality with consid-erable equanimity. Referring to Korzybski's critique of Aristotelian *either/or* logic, Burroughs dismisses "such polarities as intellect *or* emotion, reason *or* instinct," on the grounds that "every action is *both* instinctive *and* intellectual" (1985b, 159–60). In much the same way, Cage seems undisturbed by the hypothetical time-walls and cultural chasms discerned by Europeans such as Müller and Baudrillard. Like Ginsberg, Cage confidently asserts the interchangeability of Eastern and Western values. Rejecting the xenophobic objection that Zen "won't work for us . . . it's Oriental," Cage posits that "there is no longer a question of Oriental and Occidental. . . . All of that is rapidly disap-pearing" (1983, 143).

This is not to suggest that Cage shares Jameson's vision of a high capitalist global village in which everything is *negatively* identical, in the sense that the global village idiot "eats McDonald's food for lunch and local cuisine for dinner, wears Paris perfume in Tokyo and 'retro' clothes in Hong Kong" (Jameson 1984, 76). On the contrary, Cage argues that enlightenment assumes a more international character. Hence his enthusiasm for the transparency of a culture in which "we see several things at once" (Cage 1987, 6).

Cage's Zen-inspired musical experiments find their literary coun-terparts in the cut-up and permutated poems of the Paris-based Amer-ican painter Brion Gysin. Inspired by superimposed Arabic calligra-phy, Gysin's "Statement on the Cut-up Method and Permutated Poems"

(1958) argued that writers should "cut right through the pages of any book or newsprint . . . shuffle the columns of text [and] put them together at hazard" (Gysin and Burroughs 1979, 34). Gysin's introduction to his permutated poems still more interestingly observes:

> Words have a vitality of their own and you or anybody can make them gush into action. The permutated poems set the words spinning off on their own. . . . The poets are supposed to liberate the words. . . . Who told poets they were supposed to think? Poets have no words "of their very own." Writers don't own their words. Since when do words belong to anybody?   [34]

Cage's and Gysin's experiments with random and systematic texts designed to "set the words spinning off" without authorial intervention anticipate the French structuralists' preoccupation with postauthorial discourse by at least a decade. But whereas structuralist theory dogmatically asserted the death of the author and the impossibility of originality, Cage and Gysin rapidly revised their initial antiauthorial assumptions. Cage, for example, generously applauds the work of younger writers, such as the Australian composer Chris Mann, as being "fresh and a new direction in poetry" (1987, 6). Gysin acknowledged that the notionally impersonal cut-up texts made by his collaborator William Burroughs remained inimitably Burroughsian, noting: "One sniff of that prose and you'd say, 'Why, that's a Burroughs'" (Gysin and Wilson 1982, 191). More generally, Cage and Burroughs equate the avant-garde with "flexibility of mind" (Kostelanetz 1987, 238) which "enriches the whole aesthetic experience" (Burroughs 1965, 27). In Gysin's terms, such experiments help remedy the fact that most writing is "fifty years behind painting" (Gysin and Burroughs 1979, 34).

As one might imagine, Beckett's response to Burroughs's cut-ups was less than enthusiastic. Referring to their first meeting in Paris, in 1959, Burroughs reports that Beckett protested, "that's plumbing, not writing," becoming quite upset that Burroughs's cut-ups used other people's words (Bockris 1981, 214). Nevertheless, by the early seventies, Beckett himself permutated sections of *Lessness* (1970) and *The Lost Ones* (1972), on the grounds that it was "the only honest thing to do" (Pountney 1987, 55), a remark that seems to suggest that he felt that random composition would suit his themes more effectively than linear narrative. Thereafter this enthusiasm seems to have waned, "because of intractable complexities" (Admussen 1979, 22).

Beckett's and Burroughs's use of cut-up composition shares quite similar motivation. As Allen Ginsberg explains, Burroughs's cut-ups were at least partially prompted by the wish to defuse certain obsessive images—in this instance, "his most personal, romantic images" (Leyland 1978, 124), in the sense that they "cut through rehearsed habit ... cut through conditioned reflex ... cut out into open space, into endless blue space where there is room for freedom and no obligation to repeat the same image over and over again" (124).

Employing remarkably similar imagery, *Lessness* evokes desire for a state where all is "calm all white all gone from mind," or where the mind enjoys "the blue celeste of poesy" (Beckett 1970, 13). But this is not to be; "unhappiness will reign again" (11), the protagonist "will live again" (10) and will therefore "curse God again" (8). The same dilemma informs *The Lost Ones,* where sporadic references to indefinable conventions and laws (Beckett 1972, 21), such as "a certain interval difficult to assess, but unerringly timed by all" (23), give way to such potent images of distressed introspection as the final evocation of "a man in some unthinkable past for the first time" (63).

While Cage and Burroughs employ chance composition to diminish their own presence in the text and to generate new aesthetic experience, Beckett's use of fragmented narration consistently deplores the impossibility of reducing self-awareness or producing adequate art. Beckett's insistence upon his work's failure is perhaps beside the point; like Cage and Burroughs he is the author of inimitably individual texts. More significant here is Beckett's continual emphasis upon the impossibility of neutralizing painful self-awareness, be this by fragmenting narrative or by contorting narrative into "soothing" structures, like "a carefully folded ham-sandwich" (Beckett 1983b, 19).

Considered in Beckettian terminology, the fifth main postmodern mentality seems definable as the French structuralists' attempt to transform textual studies into analyses of soothing, carefully folded, narrative codes, purged of all authorial contamination. Resisting the temptation to consider texts in terms of crises of language, existential crises, national crises, or theories of chance-based creativity, structuralists such as Barthes initially argued that narrative "is not a matter of art (on the part of the narrator), but of structure" (1977, 89). Accordingly, "'What takes place' in a narrative is from the referential (reality) point of view literally *nothing;* what 'happens' is language alone" (124).

Taken to extremes, Barthes's melodramatic enthusiasm for "suppressing the Author" (143), for "deriding the Author" (144), for "the desacralization ... of the Author" (145), and so on, until one has symbolically "buried the Author" (146), leads to the assertion that the writer is never original and may only ever mix writings taken from a ready-made dictionary (146). Championing new novelists such as

Robbe-Grillet, Barthes enthusiastically applauded their intention "to assassinate the classical object" by asserting "the rapture of ... surface" in a world "stripped of its pathos" (1972, 16, 14, 21). Once again, Barthes's emotive rhetoric virtually bursts at its seams. Similarly, Robbe-Grillet's supposed attainment of fiction with "no alibi, no density, no depth" (Barthes 1972, 14) continually seems on the point of erupting with images of pathos, violence, and eroticism—images that Robbe-Grillet subsequently discussed in terms of his fiction's "fantasms" (Robbe-Grillet 1986, 10).

Some twenty years before the advent of structuralism and the new novel, Beckett's *Watt* (written in the mid-forties and first published in 1953) similarly charted the conflict between comforting face values and series of hypotheses rendering reality innocuous (Beckett 1963, 70, 75) and the disturbingly indefinable meticulous "phantoms" (74) "that resisted all Watt's efforts to saddle them with meaning, and a formula, so that he could neither think of them, nor speak of them, but only suffer them" (75–76).

Barthes himself subsequently discusses modes of photographic fantasm in *Camera Lucida* (1981), where he differentiates between the neutral realm of *studium,* or coded reality, and more mysterious and more valued modes of *punctum,* which he claims "*holds* me, though I cannot say why" (1981, 51).

Although Barthes acknowledges that certain photographs are based upon a structural rule (23) and therefore only provoke "a general, and, so to speak, *polite* interest" (27), he also insists that other images affect him "at a depth and according to roots which I do not know" (38), appealing to "a stilled center, an erotic or lacerating value buried in myself" (16). At this point, then, Barthes rediscovers and reasserts precisely the kind of subjective profundity that his earlier essays trivialized. Pondering upon a particularly moving photograph of his mother, Barthes's rhetoric glides into an elegiac, more or less symbolist register, as he describes himself as "a bad dreamer who vainly holds out his arms towards the possession of the image" (100). As he abandons his initial structuralist values, Barthes's argument and imagery become remarkably similar to the theme and scene of such late Beckettian plays as *Ohio Impromptu* and *Nacht und Traüme* (1982, in Beckett 1984), where other lost souls harken after traces of unspoken words heard in dreams (Beckett 1984, 286), and hold out their arms toward the comforting gestures of "Dreamt hands" (305). As I shall suggest, Beckett's images of ghostly affection typify the prevailing mood of rediscovered harmony and depth characterizing the seventh, most recent phase of postmodernism.

The sixth phase of postmodernism seems characterized above all by the poststructuralists' relativization and replacement of the structuralist project of tracing a line, by foregrounding "discontinuity . . . rupture, break, mutation, transformation" (Foucault 1972, 5)—all of the processes, in fact, that frustrate Watt's attempts to saddle existence with meaning (Beckett 1963, 75–76). Exemplified in terms of Foucault's discussion of his altered approach to the historical document, this poststructuralist emphasis takes as its task

> not the interpretation of the document, not the attempt to decide whether it is telling the truth or what is its expressive value, but to work on it from within and to develop it: history now organizes the document, divides it up, distributes it, orders it, arranges it in levels, establishes series . . . defines unities, describes relations. [6–7]

Alternatively, considered in terms of Derrida's writings, this diversification of focus can be seen in the shift from tangible textual structures to less tangible "traces of traces" (Derrida 1981, 26). Discussing this play of differences (27) in tandem with his concept of *différance,* Derrida explains:

> *Différance* is the systematic play of differences, of the traces of differences, of the *spacing* by means of which elements are related to each other. . . . Differences are the effects of transformations, and from this vantage the theme of *différance* is incompatible with the static . . . concept of *structure*. [27]

Taking this proliferation of perspectives one step further by considering the impact of the postmodern mass media upon the contemporary sensibility, Baudrillard has diagnosed the present as the age of simulation, characterized by "a liquidation of all referentials—worse: by their artificial resurrection in systems of signs, a more ductile material than meaning, in that it lends itself to all systems of equivalence . . . substituting signs of the real for the real itself" (1983a, 4). In such circumstances, Baudrillard argues that "the whole system becomes weightless, it is no longer anything but a gigantic simulacrum . . . never again exchanging for what is real, but exchanging in itself, in an uninterrupted circuit without reference or circumference" (10–11).

Having pushed the relativistic focus of poststructuralism beyond all referentials, Baudrillard's writings assume an increasingly literary register. Like John Cage's *Indeterminacy,* Baudrillard's *Amérique* (1986) and *Cool Memories* (1987) collect whimsical impressions of technological paradox and illusion, such as his glimpse of American television, "with its twenty-four-hour schedules, often to be seen functioning like an hallucination in the empty rooms of houses or vacant hotel rooms" (Baudrillard 1988b, 50). At this point, Baudrillard's prose virtually attains the poetic tone of Pierre Reverdy's mysterious images of such deserted interiors as the room in which someone "has left a sigh," or "The house no one enters" (Reverdy 1970, 22).

It is precisely this sense of hallucinatory wonder that seems to characterize the seventh, most recent postmodern mentality. At times this sensibility assumes an air of revived surrealism or symbolism. Baudrillard's memories of America refer quite explicitly to "the surrealist qualities of an ocean bed in the open air," and to the ways in which the surreality of magical metamorphic forms eliminates nature's more mundane picturesque qualities (1988b, 3, 8–9). Barthes's self-conscious reference to "a sentiment as certain as remembrance, just as Proust experienced it" (1981, 70) similarly aligns his vision with a modernist precursor.

Cage's and Burroughs's investigations of the chance intersections between their materials beg a slightly different definition. As Baudrillard very perceptively remarks, American culture appears to be characterized by a pragmatic, paradoxical humor and by an odd, everyday sense of extravagance (1988b, 79, 86). Baudrillard interestingly adds that this oddness is not surrealistic, insofar as "surrealism is an extravagance that is still aesthetic in nature and as such very European in inspiration" (86). While Cage and Burroughs refer at times to European precursors such as Duchamp and Tzara, their experiments with chance diverge from European modernism in at least three ways.

First, as Baudrillard suggests, there is something relatively dispassionate about Burroughs's and Cage's work—something pragmatic or everyday in the sense that their art is conceived of as part of life rather than part of some extraordinary realm beyond the everyday. Burroughs's essays, for example, treat chance relationships with a mixture of reverence and irreverence. Noting that "telepathic contact [is] used every day by ordinary people" and that "the unconscious was much more unconscious in Freud's day than ours," they offer the reader such odd, everyday advice as "certain pragmatic observations . . . useful for travellers in the magical universe" (Burroughs 1985b, 89, 100). As noted, Cage similarly equates his chance compositional practices with "the very life we're living" (1983, 12). Second, whereas Baudrillard associates the European aesthetic sensibility with those trapped within "the nineteenth-century bourgeois dream" (1988b, 73), Cage and Burroughs work within wider cultural frameworks, amalgamating American and European traditions with the tradition of the Orient

(Kostelanetz 1974, 84), and the world of "magic in Morocco" (Gysin and Wilson 1982, 127). Third, Cage's and Burroughs's contemporary influences tend to give their thinking a peculiarly contemporary streetwise quality.

Cage, for example, attributes his interest in such concepts as transparency to the way in which "a great deal of our experience comes from the vast use of glass in our architecture" (1987, 6). Rather than surrendering to the Jamesonian temptation of retreating from the present—Jameson complains that glass-fronted urban centers have "absolutely no perspective at all" (1986, 70)—Cage employs the new architecture to reorient his perceptions. Likewise in contrast to Jameson, who complains that "global multinational culture [has become] decentered" (1986, 70), Burroughs maintains that the traveler may discover extraordinary correspondences between memories, reading matter, and passing events, "if you really keep your eyes open." He amusingly explains: "I was reading Raymond Chandler, and one of his characters was an albino gunman. My God, if there wasn't an albino in the room" (1965, 28).

The anticlimactic detail "He wasn't a gunman" (28) deflates this hypothesis a little. Burroughs's exemplifications of his "psychosensory" (26) investigations are obviously both pragmatic and paradoxical. Nevertheless, for all their eccentricities, Burroughs's and Cage's chance experiments have the considerable advantage of precipitating extremely inventive creativity in an era in which theorists such as Jameson lament the dissolution of things (1986, 70) rather than exploring the "new connections between images" and the "merging of art and science" (Burroughs 1965, 25, 29).

Beckett's representations of the kind of harmony and coherence contributing to this seventh postmodern mentality are neither nostalgically modernist nor pragmatically paradoxical. Rather, Beckett seems to have abandoned his early images of partially resigned, partially grotesque, and partially impassioned anguish for carefully crafted images of affection, grace, and harmony. Whereas an early play such as *Endgame* (1958) is discussed by Beckett in terms of "the power of the text to claw" (1983b, 107), recent texts such as *Company* (1980), *Ill seen ill said* (1982), *Worstward Ho* (1983a), and *Nacht und Träume* (1982) all evoke what one might perhaps define as Beckett's antithetical power to becalm and console. These works are all quite different from Beckett's previous attempts to find a form to accommodate the mess, insofar as they progressively register maximal form with minimal mess; maximal form without any mess; and finally, the synthesis of what one might think of as "form" and "*mass,*" in the sense that their content suggests mysterious communion between the living and the dead.

Despite final reference to its narrator's inevitable suffering, "as you always were...Alone" (Beckett 1980, 89), *Company* hints at modes of peaceful presence in the company of others when, temporarily relieved from "the woes of your kind" (80), the narrating consciousness remembers, or imagines, a disintegrating idyll with some lost loved one. "Eyes in each other's eyes" (67), he feels "the fringe of her long black hair stirring in the still air" as they gaze at one another, "Within the tent of hair" (66). Significantly, this memory emerges "In your dark" (66), to a narrator who himself seems to be more dead than alive, "on his back in the dark" (7).

Commenting upon this otherworldly realm of discourse and dream, in which "A voice comes to one in the dark" (7), the American poet Robert Lax defines Beckett's world as deep sleep (1987, 34)—a zone that Beckett's *A Piece of Monologue* (1982) associates with existence "Beyond that black beyond," "Buried in who knows what profounds of mind" (Beckett 1984, 269, 288). Put another way, Beckett's accounts of deep memories, insights, and imaginings probe precisely the kind of deep time that Jameson finds irrelevant to our present existence (1986, 70). Lax movingly observes: "It is down there in deep sleep that Beckett lives, and where all of us live, but few in our time have been so expert in visiting that region, in staying there, and in bringing back a living report" (1987, 34).

As I have suggested, the most interesting aspect of these "reports" is their increasing emphasis upon harmonious, conciliatory visions. Like *Company, Ill seen ill said* concerns the attempt to look beyond the solitude and "old nausea" (Beckett 1982, 38) of existence, and offers brief glimpses of something more positive than the general "misfortune to be still of this world" (8). At its most elegiac, this text evokes occasions when "the eye closes in the dark and sees" the calm carefully balanced vista of a mysterious she, who, "in a twin movement full of grace," drinks from a bowl which "she slowly raises . . . toward her lips while at the same time with equal slowness bowing her head to join it" (35).

Beckett's *Worstward Ho* (1983a), another narrative located within a dim void animated by dim light (Beckett 1983a, 10), and evoking a consciousness vainly "gnawing to be naught" (46), similarly pauses to contemplate two adjacent figures, bowed in unison, and moving with equal plod. Peering into the dim void, the narrator "bit by bit" distinguishes an old man and child (12), observing: "Hand in hand with equal plod they go...Backs turned both bowed with equal plod they go. The child hand raised to reach the holding hand. Hold the old holding hand. Hold and be held" (13). Subsequent meditations attempt to minimize the impact of this image, by converting "the twain" (14) to "Topless baseless hind-trunks" (43). For all its formal felicity, this vision still seems to strike the narrator of *Worstward Ho* as being too poignant for comfort.

Nevertheless, Beckett's *Nacht und Träume,* a play for television first produced in 1982 and published in 1984, focuses yet again on the image of the benevolent "holding hand," offering one of Beckett's most explicit representations of form *without* mess. Set, once again, within the dark of an "empty room lit only by evening light" (Beckett 1984, 304), *Nacht und Träume* evokes the process by which a Dreamer contemplates rituals of comfort within the realm of a "kinder light," as "Dreamt hands" minister to his "dreamt self" (305). Mysteriously emerging from the "dark beyond and above," these hands rest gently on the dreamt self's head, convey a cup gently to the dreamt self's lips, and gently wipe the dreamt self's brow (305), to the accompaniment of softly hummed and softly sung versions of Schubert's *Nacht und Träume:* a song concluding *"Holde Träume, kehret wieder!"* — "Tender dreams, return!" (O'Brien 1987, 35).

Like Cage's emphasis upon the "co-being [of] elements paradoxical by nature [within] organic unity" (Kostelanetz 1974, 84), and Burroughs's recent references to the way in which the artist may locate those points where "inner and outer reality intersect" and reveal "the underlying unities of disparate elements" (Burroughs 1985a, 66), Beckett's celebrations of twin movements "full of grace" epitomize the unexpected coherence and confidence of much recent postmodern creativity. The significance of this positive creativity is at least twofold. First, it reminds us that postmodernism's poetics do not stagnate in the sixties and are not simply preoccupied with the crises of language, the crises of the self, and more collective national crises. Second, this creativity makes it evident that the postmodern sensibility is not simply reducible to the philosophical crises associated with poststructuralist relativism.

It may well be the case that "post-structuralists like Foucault, Derrida and Lyotard are postmodernists" (Sarup 1989, 131), in the sense that their work constitutes one of the seven postmodern mentalities outlined in this essay. But it seems oversimplistic to conclude that "there are so many similarities between post-structuralist theories and postmodern practices that it is difficult to make a clear distinction between them" (131). For all Jameson's assertions to the contrary, there appear to be few reasons for arguing that postmodern culture as a whole lacks "interpretive depth ... *philosophic* notions of depth ... historical depth [and] visual depth" (Jameson 1986, 69). On the contrary, the most recent works of postmodernism frequently assert a cohesion and a depth of significance quite at odds with the dominant claims of poststructuralist theory.

Significantly, there are already certain indications—such as Barthes's meditations upon *punctum* in *Camera Lucida,* and Baudrillard's celebration of magical vistas in *America*—that poststructuralist perspectives are themselves returning to the harmonious subjective concerns evoked by Beckett, Burroughs, and Cage. As the American artist Jenny Holzer breezily suggests in her dictum "I'd rather be reconstructivist than deconstructivist" (1986, 72), the attractions of postmodern creativity's innovations are perhaps even more interesting than its theoretical hesitations and recriminations.

To be sure, the reconstructivist impulse in postmodern creativity usually takes the form of predominantly literary or extrarational notions, such as Cage's concepts of purposeful purposelessness (Cage 1983, 12) and the omniattentive electronic soul (Kostelanetz 1974, 167), rather than satisfying Jürgen Habermas's appeal for communicative rationality and a purposive rational conduct of life (Habermas 1981, 8, 6). According to Habermas, aesthetic or conceptual experimentation is inadequate to the task of resolving the general cultural discontent that he associates with "deep-seated reactions against the process of *societal* modernization" (7). Put another way, "A rationalized everyday life ... could hardly be saved from cultural impoverishment through breaking open a single cultural sphere—art—and so providing access to just one of the specialized knowledge complexes" (11).

Habermas refers here to what he terms the failure of the surrealist rebellion (6), but his comments also raise crucial questions regarding the potential success or failure of the different modes of postmodern rebellion—be these the apocalyptic fictions of Baudrillardian theory or the apocalyptic theories of Burroughsian fiction. As becomes apparent, these facets of postmodernism both generate modes of communicative extrarationality. Baudrillard and Jameson, for example, succumb to the compulsion to write panic science fictions about the perils of being lost in hyperspace (Baudrillard 1988a, 36; Jameson 1986, 70), a term that becomes an all-purpose catchword for whatever aspects of contemporaneity they no longer feel sufficiently confident to confront.

In such circumstances, it is surely salutary that Habermas's more rational arguments for social and moral betterment are complemented by Beckett's, Burroughs's and Cage's visionary multimedia accounts of ethical, aesthetic, and existential coherence. Proposing a welcome positive alternative to the poststructuralist concept of hyperspace, Burroughs gives the term utopian rather than dystopian connotations when he asserts: "What you experience in dreams and out of the body trips, what you glimpse in the work of writers and painters, is the promised land of space" (1985b, 103).

While it is too early to assess the impact and influence of such creativity beyond the single cultural sphere of art, it seems appropriate to quote Burroughs's conviction that "artists and creative thinkers lead the way into space because they are already writing, painting and filming space" (102). Burroughs stirringly concludes:

> *We are not setting out to explore static pre-existing data.* We are setting out to *create* new worlds, new beings, new modes of consciousness. As Brion Gysin said, when they get there in their trillion dollar aqualungs they may find that the artists are already there. [1985b, 102]

References

Admussen, Richard L. *The Samuel Beckett Manuscripts: A Study.* Boston: G. K. Hall, 1979.

Barthes, Roland. *Critical Essays.* Translated by Richard Howard. Evanston, Ill.: Northwestern University Press, 1972.

————. *Image-Music-Text.* Translated by Stephen Heath. Glasgow: Collins, 1977.

————. *Camera Lucida.* Translated by Richard Howard. New York: Hill and Wang, 1981.

Baudrillard, Jean. *Simulations.* Translated by Paul Foss, Paul Patton, and Philip Beitchman. New York: Semiotext(e), 1983a.

————. "The Ecstasy of Communication." Translated by John Johnston. In *The Anti-Aesthetic,* edited by Hal Foster. Port Townsend, Wash.: Bay Press, 1983b.

————. "The Year 2000 Has Already Happened" (1985). Translated by Nai-dei Ding and Kuan-Hsin Chen. In *Body Invaders: Sexuality and the Postmodern Condition,* edited by Arthur Kroker and Marilouise Kroker. London: Macmillan, 1988a.

————. *America.* Translated by Chris Turner. London: Verso, 1988b.

Beckett, Samuel. "Dream of Fair to Middling Women." Unpublished typescript (Reading University [England] Library, Samuel Beckett Collection, MS 1227/7/16/8), 1933.

————. "Moody Man of Letters." Interview with Israel Shenker. *New York Times,* 6 May 1956.

————. "Beckett by the Madeleine." Interview with Tom F. Driver. *Columbia University Forum* 4 (1961): 21–25.

————. *Watt* (1953). London: John Calder, 1963.

————. *Proust and Three Dialogues with Georges Duthuit.* London: Calder and Boyars, 1965.

————. *Waiting for Godot* (1956). London: Faber, 1968.

————. *Lessness.* London: Calder and Boyars, 1970.

————. *The Lost Ones.* London: Calder and Boyars, 1972.

————. *Malone Dies* (1958). London: Calder and Boyars, 1975.

————. *Company.* London: John Calder, 1980.

————. *Ill seen ill said.* London: John Calder, 1982.

————. *Worstward Ho.* London: John Calder, 1983a.

————. *Disjecta: Miscellaneous Writings and a Dramatic Fragment.* Edited by Ruby Cohn. London: John Calder, 1983b.

————. *Not I* (1973). *Nacht und Träume* (1982). *Ohio Impromptu* (1982). *A Piece of Monologue* (1982). In *Collected Shorter Plays.* London: Faber, 1984.

Bockris, Victor. *With William Burroughs: A Report from the Bunker.* New York: Seaver Books, 1981.

Burroughs, William. "The Art of Fiction XXXVI." Interview with Conrad Knickerbocker. *Paris Review* 35 (1965): 13–49.

————. "Robert Walker's Spliced New York." *Aperture* 101 (1985a): 66.

————. *The Adding Machine: Collected Essays.* London: John Calder, 1985b.

Cage, John. "Notes on *Indeterminacy.*" Unpaginated notes, published with recording of *Indeterminacy* (1959).

————. *Silence.* Middletown, Conn.: Wesleyan University Press, 1983.

————. "Interview with Nicholas Zurbrugg." *Eyeline* 1 (1987): 6–7.

Derrida, Jacques. *Positions.* Translated by Alan Bass. Chicago: University of Chicago Press, 1981.

Eagleton, Terry. "Capitalism, Modernism and Postmodernism." *New Left Review* 152 (1985); 60–73.

Eco, Umberto. *Travels in Hyper-Reality.* Translated by William Weaver. London: Picador, 1987.

Federman, Raymond. "Fiction Today or the Pursuit of Non-Knowledge." *Journal of Art, Performance and Manufacture* 1 (1977): 9–16.

Foucault, Michel. *The Archeology of Knowledge* and *The Discourse on Language.* Translated by A. M. Sheridan-Smith. New York: Pantheon, 1972.

Ginsberg, Allen. *Howl* (1956) and "Notes for *Howl* and Other Poems." In *The New American Poetry,* edited by Donald M. Allen. New York: Grove Press, 1960.

Grass, Günter. *Headbirths: or The Germans Are Dying Out.* Translated by Ralph Manheim. New York: Penguin Books, 1984.

Gysin, Brion, and Burroughs, William. *The Third Mind.* London: John Calder, 1979.

Gysin, Brion, and Wilson, Terry. *Here to Go: Planet R-101.* San Francisco: Re/
Search Publications, 1982.

Habermas, Jürgen. "Modernity versus Postmodernity." Translated by Seyla
Ben-Habib. *New German Critique* 22 (1981): 3–14.

Holzer, Jenny. *Signs.* Des Moines, Iowa: Des Moines Art Center, 1986.

Jameson, Fredric. "Postmodernism, or the Cultural Logic of Late Capitalism."
New Left Review 146 (1984): 53–92.

————. "Interview with Anders Stephanson." *Flash Art* (international edition)
131 (1986): 69–73.

Janco, Marcel. "Dada at Two Speeds." Translated by Margaret I. Lippard. In
Dadas on Art, edited by Lucy R. Lippard. Englewood Cliffs, N.J.: Prentice-
Hall, 1971.

Jencks, Charles. *Post-Modernism: The New Classicism in Art and Architecture.* London: Academy Editions, 1987.

Kostelanetz, Richard. *John Cage.* London: Allen Lane, 1974.

————. *The Theatre of Mixed Means.* New York: RK Editions, 1980.

————. *Conversing with Cage.* New York: Limelight Editions, 1987.

Kroker, Arthur, and Kroker, Marilouise. "Theses on the Disappearing Body in
the Hyper-Modern Condition." In *Body Invaders: Sexuality and the Post-
Modern Condition,* edited by Arthur Kroker and Marilouise Kroker. London: Macmillan, 1988.

Lax, Robert. "Beckett and *Deep Sleep.*" *Review of Contemporary Fiction* 2
(1987): 34.

Leyland, Winston. *Gay Sunshine Interviews.* San Francisco: Gay Sunshine
Press, 1978.

Lyotard, Jean-François, and Thébaud, Jean-Loup. *Just Gaming.* Translated by
Wlad Godzich. Manchester [England]: Manchester University Press, 1985.

Müller, Heiner. "Reflections on Post-Modernism." *New German Critique* 16
(1979a): 55–57.

————. "An Interview with Heiner Müller." Interview with Ingrid Eggers. *Theater* 1 (1979b): 83–84.

————. "The Walls of History." Interview with Sylvère Lotringer. *Semiotexte*
2 (1982): 36–76.

————. *Hamletmachine and Other Texts for the Stage.* Translated by Carl
Weber. New York: Performing Arts Journal Publications, 1984.

O'Brien, Michael. "A Note on *Ill Seen Ill Said* and a Note on Criticism." *Review
of Contemporary Fiction,* 2 (1987); 35–39.

Poggioli, Renato. *The Theory of the Avant-Garde.* Translated by Gerald Fitz-
gerald. Cambridge, Mass.: Harvard University Press, 1968.

Pountney, Rosemary. "The Structuring of *Lessness.*" *Review of Contemporary
Fiction* 2 (1987): 55–73.

Reverdy, Pierre. "Sun" and "Nomad." Translated by Anna Balakian. In *Modern
European Poetry,* edited by Willis Barnstone. New York: Bantam, 1970.

Robbe-Grillet, Alain. "Confessions of a Voyeur." Interview with Roland Caputo.
Tension 10 (1986): 10–11.

Sarup, Madan. *Post-Structuralism and Postmodernism.* Athens: University of Georgia Press, 1989.

Steiner, George. *Language and Silence* (1967). New York: Penguin Books, 1969.

Weber, Carl. "Heiner Müller: The Despair and the Hope." *Performing Arts Journal* 12 (1980): 135–40.

Zurbrugg, Nicholas. "Postmodernity, *Métaphore manquée,* and the Myth of the Trans-avant-garde." *SubStance* 48 (1986): 68–90.

4   A Cryptanalysis of Beckett's *Molloy*

Angela Moorjani

I n puzzling over the patterns of repetition in *Molloy,* readers might want to keep in mind two passages on decrypting that Beckett embedded into the novel. For like Dante's *Commedia* and Proust's *Recherche*—to mention only two of an illustrious tradition—*Molloy* is an exploration of writing as reading a cryptic text inscribed within. I am thinking of the two instances when the narrators Molloy and Moran, who rarely give way to affection or rapture, do so on being faced with an indecipherable artifact or code. In these passages, the contemplation of two enigmas—Molloy's knife rest and Moran's dance of the bees—whose formal patterning of horizontal and vertical repetitions, variations, and reversals echo the novel's construction, leads to the narrators' jubilant mediations on the ultimately indeterminable.

The rapture of unreadability—what Barthes terms the *jouissance* of the writerly text—by no means precludes the pleasure of repeated attempts at understanding (1974, 1975). Thus Molloy and Moran study the figures that will continue to baffle them, and according to their diverse ways the first gives a formalist reading, the second, a functional analysis. These miniature replicas of the novel, a technique of interior duplication already amply evident in *Murphy* and *Watt,* suggest that writers as readers and their readers in turn engage in multiple bids at understanding cryptic texts against a horizon of unknowingness. It is within this purview that I link the novel's writerly explorations to a number of theories concerning cryptanalysis and aesthetic process.

This essay is dedicated to P.G.

53

Self-division and Cryptanalysis

For *Molloy,* Beckett adopts the labyrinthine and circular form of novels of reminiscence, such as Proust's *Recherche,* only to explode the
genre by infinite duplication on the one hand and negation on the
other. Parodied too, or so it would seem, are most of the poetic alle-
gories of self-discovery to which writers have repeatedly turned, such
as the descent into the underworld, followed by rebirth, resurrection,
or paradise; the fall and redemption; the odyssey out and back; family
romances and quest narratives, particularly oedipal mysteries in
which seeker and sought are one. These are mocked in the manner
familiar to spectators of *Godot,* where waiting is endless, for in the
earlier *Molloy,* it is the wanderings that are deprived of a reachable
goal and ultimately annulled. With *Molloy,* then, Beckett has at the
same time given us another turn in the mystic quest for self with
which modernism replaced the religious ascent of the soul and pulled
off a postmodern spoof on the entire tradition.

    Molloy, of course, is also a self-reflexive fiction about how it came
to be written. The novel contains three first-person teller/told pairs,
the first of which is the extradiegetic writer of the preamble, who
situates himself in his mother's room. This anonymous writer, who
composes quite unwillingly the work imposed on him from without,
presents himself to the reader as unknowing and unable. His is the
famous Beckettian predicament of the writer obliged to write, who,
unable to write, writes. The previously composed narrative that he
introduces is divided into two fragments of equal length; the first recounts Molloy's vain quest for his mother, the second, Jacques Moran's
equally vain hunt for Molloy.

    So many views have been put forward on the relation between the
two parts of *Molloy* that it is quite impossible to summarize them
here. Exegetes have in particular argued about the simultaneity or
sequencing of the two segments, with many adopting Edith Kern's
contention that Molloy's part follows Moran's chronologically (1959,
188–89). According to my view, the preamble's writer, in a series of
proliferating schisms, has split himself into two opposing surrogates
(Molloy/Moran), who in turn divide into pairs and pairs of pairs, two
becoming four becoming eight, and so on, in an unending sequence
of doublings. At the same time, the Molloy segment is contained
within the Moran text in the manner of the unconscious within the
conscious, with this double story or palimpsest forming only a part of
an infinite series of texts within texts (Moorjani 1982, 39–46, 108).

    It is striking to what extent *Molloy*'s nonlinear topology of infinite bifurcations and duplications corresponds to what mathematicians term "period doublings" and identify with the dynamic order within chaos.[1] Continuing presocratic and romantic meditations on chaos, and at the same time anticipating the detailed mathematical theories worked out in the seventies, Beckett's novels of the forties show an astonishing intuitive understanding of this engrossing phenomenon. For in *Molloy,* Moran's orderly and Molloy's disorderly texts exist as aspects of the artistic process in the manner of the orderly disorder of chaos.

The self-division into opposites that the novel stages is further emphasized by two interior duplications: in the first, Molloy sees two figments, A and C, walk in opposite directions, and in the second, Moran is accosted by the same antithetical specters, with whom he identifies. The duality of the artistic imaginary, which is here being repeatedly reenacted, has behind it an extensive history in aesthetic theory. Among the most influential, since it continued a long tradition and launched another, is the theory of art Schelling developed in 1800 in his *System of Transcendental Idealism* (part 6). Indeed, Schelling's influence on the work of Hegel, Schopenhauer, Nietzsche, and Heidegger and on subsequent theories of aesthetics would be hard to overestimate. Schelling's dialectical treatment of artistic consciousness is particularly apropos for a reading of *Molloy* (among other modern works of art), for the philosopher depicts artistic process as a self divided from self, contemplating its otherness and harmonizing or synthesizing the conscious and the unconscious. It is well recognized that Schelling's theory in turn owes much to Jacob Boehme, the mystic philosopher, who in the early 1600s conceived the doctrine of god's self-differentiation into opposing forces. How much Boehme in turn owes to cabbalist thought, and that in turn to gnosticism's notion of divine self-division, is difficult to determine. Important, though, is that mystic thinkers, philosophers of art, psychoanalysts, and artists themselves concur that the experience of the exile of self from self is the basic experience of the creative or aesthetic process. Since this vision of exteriority is particularly identified with the gnostics, it is not surprising that artists—among whom Beckett, as we shall see—continue to be drawn to their speculations.

If we return to Schelling's manipulation of these dualistic concepts, it is the contradiction within the self between the conscious (spiritual) and the unconscious (sensual) that is at the origin of the artist's involuntary activity: "It can only be the contradiction between conscious and unconscious in the free act which sets the artistic urge in motion; just as, conversely, it can be given to art alone to pacify our endless striving, and likewise to resolve the final and uttermost contradiction within us" (1978, 222). The reconciliation of the inner conflicts is made possible by an unknown absolute containing "the common ground of the preestablished harmony between the conscious and the unconscious" (221). This "dark unknown force," radiating back from the work of art and fleetingly visible in the work's interstices, cannot appear as such (222). Although Schelling tends to suggest that it is within art's power to attain the absolute, his transcendent ground is ultimately akin to the gnostics' absent god and Boehme's divine indeterminacy ("Nothing is nothing but a *stillness* without stirring"),[2] which can only stand behind artistic or mystic odysseys as a postulate (Vater 1978, xxxi–xxxv).

In psychoanalytic thought, these religious and philosophical conceptions of self-differentiation and exile find an echo particularly in the topology of mourning. I am thinking of the permanent incorporation of the lost one into an ego divided from itself that Freud hypothesized for abnormal mourning (*S.E.* 14:249) and of the *fort/da* game and its interconnections with what in *Molloy* is termed the "fatal pleasure principle" (Beckett 1965, 99). The Freudian splitting of the ego has recently been extended by Maria Torok and Nicolas Abraham's concept of encrypting. In their work on incorporation, discussed by Derrida in "Fors," the lost one, a living dead with whom the mourner identifies, is encrypted into an "artificial unconscious," a place of exile marked out within the ego (Derrida 1986, xix). This inner crypt's paradoxical status as an exterior interiority or an interior exteriority is emphasized by Derrida's reading in "Fors" and recalls the gnostic/cabbalist versions of fracture and creation. Similarly, in *Glas,* in commenting on the inner crypt that Jean Genet in his essay on Giacometti describes as "a secret wound" within each subject, Derrida identifies it with the artist's splintered signature that is at the origin of a work of art (Genet 1979, 42; Derrida 1981, 2:257).

It is Melanie Klein, though, who most insistently linked artistic process to the subject's mourning of early loss (beginning with birth). According to Kleinian psychoaesthetic theory, the mourner and the artist both rehearse or repeat the infant's earliest ties and experiences of grief, first the fantasmatic loss of self because of a destructive (m)other, and then, in reverse, the loss of the (m)other because of a destructive self. Such aggressive fantasies of death and fragmentation bring with them a depressive load of guilt toward an object both hated and loved and the desire to make reparation (Klein 1975, 210–18, 262–89). In *The Hidden Order of Art,* Anton Ehrenzweig, following Melanie Klein, posits a similar confounding of contrary forces in artistic production—the projection of death and fragmentation yields to libidinal fusion in an oscillatory swing typical of the child's earliest fantasies. The function of artistic work is to shape or harmonize this ordered disorder of the unconscious into the disordered order of a work of art.

What these psychoanalytic theories share with Schelling and his mystic predecessors is the schema of psychological self-division; in the manner of the horizontal and vertical schisms postulated for *Molloy,* this schema may be envisioned as both a conscious/unconscious layering and as a dialectic of opposing forces that, beyond the repetition of pendular swings to and fro, *fort* and *da,* it is the function of art to confound. Outside or beyond the dialectic lurks the nothingness that is Beckett's most fervent attraction, akin to the Freudian "Nirvana" principle and to Schelling's and the mystics' absolute ground.

The conscious/unconscious textual duality that the above theories posit, particularly the concept of encrypting, require intricate decrypting maneuvers to translate from one level to the other. Of course, just such conscious/unconscious layering in dreams, narrative reminiscences, jokes, and artworks led Freud to develop a method of cryptanalysis in *The Interpretation of Dreams.* Instead of the terms he used—that is, *manifest* and *latent* for *dream content* and *dream thoughts*—I will use *conscious discourse* and *subtext* in line with Freud's insistence on the materiality of the text and the decipherment of signs. (Subtext here has the double meaning of an already constituted text occurring in a new one; and an indirect message subtending what is literally expressed, both of which apply to "latent thoughts.")

In *The Interpretation of Dreams,* Freud would have the dream discourse read in the manner of a written (hieroglyphic) text whose code the reader must break in order to understand the message. This, then, is a lesson in decrypting a text that, unlike the transparent pictographic narrative it might be taken to be, is coded in an unfamiliar script. In the distinction made by Roman Jakobson, Freud proceeds not in the manner of a "decoder" who already knows the language, but in the manner of a "cryptanalyst" who must first break the code in order to decipher the message (Jakobson and Halle 1971, 28).

Abraham and Torok's extension of Freud's splintered ego into the concept of the inner crypt also includes further meditations on cryptanalytic or "cryptonymic" techniques. In *The Wolf Man's Magic Word,* they define "cryptonyms" as fetish words that cover up or screen one key word, a secret word that remains lost in the fractured ego's artificial unconscious or crypt (1986, 16–19). The link between cryptonyms and the unconscious word is partly phonological, that is, involving a homonymic or punning multiplicity of meanings, and partly semantic, that is, involving numerous synonyms for the one hidden word. The secret term can be traced, albeit with great difficulty, by recording such recurring phonological and semantic substitutions across several languages. (It is not surprising that "cryptonymy" in turn recalls gnostic and cabbalist disguises of secret words.)

The stage has now been set for a cryptanalysis of *Molloy,* in which Moran's part may be taken as the conscious discourse and Molloy's segment as its unconscious subtext, these being only two in an infinite sequence of embedded archives. According to this view, multiple instances of displacement, identification, composites, and cryptonyms serve to associate one text with the other. And since it is the unconscious subtext that the conscious discourse disguises and transforms, the Molloy section precedes the Moran narrative in the novel's presentation.

In *The Interpretation of Dreams,* Freud had given a perspicacious linguistic analogy for the splitting of the dreamer's self or "I" into several "I"s in the manner of *Molloy*'s three first-person narrators: "The fact that the dreamer's own ego [*Ich*] appears several times, or in several forms, in a dream is at bottom no more remarkable than that the ego [*Ich*] should be contained in a conscious thought several times or in different places or connections—e.g. in the sentence 'when *I* think what a healthy child *I* was'" (*S.E.* 4:323). The English translation of the German *Ich* into "ego" unfortunately obscures Freud's thoughtful link of oneiric identification with the shifting or deictic terms of discourse and the speaking of self as divided from self. In *Molloy,* the fracturing of the "I" is multiple, since not only is the narrative "I" of the preamble divided into Molloy's "I" and into Moran's "I," but each of the latter two, in the manner of retrospective self-narrations, is splintered into teller/told "I"s (as in Freud's example). The extent to which the "I"s are but disguises (as are the personages' names) becomes more and more obvious in the subsequent volumes of the Trilogy, where the narrators attempt to dispossess themselves of the first person, as in the Unnamable's contention, "I seem to speak, it is not I, about me, it is not about me" (Beckett 1965, 291).

In line with the construction of Beckett's novel, let us look first at Molloy's narration, which at its outset stages the oneiric descent into the inner depths, suggesting an "unreal" excursion of the artist's imaginary in a "mythological present" or mythic temporality (Beckett 1965, 16, 26). Sounded at the very beginning of the journey within is the refrain of transgression and guilt that Melanie Klein locates on the path from aggression to sublimation: "Fault? That was the word. But what fault?" (8). Not surprisingly, then, within a Kleinian perspective, Molloy's body is falling to pieces, as he commences his journey toward the maternal figure.

Molloy's description of the imaginary mother is surely among the most repulsively aggressive (and burlesque) of modern literature. He calls her "Mag"—perhaps a blend of "Ma" and "hag"—because the "Ma" satisfies his desire for his mother, and the "g" his need to deny her (17). It's the love/hate relation to the mother expressed in a short clipped syllable. Then, in a vengeful reversal of fantasized maternal cruelty, Molloy projects the early suffering image of self onto Mag: she is a monstrous infant, incontinent, babbling, incapable of understanding. To get money out of her, Molloy resorts to nonverbal pounding on her head, only to end up stealing from her instead. It's a striking instance of vengeful greed directed against a maternal ogre reduced to a fantasmatic mirror image of the early shattered self.

On his way to this loved/hated figure of life and death, Molloy is hindered not only by physical disintegration but by phallic and matric figures of the law (and by inner imperatives) that enigmatically—in the manner of the double bind—both deter him and launch him in the direction of his mother. Looming much larger than the oedipal figures of the policeman and sergeant who first stop and threaten him, then send him on his way, or than the charcoal burner whom Molloy attacks when he bars his way to his mother, is Sophie Loy or Lousse, a figuration of the matric law (and a reminder of *loi,* the French for "law"). The oedipal law of the father is overshadowed by the pre-oedipal law of the mother. Thus, in Lousse's domain, as much paradise as inferno, Molloy spends a year or so. This central episode of the Molloy script multiplies mythic references to the androgynous Great Mother in a ferociously ironic vain. In a striking instance of a composite formation, Loy-Lousse suggests Hecate, the triple moon goddess of the underworld, who with her hounds guards the gates of Hades; Cybele, the Phrygian *Magna Mater,* whose son and lover Attis bleeds to death after castrating himself under a pine tree; and the gnostic Sophia, divine wisdom and creator in female form, and according to one tradition, the emanation of an unknowable, hidden divinity.

Within this cryptic underworld, in which the maternal figure/Muse is both male and female, hated and loved, spectral and alive, Molloy details the buried aliveness of the artistic imaginary. (For a detailed discussion of the mythic subtexts, see Moorjani 1987, 149–54.) As hypothesized by Klein, Ehrenzweig, and others, Molloy oscillates between the aggressive/libidinal polarities of artistic process in relation to the (m)other. On the one hand he imagines himself the dismembered victim of the Great Mother of life, death, and rebirth, who holds him prisoner, and on the other he depicts a manic fusion or enwombing with Loy/Lousse's paradisiacal garden, a oneness further underscored by the names Molloy/Loy.

Missing, however, from the Lousse episode, which is staged like a descent into the underworld, embedded within the descent into the underworld that is Molloy's "unreal journey" to his mother (or like a dream within a dream), are the pardon, enlightenment, and rebirth that other travelers have gained from their travails. Instead, at the end of a year's turn of seasons in Lousse's garden, Molloy hears a "small voice" telling him to leave (59).

Similarly, in the narrative surrounding the central Lousse episode, which doubles his journey to his mother, Molloy chronicles his failure to reach her. He ends instead in a ditch at the rim of the forest, suggesting both the womb and tomb, the in-between realm of artistic gestation, but outside of sacred maternal enclosures. There he teeters on the edge of beginning or ending, in the cryptic exiled state of lifelessness and death-lessness from which in Beckett there is no redemption.

That Beckett would have placed the unconscious subtext before its conscious transformation is not surprising, since it is this procedure that permits readers to recognize the multiple instances of displacement and overdetermination that crisscross from one narrative to the other. Or in terms of Ehrenzweig's *Hidden Order of Art,* it permits shifting back and forth between the "hidden order" of the artist's chaotic unconscious and the hidden disorder of conscious ways of seeing (1967, 4–5). Or to use a musical model, as Beckett is fond of doing, for instance by embedding into *Watt* compositions echoing the novel's polyphonic structure, the Molloy and Moran texts are akin to two-part counterpoint, in which the theme may appear in the upper voice in inverted form, with the motifs undergoing further variations by diminution and augmentation in the manner of Freudian condensation and displacement. And like the structure in Schönberg, to whose work Beckett has stated his affinity (Gruen 1969, 210), *Molloy* lacks a (tonal) center to which the other elements refer. It is up to the reader to align the two parts vertically as well as to trace the horizontal (melodic) variations in order to work through the novel's complex contrapuntal texture against an ultimate horizon of silence.

In the most immediately apparent instance of inversion at work in the two-part novel, Moran rewrites Molloy's maternal subtext in terms of the paternal. In general, Molloy's son/mother relation is recast as Moran's son/father identification and rivalry, with each duality screening the third figure of the oedipal triangle. Whereas Molloy merges with the mother, Moran identifies with Youdi, who, it will now become clear, is the patriarchal equivalent of the first part's Sophia. The garden episodes of the two narratives are maternal/paternal variations parodying Eden and the gnostics' degraded creation myth. (More on this later.)

The Molloy/Moran double story is thus a mother-father palimpsest, with the more archaic maternal order everywhere legible within the paternal. And in the manner of cryptanalysis, the occulted Molloy subtext can be decrypted from the Moran narrative. This may be illustrated by focusing on Martha (one can't help notice the "Ma"), who functions as the servant in Moran's patriarchal domain. This peripheral personage of the Moran narrative screens the formidable composite Loy/Lousse of the Molloy subtext, in whose matriarchal realm, by contrast, it is males who serve. By displacement, the patriarchal marginalization of the maternal so obvious in the Moran narrative conceals and reveals the matric power foregrounded in the Molloy part.

Smaller motifs further associate the two domains and their figures. For example, along the lines of the bad oral mother fantasy, both Molloy and Moran suspect Lousse/Martha of tampering with their beer and poisoning their food; Moran/Molloy are voyeurs spied upon by voyeurs; both allude to contradictory imperatives, guilt, and divine messengers; they describe their own tombs and being buried alive, and refer to a number of objects, such as a lacquered tray and a silver knife rest with which Moran toys and which Molloy describes as an object over which he could puzzle endlessly. In the manner of oneiric condensation, the two garden narratives are identical and opposite.

These examples related to the two garden sequences, which emphasize female/male inversions, are only a few among multiple instances of overdetermination in the double text pointing to the two in one of the artistic imaginary. Once the reader is convinced of the novel's conscious/unconscious layering, the textual repetitions that many commentators have pondered can be related to the subject's split into two conflicting selves. Of the many reiterations that emphasize the identity of the two personages, their progressively disintegrating bodies (especially the legs) and oedipal and preoedipal fusions and aggressions, the endless questing, and the lyrical outpouring about hats, dogs, and bicycles are most immediately evident. As narrators, both fuss about verb tenses, names, and namelessness, and speculate about the ultimate status of their discourse as a texture of lies. Of those repetitions that point to Molloy/Moran as opposites, one might mention that Molloy's manipulation of sixteen sucking stones

and Moran's reflection on sixteen disconcerting theological questions suggest the sensual/spiritual contradiction. And the much-
commented-upon encounter with a shepherd and his dog, in whose
midst Molloy casts himself as a victim and Moran sees himself as the
butcher, stages the tormentor/tormented, saved/damned two-in-
oneness that recurs throughout Beckett's work and which he repeatedly links to symmetrical figures such as Cain and Abel (the "A" and
"C" in *Molloy*'s English version) and the two thieves (in the French
Molloy [1951, 61]). Indeed, there are hints that Beckett meant to emphasize the Molloy/Moran opposition by associating them to the gnostic revision of the Cain and Abel story. Not only are the two figments
at the beginning of the Molloy narrative designated as A and C (in the
English version), with A for Moran's mirror image and C for Molloy's,
but the emblems associated with the novel's dual persona are those
the gnostics applied to Cain and Abel. Cain-Molloy is linked to the
lower elements of water and earth, whereas Abel-Moran is associated
with the upper element of fire (Jonas 1963, 205). In the kind of po-
lemical reversal of usual religious doctrine in which the gnostics de-
lighted (and Beckett with them), it is Cain (or C), the fugitive vaga-
bond, who is an agent of *gnosis,* of the divine spirit, and a symbol of
Christ, all of which is echoed in Moran's description of the man with
the stick and his own subsequent inner metamorphoses (Jonas 1963,
95; Beckett 1965, 145–49). In contrast, since the gnostics devalued
fire, the Heraclitean primary material, a step leading eventually to the
conception of fire as the hellish element, Abel and his burning sacri-
fice are particularly condemned (Jonas 1963, 198–99). In *Molloy,* the
attacks on demonic fire figures include the patriarchal thunder god
(Youdi), the charcoal burner, and the Abel surrogates, among which is
the specter Moran kills in the hallucinatory meeting with the A and C
doubles.

In accordance with the conscious/unconscious schism, when on
descending into his psyche in search of Molloy, Moran comes upon
the disordered opposite to his ordered self, he denies any relation. He
emphasizes that Molloy fills him with confusion and causes him to
dissolve from solid into liquid (1965, 148–49), a process that the
reiterated play on the word *mollify* underscores. Instead of recognizing himself in Molloy, Moran represses this negative mirror image and
projects it onto his son. In this manner, Molloy is legible not only by
focusing from text to subtext but by tracing within the Moran narrative the protagonist's denials and projections. As one follows this decrypting process, it becomes apparent that in the manner of conden-

sation, in which one figure may stand for many or many may stand for one, Moran's son is another transformation of Molloy.

Perhaps the most astounding instance of the process of denial and projection is to be found in the reiterated death-of-god theme. On the conscious level, Moran is a meticulously practicing Catholic who denies his godlessness. But when he receives communion, he notices that the host has no effect on him; indeed, when he thanks Father Ambrose for the exceptional communion, the priest replies, "Peuh . . . des bêtises" in the original French (1951, 156), which is translated as "Pah! . . . it's nothing" (1965, 101). Such light bantering occults the "dying god" motif of the Molloy subtext, which is staged in the fantasmatic scene of the killing and burial of Teddy, Lousse's dog. This incident suggests an oneiric equivalent of Moran's loss of religious anchors by its cryptonymic play on words—*dog* in English is an anagram of *god,* and "Theodore" means "gift of god" in Greek—and by its multiple mythic echoes, particularly the biblical Fall and Frazer's "dying god" motif associated with the "burying mother."

The amplified "dying god" theme of the Molloy subtext—whose ubiquity in the artistic imaginary was pointed out by Ehrenzweig (1967)—is further screened by the frequent peripheral asides in the Moran narrative that juxtapose an animal or a dog with god. When the narrating Moran recalls the dog Zulu who disgusts him, he writes, "It's a strange thing, I don't like men and I don't like animals. As for God, he is beginning to disgust me" (105). Since the French version of the dog's name, "Zoulou," is a close anagram of "Lousse," it points to another instance of inversion between the two parts. At first refusing to recognize his godlessness, Moran not only represses it into his unconscious, where it receives amplification, but projects it onto Jacques, whom he suspects of skipping mass to play behind the slaughterhouse. This dizzying dispersal of a number of mythological and biblical stories into reverberating fragments is an example of one of Beckett's fiercest attacks on the obsessive fantasy of the artistic imaginary knotting artistic process to the family romance and parental (superego) narratives.

Ultimately, Moran's quest for Molloy, although taking him in the direction of the chaotic other into whom he would seem to be dissolving, is as tentative as Molloy's melding with cosmic turmoil: "And there was another noise, that of my life become the life of this garden as it rode the earth of deeps and wildernesses" (49). Such manic fusions are only moments of the artist's itinerary that reverse to anxious dispersions of self, and then back again, unless confounded or harmonized. For Beckett, though, there is no resolution of conflicts but an endless to-and-fro between contradictory forces within. All that his writer/narrators might hope to do is unwrite themselves in the direction of anonymity and dissolve the contraries into silence. As Moran puts it, what he was doing was neither for Molloy nor for himself but for a cause that was "in its essence anonymous" (114). Likewise Molloy, who has great difficulty recalling names, including his own, writes that his "sense of identity was wrapped in namelessness" (31).

Anonymity, Exteriority, and a Gnostic Aesthetics

Although at times it would seem that Moran is merging with Molloy and Molloy with the (m)other in an unending sequence of displacements, these are but illusory fusions soon again split apart. Molloy and Moran's double quest only appears to take them in the direction of self-knowledge and an authentic self, for finally it is just this teleology that the novel denies for a radical exteriority. Thus, the patriarchal law (Youdi/Yahweh) that commands Moran to find Molloy and the matriarchal law (Sophie Loy/Lousse) that demands that Molloy join his mother—these two inverted oneiric figurations—are but fantasmatic (nightmare) variations on the ultimately unnameable. Similarly, Molloy/Moran's lying texts detailing falsely circular journeys fail to return to the beginning or to end. What remains at the end of Moran's report, which he terms a lie just as Molloy does his own quoting from "something gone wrong with the silence" (88), is the call to an exteriority not yet tried. In a reference akin to Molloy's "small voice," Moran speaks of a language—not to be confused with angel messages or human speech—yet to be decrypted.

Beckett thus would demystify artistic process by wrenching it free from the sacred mother-father inscriptions with which it has been entangled at least since late classical antiquity, when artists began to identify their activity with a divine maternal muse and divine generativity (Kris and Kurz 1979, 43ff.). Accordingly, he devised *Molloy*'s illusory play of figments over an unknowable ground of chaos or silence. Unlike Rilke, whom he criticized in a 1934 review, Beckett refuses to identify the writer's "fidgets," so wonderfully exemplified by the self-annihilating journeys of Molloy/Moran, with "God, Ego, Orpheus" (Beckett 1984, 67).

In order to emphasize the nonanthropomorphic nature of the anonymous voice heard by his double persona, Beckett multiplies allusions to bird song and the dance of the bees. (That honeybees and birds are generally associated with artistic productivity and sublimation is clearly apropos.) Moran insists, "I would never do my bees the wrong I had done my God, to whom I had been taught to ascribe my angers, fears, desires, and even my body" (169), and specifies that in order to understand the language of the birds he would have no recourse to his own (175). Finally, like the threne, descant, and rhythmic frog croaking in *Watt,* the bees' dance and bird song are "musical" echoes of the novel's composition. Moran finds that the buzzing accompanying the figures traced by his bees serves not to emphasize but to *vary* the dance, as do the three or four levels at which the dance is being performed. Molloy, too, compares the words he utters without understanding their meaning to the buzzing of an insect (50). This foregrounding of signifiers (without signifieds), which Molloy extends to signs in all sensory modalities, is further reenforced by Moran's rapturous conclusion, "Here is something I can study all my life, and never understand" (169), which is a lesson in not knowing, not understanding. And although the novel's transformation of divine imperatives into inner voices that are associated in turn with natural languages brings to mind romantic nature and identity philosophy, especially Schelling's notion of an absolute identity behind both the psyche and nature, Beckett is intent on reversing Schelling's eventual designation of the indeterminate as absolute "I" (ego) and later as god.

As an aside, it is interesting to note to what extent Beckett follows and deviates from Karl von Frisch's decipherment of the bees' code. Moran's first hypothesis—the hum emphasizes the dance—is the correct one according to von Frisch, since both the wagging dance tempo and the number of bursts of sound produced by the flapping wings indicate the distance to the food source (1971). Nor have the levels at which the bees dance been found to vary the message. Moran's version of the dance of the bees, then, is an imaginary construction corresponding to Beckett's polyphonic novel about artistic process.

One of the most pleasurable aspects of Beckett's writing is its force of reverberation with philosophical thought. But somewhat like certain eighteenth-century *philosophes* who approached philosophical inquiry with serious playfulness, he does anything but flaunt the philosophical import or intertexts of his works. (The early writing is an exception.) In relation to the demythologizing of the artistic process in *Molloy,* I find of particular relevance the projects of Anaximander and other presocratic thinkers, who set out to describe genesis in (abstract) material terms, outside mythic and religious (mother-father) categories. Moreover, the parallels between Anaximander's concept of the indefinite and Beckettian silence are striking. According to Anaximander, pondering in the sixth century B.C., the indefinite is the primary stuff from which everything comes into being and into which everything returns as a result of the continuous strife of opposite forces (Kirk et al. 1983, 105–20). In his *Philosophy in the Tragic Age of the Greeks,* in which he quotes the following formulation of Anaximander's thought—"Where the source of things is, to that place they must also pass away, according to necessity, for they must pay penance and be judged for their injustices, in accordance with the ordinance of time"—Nietzsche found the presocratic philosopher to be a "true pessimist" (1962, 45–46). Indeed, Nietzsche gives a Schopenhauerian (or ultimately gnostic) explanation of Anaximander's injustice by interpreting it in the light of Schopenhauer's guilt of birth and all coming into being, for which penance is exacted by living and dying (Nietzsche 1962, 46–48). (Other interpreters see in the presocratic notion of injustice a constant process of encroachment and restoration between opposites [Burnet 1930, 52–55; Kirk et al. 1983, 119–20].) To what extent Beckett is in agreement with this Schopenhauerian version of existential guilt is apparent as early as his 1931 *Proust* essay, in which the declaration that tragedy is not concerned with human justice but is an expiation of the original sin of having been born is taken (with a Calderón quotation included) directly from Schopenhauer (Beckett 1931, 49; Schopenhauer 1969, 1:254 [§51]).

In addition to Anaximander's indefinite, the other presocratic versions of primal material from which the world was generated—particularly water (Thales), night (Orphic cosmogony), cosmic breath or wind (Anaximenes), chaos (Anaxagoras), and fire (Heraclitus)—enter into the Beckettian *fort/da* between coming into life and returning into death. However, it might be more accurate to say that these primary materials and the repetition of the universal in the human occur in Beckett's work in their gnostic reformulations—as, for example, the emblems attached to Cain and Abel. Thus, in accordance with the Molloy/Moran opposition, Molloy's elements are night, water, breath, and chaos, whereas Moran's element is fire. Molloy writes of being born into darkness and being made of night (31, 67), describes an inner chaos (39), an inner breath—*souffle* in the French version (1951, 60), which is translated as "whisper" in the English (1965, 40)—and imagines putting out to sea never to return (69); Moran sees himself consumed by fire (147). But it is the unnameable indefinite that appears to be the closest approximation of Beckettian silence. As Nietzsche saw so well, the indefinite "womb of all things" can be linguistically referred to only as a negative—one, moreover, that he compares to the unattainable Kantian thing in itself (Nietzsche 1962, 47).

Since Beckett has frequently hinted that if anything has explanatory force for his work it is Democritus's "nothing is more real than nothing," which he quotes again in *Malone Dies* (1965, 192), it may make sense to link this particularly paradoxical formulation of presocratic cosmogony to the tradition of material transcendence. The void of Democritus is taken to be an empty space, which exists only where atoms are not, thus forming gaps between them (Kirk et al. 1983, 415, 416 n. 3). It is such gaps of nothingness that, together with Anaximander's indefinite and the etymological meaning of *chaos* as "empty space" or "gap," relate to Schelling's mute ground and to *Molloy's* silence, of which Moran writes "the universe is made" (121). Beckett, though, resolutely denies to silence not only mythological and anthropomorphic associations but especially theological conceptions. On these he turns with daunting irony.

This is where *Molloy* may be said to posit a gnostic aesthetics. The gnostic heretics of the first centuries of the Christian era developed a negative theology to describe their unknowable god, conceived in terms of an unnameable abyss or silence or nothingness (Jonas 1963, 199, 288). This ineffable is radically distinct from the cosmos, a split that some gnostics, such as Valentinus in the second century, thought to explain by divine self-division or exile, an idea that was to be taken up by the cabbalist Isaac Luria and by the Protestant mystic Jacob Boehme and that we have found at work in psychoanalysis, aesthetic theory, and Beckett. It is surely not by chance that this notion is particularly charged for those who by choice or necessity take up their stance outside the social order into which they were born—the gnostic or Protestant heretic, the Jewish exile, the romantic outsider, the modernist expatriate, the writer who uses a second language.

Emphasizing the rift they perceived between an unknowable god and the created world, the gnostics turned to light/dark and up/down imagery to differentiate an unfallen realm of light from a fallen world of darkness. Earthly existence is likened to an underworld realm of death, a tomb, a labyrinthine prison, a dark place of exile, a turbulent sea, or alternately a state of anxiety or of numbness, sleep, and drunkenness (Jonas 1963, 52–99, 204, 224). To readers of Beckett these are familiar images of the inner crypt of exile from which the Beckettian voices ultimately speak. The creators of the gnostics' fallen world are likewise devalued divinities in contrast to the ineffable. Valentinus, for example, wrote of silence as the womb of all things (partly because of the feminine gender of the Greek word) and imagined an entire genealogy of male/female emanations, including Sophia, "wisdom," the first universal creator of this defective world, and her son the demiurge (Greek for "creator"), whom she set over her creation, to which the Sophie and Youdi figures of *Molloy* correspond (Pagels 1981, 59–65). In the words of Plotinus, the third-century neoplatonic philosopher, gnostics are those "who say that the Creator of the World is evil and that the World is bad" (quoted in Jonas 1963, 38). Because of the debased nature of the creator-god, gnostic initiatives must learn to participate as little as possible in the demiurge's projects and to reject his arrogant (and, in some versions, diabolical) authority in order to recognize the true call of "the depth" (Pagels 1981, 43–44, 64–70). In listening to the call from without, they free themselves from their bonds to an evil order. This disengagement can take the form either of asceticism or of what Jonas calls gnostic "libertinism," the freedom from the law of the tyrannical creator (1963, 46). The gnostics, then, posit an extreme otherness, a divine principle of radical exteriority from which the world and bodily self exist in a fallen state of exile.

When Molloy shakes off the sleepy and drugged state in which he was languishing and flees Sophie Loy/Lousse's garden by listening to the "small voice," or when Moran begins to hear a voice that is neither Youdi's nor a human language, the parallels with the gnostic call become apparent. Molloy/Moran's reiterated questions concerning their freedom (36, 176), too, appear to echo gnostic disengagement from the debased creators' imperatives.

Reiterating the gnostics' dualistic theology and cosmology, gnostic psychology posits a radical split within the self. In a conception akin to that visualized by Klein regarding the first stage of development, which is reactivated by mourning and artistic activity, the gnostics insist that the self's original experience of evil involves internal suffering, the fear of death and dissolution, confusion, and grief. It is consequently a repetition of this experience of anguish and loss that is placed at the outset of the gnostic's search, just as it is the first stage of the artistic process. The gnostics' well-known aversion for the body, which includes the condemnation of procreation, follows from this early experience of dread and loss (as do the fantasies of fragmentation and dissolution to which Klein points). The gnostics' abhorrence, though, is not counterbalanced, as it is in Klein, by a "good (bodily) object" and a sublimating reparation, for the sensual body is part of the fallen and dark world of degradation, which is irredeemable. Redemption is entirely spiritual and to be attained by a mystic ascent to the divine light within (Pagels 1981, 172–75). What Kleinian psychoaesthetics has in common with gnostic mysticism, though, is the dualism of destructive and ideal forces, of death and life within, based on the experience of early loss and exile.

The indictment of bodily processes in *Molloy* is surely among the most ferocious in literature, beginning with birth, which Molloy finds unforgivable, and including oral gratifications that he disdains and forgoes for sucking stones; anal disgust and fantasies that he entertains at length, albeit unwillingly; and a genitality consisting of the burlesque coupling with an androgynous hag, with whom he merges the figure of his mother, and to which finally he prefers masturbation. Moran, too, is intent on instilling in his son "that most fruitful of dispositions, horror of the body and of its functions" (118). To this, of course, is to be added the body's progressive disintegration, noted at length in both narratives. Not surprisingly, given an antagonism to the body that any gnostic would have applauded, Molloy indicates that he was born into a fallen state of darkness and exile from which there is no redemption.

The extent to which Beckett knowingly manipulates gnostic notions is apparent from two pages of notes written for his 1969 production of *Krapp's Last Tape* at the Schiller Theater Werkstatt in Berlin.[3] In these pages, there are lists of "light emblems" and "darkness emblems" and references to an "ascetic ethics, particularly abstinence from sensual enjoyment." One passage, in accordance with Manichaean myth, speaks of the creation of human beings by Satan and designates Cain and Abel as the sons of Satan and Eve. In relation to the play there is a dense passage about Krapp's punishment for his intellectual reconciliation of the irreconcilable light (spiritual) and dark (sensual). The "aeons" Beckett mentions in connection with Krapp's punishment most likely refer to Mani's five aeons that are part of the evil principle: smoke, fire, wind, water, and darkness (Jonas 1963, 210). Just as these emblems are divided between *Molloy's* double persona, they are scattered over Krapp's past selves or "I"s. At thirty-nine, for instance, Krapp reminisces about his mother's death, "There I sat, in the biting wind, wishing she were gone," and thirty years later, he recalls his own longing for death, "Sat shivering in the park, drowned in dreams and burning to be gone" (1960, 19, 25).

Finally, the gnostic road to spiritual knowledge within is in *Molloy* reduced to a wandering along the borders of uncertainty, and ultimately in Beckett's work, as in *Watt*, to a path abandoned, a journey denied. Valentinus called such roadlessness "aporia" (Pagels 1981, 172), a term adopted by Beckett on the first page of *The Unnamable*, so that steps forward reverse to steps backward, affirmations become denials, annulling all progress anywhere. It is, consequently, in unraveling all they have fabricated that *Molloy*'s narrators approximate the silence and nothingness on which all utterances are a stain.

In returning now to the writing subject of *Molloy*'s preamble, it becomes obvious, as has often been pointed out, that his situation is that of Malone of the next work of the Trilogy, who is waiting to be born into death from the tomblike womb of the artistic imaginary. Instead of self-generation, though, the last pages of *Malone Dies* stage an elaborate spoof on the splintered doubles of the writer's encrypted self. Two by two by two these six characters in search of an author file into a boat that puts out to sea and fades into darkness. It is another version of the reiterated come and go of textual fragments of self, which is the pain and the pleasure of the writing of exile.

That Beckett's Trilogy and *Godot* were composed soon after a harrowing war in which he was active in the Resistance surely plays a role in their gnostic pessimism. For, although a constant of the artistic imaginary, the fantasms of dissolution surface with particular force at moments of social horror and grief. Thus, in a 1946 radio address on Radio Erin concerning his work at the Irish Hospital at St. Lô, Beckett speaks of the "vision and sense of a time-honoured conception of humanity in ruins" and of the deriding smile at its contradictory ways (1986, 74–76). It is the reiteration of this vision and smile that suggests the affinity Beckett feels for a long line of pessimists, laughing or not, and for an aesthetics of cryptic exteriority.

Notes

1. For a description of modern theories of chaos, see Gleick (1987).

2. Quoted in Brown 1977, 48, n. 41, from Boehme's *Threefold Life.*

3. The two pages are published in photofacsimile at the end of James Knowlson's *Light and Darkness in the Theatre of Samuel Beckett* (1972). See also Morot-Sir's illuminating discussion of Beckett's use of the categories of Manichaean gnosticism in "Samuel Beckett and Cartesian Emblems" (1976, 81–104); and Frederick Busi's analysis of *Godot*'s Pozzo in the light of Marcion's identification of the Old Testament's god with the devil (1980, 77–78). It is surprising, though, that Busi does not apply the gnostic notion of the alien, unknowable god to the play's Godot.

References

Abraham, Nicolas, and Torok, Maria. *The Wolf Man's Magic Word: A Crypto-nymy*. Translated by Nicholas Rand. Minneapolis: University of Minnesota Press, 1986.

Barthes, Roland. *S/Z*. Translated by Richard Miller. New York: Hill and Wang, 1974.

———. *The Pleasure of the Text*. Translated by Richard Miller. New York: Hill and Wang, 1975.

Beckett, Samuel. *Molloy*. Paris: Minuit, 1951.

———. *Proust* (1931). New York: Grove Press, 1957.

———. *"Krapp's Last Tape" and Other Dramatic Pieces*. New York: Grove Press (Evergreen), 1960.

———. *Three Novels: "Molloy," "Malone Dies," "The Unnamable."* New York: Grove Press (Black Cat), 1965.

———. *Disjecta: Miscellaneous Writings and a Dramatic Fragment*. Edited by Ruby Cohn. New York: Grove Press, 1984.

———. "The Capital of the Ruins." In *As No Other Dare Fail: For Samuel Beckett on His 80th Birthday by His Friends and Admirers*. New York: Riverrun Press, 1986.

Brown, Robert F. *The Later Philosophy of Schelling*. London: Associated University Presses, 1977.

Burnet, John. *Early Greek Philosophy*. 4th ed. London: Adam and Charles Black, 1930.

Busi, Frederick. *The Transformations of "Godot."* Lexington: University Press of Kentucky, 1980.

Derrida, Jacques. *Glas*. 2 vols. Paris: Denoël-Gonthier, 1981.

———. "Fors: The Anglish Words of Nicolas Abraham and Maria Torok." Translated by Barbara Johnson. In Abraham and Torok (1986, xi–xlviii).

Ehrenzweig, Anton. *The Hidden Order of Art: A Study in the Psychology of Artistic Imagination*. Berkeley and Los Angeles: University of California Press, 1967.

Freud, Sigmund. *The Standard Edition of the Complete Psychological Works of Sigmund Freud*. Edited and translated by James Strachey. 24 vols. London: Hogarth Press, 1953–74.

　　The Interpretation of Dreams (1900–1901), vols. 4, 5.

　　"Mourning and Melancholia" (1917), vol. 14.

Frisch, Karl von. *Bees: Their Vision, Chemical Senses, and Language*. Ithaca: Cornell University Press, 1971.

Genet, Jean. *L'Atelier d'Alberto Giacometti*. In *Oeuvres complètes*. Vol. 5. Paris: Gallimard, 1979.

Gleick, James. *Chaos: Making a New Science*. New York: Penguin Books, 1987.

Gruen, John. "Samuel Beckett Talks about Beckett." *Vogue* (December 1969): 210.

Jakobson, Roman, and Halle, Morris. *Fundamentals of Language.* 2d ed. The Hague: Mouton, 1971.

Jonas, Hans. *The Gnostic Religion.* 2d ed. Boston: Beacon Press, 1963.

Kern, Edith. "Moran-Molloy: The Hero as Author." *Perspective* 11 (1959): 183–93.

Kirk, G. S., Raven, J. E., and Schofield, M. *The Presocratic Philosophers: A Critical History with a Selection of Texts.* 2d ed. Cambridge: At the University Press, 1983.

Klein, Melanie. *Love, Guilt and Reparation and Other Works, 1921–45.* London: Hogarth Press, 1975.

Knowlson, James. *Light and Darkness in the Theatre of Samuel Beckett.* London: Turret Books, 1972.

Kris, Ernst, and Kurz, Otto. *Legend, Myth, and Magic in the Image of the Artist: A Historical Experiment.* New Haven: Yale University Press, 1979.

Moorjani, Angela. *Abysmal Games in the Novels of Samuel Beckett.* North Carolina Studies in the Romance Languages and Literatures. Chapel Hill: University of North Carolina Press, 1982.

———. "The *Magna Mater* Myth in Beckett's Fiction: Subtext and Subversion." In *Beckett Translating / Translating Beckett,* edited by Alan Warren Friedman, Charles Rossman, and Dina Sherzer. University Park: Pennsylvania State University Press, 1987.

Morot-Sir, Edouard. "Samuel Beckett and Cartesian Emblems." In *Samuel Beckett: The Art of Rhetoric,* edited by E. Morot-Sir et al. North Carolina Studies in the Romance Languages and Literatures. Chapel Hill: University of North Carolina Press, 1976.

Nietzsche, Friedrich. *Philosophy in the Tragic Age of the Greeks.* Translated by Marianne Cowan. Chicago: Regnery Gateway, 1962.

Pagels, Elaine. *The Gnostic Gospels.* New York: Vintage, 1981.

Schelling, Friedrich W. J. *System of Transcendental Idealism (1800).* Translated by Peter Heath. Charlottesville: University Press of Virginia, 1978.

Schopenhauer, Arthur. *The World as Will and Representation.* Translated by E. F. J. Payne. 2 vols. New York: Dover, 1969.

Vater, Michael. Introduction, in Schelling (1978, xi–xxxvi).

5   The Whole Story

Robert Winer

Over the past few years, influenced by Donald Spence (1982) and Roy Schafer (1980), I have begun to think of the heart of the psychoanalytic process as the unfolding of narrative—actually the unfolding of two narratives, the story of the patient's life and the story of the relationship between analyst and patient. The analytic process works on the relationship between those two narratives, a seemingly old story and a seemingly new one. This way of thinking about analysis has led me to reflect on the narrative structures of my patients' lives, and of my own, and to consider the ways in which we fracture, fictionalize, plagiarize, and disassemble our stories. One way we disrupt our narratives is to break the connections and continuities of past, present, and future. In depression, for example, I insist that the past constitutes the present as I refuse to mourn a loss and place it in historical perspective; I both deny that the past is past and turn away from the freshness of the present moment and its new frightening possibilities.

I think that part of the appeal of Beckett's plays for me is that he evokes so compellingly this destruction of connection in contemporary life, in my life and the lives of my patients—what we might call our schizoid existence. It is a destruction that I understand to be not only a defense, in the service of avoiding the greater pain that connection can threaten us with, the pain of guilt or hurt or longing, but also a response to living in the preapocalyptic age (which I do not consider a nonanalytic concern). But Beckett would not be so fascinating

Based on a talk given at the Smithsonian Beckett Symposium in Washington, D.C., on 3 March 1989.

to me if he were simply a chronicler of our, and my, times. I volunteered to prepare these comments with the expectation that doing so might help me to discover why Beckett so deeply engages me.

Everyone seems to agree that Beckett's plays do not tell stories, and I will review the ways in which Beckett deconstructs narrative. I find Beckett to be profoundly concerned with our schizoid condition (and "our" here must include Beckett's own). I will be arguing that Beckett, both in the content and form of his writing, points us toward help. I will be proposing, first, from the point of view of content, that *Eh Joe* (1967) and *Ohio Impromptu* (1981), two of Beckett's shorter plays, have embedded in them implied narratives, through which Beckett is suggesting that the opening up of desire and the acceptance of mourning are the remedies that heal fractured narrative. I will also be speculating that these were solutions Beckett was struggling with in working through certain crises in his own life. I am not implying that these plays are simply Beckett's reworking of his neurosis or that these implied narratives are what the plays "mean." I do believe, however, that great art, like any great work, including great psychoanalysis, involves in complicated ways a sublimation of personal conflict, and that paying attention to the correspondences between life and art may be of interest, even illuminating.

To go a step further, and to look at the form, the power of Beckett's writing, what I find spellbinding is not the stuff of the implied narratives (although I find them interesting). It is his focus on the immanence of the present moment, the moment into which time has collapsed, the moment in which we can accept both the futility of going on and the necessity of going on, in which we can simply rest beset with the irony that we are "born astride a grave," born to die, in which we can bear that we both want to meet Godot and won't—that's what I find compelling. Paradoxically, accepting that narrativity can also be comforting illusion, that, standing with Estragon, I am not a historian, I may be opened to discovering my historical self. So Beckett's third remedy for narrative fracture is abiding the novel's pain, the anxiety of uncertainty. And this is one way in which Beckett's art has a curative power quite different from the quest for meaning of psychoanalysis.

Finished. Finished before we've begun. That's Sam Beckett's cheerful approach to storytelling...and, perhaps, to living. But you don't have to take my word for it, I have it all right here. (Searches.) Ah! box... threee...disc...five. Sam's last CD.

Little is left to tell. More. till in the end / the day came / in the end came / close of a long day / when she said / to herself / whom else / time she stopped / time she stopped...Joe...Joe...Thought of everything?...Forgotten nothing? Finished, it's finished, nearly finished, it must be nearly finished. Nothing to be done.

In the fashion of the Golden Oldies you've seen advertised on late-night television, I've offered you a collation of the opening lines in five of Beckett's plays: *Ohio Impromptu, Rockaby* (1981), *Eh Joe, Endgame* (1958), and *Waiting for Godot* (1954). He's cautioning us to abandon hope as we enter his domicile. Actually, we've been invited to the estate sale, where we'll have a chance to sort through the paraphernalia, the flotsam and jetsam of abandoned lives, and if we want to draw some inferences, reconstruct a life, we're free to putter around but this mausoleum comes without a dozent.

Insofar as there is a future in Beckett's plays that is other than more of the same, it is, at least on the surface, a decaying contracting future that will fade into death, and even death will arrive not as a catastrophe or climax, not as something longed for or dreaded, not even as an event, but as the outcome in an inevitable seamless cessation, life fading to zero on the monitor. Consider Beckett's three major plays: *Waiting for Godot* ends in more waiting, *Endgame* in further decomposing, and *Krapp's Last Tape,* implicitly, in death. Although the present moment may be intolerable, Beckett sees to it that the future is of no interest to us. For example, only incurable optimists could think that this time Godot will appear, and they're already on the stage.

Beckett seems equally ungenerous about the past, which is ironic considering that his plays are generally either in the form of reminiscences, like *Eh Joe* and *Ohio Impromptu,* or are about reminiscing, like *Krapp's Last Tape,* or languish in reminiscence, like *Waiting for Godot* and *Endgame.* Whatever is important has already happened, but the connection between the past events and present state of affairs is unclear. It's not that we couldn't imagine explanations that would link present and past. We could imagine lots of explanations, enough to fill whole bookshelves in libraries and reams of pages of senior theses or, for that matter, psychoanalytic expositions, but our explaining would have more to do with our intolerance for the lack of narrative closure than with sounding out implications Samuel Beckett had in mind. The past that Beckett reveals to us is a fractured, degraded past, odd shards of experience, ambiguous and dislocated in time and space. The character is further dissociated from his past as Beckett places recollection in another voice. The listener is then confronted with his past, a past from which he is estranged, alienated.

For Beckett, what is important is not to be found in the past or future—importance, if it exists, is immanent in the present moment. Future and past are echoes of the present, or perhaps shadows, cast forward and back. Beckett wants his audience to be riveted by the luminous immediacy of the present experience, the presented presence. In the evolution of his technique he increasingly focuses our attention, as his dramatic structure and staging work toward simplification and intensity: one act, one character, one voice, a single spotlight. We could say that Beckett's writing is never symbolic for symbolism occurs in time. A symbol places a current perception in the context of collected experience; it depends on the linking of present and past. In this sense, in *Krapp's Last Tape* a banana is a banana.

I want to focus on the problematic side of this denial of past and future—the destruction of narrative—for it is in the nature of the story that it must occur in the passage of time. (It was in this sense that John Calder described Beckett's newer work as "more painterly than literary" [Miller and Nelson 1971, 9].) But I first want to take a detour away from Beckett's plays, although not from Beckett, and discuss this in relation to the construction of the human life.

We each have a personal history which could be assembled from photo albums, report cards, our correspondences and interviews with our friends; if someone else compiles these, it becomes our biography. For the biographer, time is linear and serves to order the data. But we each also contain a living personal history, our own accounting of the meanings and purposes of our lives, which we shift and refract, kaleidoscopically, with new experience. In this living history, time serves a linking function, to bring together past, present, and future, not as points in a continuum, but as separate dimensions or layers in a matrix of experience. Our past is what we have been, and that compellingly determines our present and our visions of the future, a truth psychoanalysts encounter each hour in their consulting rooms. (Referring to the ineluctable power of the past, I recall an aphorism attributed to Anna Freud that I heard during my training: we may treat patients as we will, but they will treat us with their transferences.) But the past, in the subjective sense in which I am now describing it, is not a static record etched in the cerebral cortex; it is a living structure reinterpreted and reshaped on the basis of new experience. The heart of the psychoanalytic process is not the archaeological uncovering of the past. It is the refinding and reinterpretation of the past, made possible by new experience. In psychoanalysis the past informs the present, the present recreates the past, and in so doing they give birth to a new vision of the future and a new story is created. As psychoanalysts we are physicians to disordered narratives.

But matters are yet more complex. We hold the past not only in the form of memories, rememberable and repressed. The past is more vividly alive in the ghosts that haunt us. I think of a patient who had a truly hateful relationship with her mother. By the time she was three she had become her mother's "miserable rotten child" and mutual torment became the format for their involvement. In each subsequent relationship that mattered to her, she recreated this interaction, at times playing the part of the mother and at other times the part of the child. And so at one moment I felt shamed and persecuted by this tyrannical mother, at another enraged with her provocative rotten hatefulness. This internal relationship between a mother and daughter united in hatred constitutes a past that my patient lived in the present. When she was not enacting it, she felt tormented by it inside her head.

Let me mention one final way in which the past is present in us: in the form of identifications. In those moments when I am carrying forward my mother's devotion by being a devoted husband or when I am exercising my father's sensible authority, I am memorializing those aspects of them in the identification. This is not the past remembered or the past hauntingly reenacted but the past transformed into present being. Hans Loewald (1980b) summed it up by describing personal historicity as "the fact that the individual not only *has* a history that an observer may unravel and describe, but that he *is* history and makes his history by virtue of his memorial activity in which past-present-future are created as mutually interacting modes of time" (146). This integration puts us "on the path to becoming a self" (172).

The selves of Beckett's characters are profoundly fractured. As clinicians, we know this rupturing as a way of avoiding pain—the pain of shame, or grief, or love, or of recognizing one's own destructiveness. If it didn't happen, if I can't remember it, if it's not worth hoping for, if I didn't do it, I am protected. As an example of the lengths to which this fragmentation can be carried, let me offer you Harold Searles's description of a patient he treated:

> There were, she was utterly convinced, numerous "doubles" of everyone, including herself. When a male aide to whom she had been attached left the sanitorium, she did not miss him, for she knew there were 13 Mr Mitchells, most or all of them still about, in various guises. She felt accused unfairly by all persons about her for her more destructive acts which, she was convinced, her malicious doubles had done.

> She once protested, "Well, there were nine hundred and ninety-seven tertiary skillion women ... associated with Chestnut Lodge; so why should *I* be blamed for everything everybody did?" She misidentified herself and others repeatedly and unpredictably.... She had only "splashes of memory" of any experiences prior to her hospitalization, asserted that she had never had a mother or father or husband or children, and once when I started to ask something about her mother, protested, "When you use the word 'mother', I see a picture of a parade of women, each one representing a different point of view." More often than not, she reacted to me with the utter conviction that she had never seen me before, and very often expressed the conviction that I was the such-and-such person who had done malevolent things to her in her childhood—raped her, murdered her, and so on.   [1972, 3]

I am now going to turn to two of Beckett's shorter plays to explore the question of what it takes to live life as a historical self. Although these plays were not written as stories, I am going to present what I take to be the implied narrative in each of them. These narratives will, in their telling, elaborate the problems that stand in the way of creating history and might direct us toward potential solutions.

Eh Joe, a television play, begins with Joe, a grey-haired man in his late fifties, garbed in an old dressing gown and slippers, leaving his bed to peer out his window and then close and curtain it, look out his door and then lock it, peer in his cupboard then lock and curtain it, look under his bed, and finally, relaxing, sit on the edge of the bed. The camera then gradually moves in on his face, which stays almost motionless throughout, as a woman's voice confronts him about his destructiveness. We learn that Joe has made a career of destroying the voices that haunt him:

> You know that penny farthing hell you call your mind...That's where you think this is coming from, don't you?...That's where you heard your father...Isn't that what you told me?...Started in on you one June night and went on for years...On and off...Behind the eyes...That's how you were able to throttle him in the end...Mental thuggee you called it...One of your happiest fancies...Mental thuggee...Otherwise he'd be plaguing you yet...Then your mother when her hour came...   [1968, 37]

> Pitying love...None to touch it...And look at him now...Throttling the dead in his head.   [37]

We learn that Joe once seduced and discarded the woman who is speaking but that she has survived to go on and find a better man. Another one wasn't as fortunate. We hear the story of her suicide, under the viaduct; still alive after failing to drown herself and cutting her wrists, she took tablets and scooped out a place for her face in the wet stones, where she died. As the play ends, the woman's voice drops to a whisper and Joe's face fades.

Joe is a paranoid serial killer. His campaign is to exterminate these haunting presences, as though that will free him from their persecution, while denying to himself that the voices and lurking threats under the bed are creations of his own mind. He's glorified this into a holy mission: the thugs of India practiced thuggee in the service of Kali, the goddess of destruction. The voice taunts him, "Why don't you put out that light?...There might be a louse watching you...Why don't you go to bed?" knowing that the darkness would bring on nightmares and that Joe must sleep with the light on, perhaps the television on. She reminds Joe that he's absolutely alone: "Anyone living love you now, Joe?...Anyone living sorry for you now?" She describes Joe's squeezing: "Squeezed down to this," "Brain tired squeezing," "That's right, Joe, squeeze away." Joe is squeezing his mind empty, but we also imagine his heart ("Dry rotten at last") trying to squeeze blood through his cadaver. And she warns him, "Watch yourself you don't run short, Joe...Ever think of that?...Eh Joe?...What'd it be if you ran out of us...Not another soul to still...Sit there in his stinking old wrapper hearing himself...That lifelong adorer."

The fantasy in her last thought is that Joe, having extinguished all the voices, would be reduced to a perfectly narcissistic state, completely disconnected from the world, left with only his own voice to listen to, which would become a living death. But the murdered voices don't actually disappear. They are transformed into unnameable menace lurking inside and outside his room. The historical past becomes primal unfocused terror. This psychic destruction is a portrayal in purified form of a process typically operating in Beckett's characters. And yet matters are more complex because the woman's voice is also a creation of Joe's mind, and the stories she tells of her own fate and of the one who didn't survive are also tales in Joe's narrative. In those tales Joe makes an accounting of his destructiveness: do not despair, one was saved; do not presume, one was damned.

In the telling of the suicide we hear an unexpected tenderness: "Scoops a little cup for her face in the stones...The green one...The narrow one...Always pale...The pale eyes...The look they shed before ...The way they opened after...Spirit made light." Joe is imagining someone who was capable of loving him, loving him enough to become hurt beyond repair, the one who could have made a difference for him. Had he been able to accept her compassion, to be open to his own vulnerable longing self, the lost child in himself, his narrative might have taken another course. The narrative he might now unfold would be something like this: I grew up with a mother too moody, too absorbed in herself, a mother unable to teach me to love. If I had had a mother like the one who died, one who could call out to me, reach out to me, open my lips, one who would die for me, I might have created that mother in myself and learned to love; instead I have become callous and estranged, I'm rotting in fear and contempt and hatred. This telling, this recognition of a narrative, could be the starting point for Joe of a path back to the living.

Samuel Beckett might have told such a story about his relationship with his own mother, that mercurial, bitter, shielded woman, and about the fate of his own early attempts to love.[1] His great first infatuation was with the fascinating, green-eyed Peggy Sinclair, the daughter of his father's high-spirited, semi-outcast, artistic sister. After he spent years of futile pursuit, she finally developed an interest in him as his own attraction to her was fading. In a remarkably hurtful act, he inserted in a story in the volume *More Pricks Than Kicks* (1972) a letter from Peggy, who was by now seriously ill with tuberculosis. Her parents, who had become something of a foster family for the struggling young Beckett, were horrified and cut him off completely. A year later Peggy died, and Beckett's biographer, Deirdre Bair, believes that her death brought Beckett to an acute awareness of the wasting of his own life (1978, 166). It seems imaginable to me (although, of course, entirely speculative) that the writing of *Eh Joe,* for all its apparent denial of narrative, may have unconsciously represented, in part, the reworking of that crisis, the facing of the destructiveness in his act of bad faith and a confrontation with his abandoned desire.

The moral of *Eh Joe,* in my expansion of it (this filling out being my project and certainly not Beckett's), is that desire, the capacity to bear wanting, is the medicine that heals dismembered narrative. Being found wanting, finding oneself wanting, is not a death sentence, terminal emptiness; it is an opportunity for discovering purpose, an invitation to life. Much of psychoanalytic work with patients these days involves the unsilencing of passion: reversing Freud, where ego was, id once again shall be. Opening up transference, both in psychoanalysis and in living, is the breathing of old desire into contemporary life, the kindling of fire (see Loewald 1980a). In his chapter on Beckett in *Tragic Drama and the Family,* Bennett Simon (1988a) articulates the relationship between the abortion of desire and fragmentation of the self. Samuel Beckett and *Eh Joe* squeeze desire in their trash compactor; in response, as audience I long to recreate desire, to breathe life into that drowning form.

Desire feels unsafe when there is too much aggression; we stanch our love when we fear it will harm. When we are very young, we are all frightened by our destructiveness, the more so for those of us who have had greater privation, who have felt more helpless. Our felt destructiveness makes us afraid—that's Joe's experience in his room. As infants and toddlers we use our parents to still those fears that we cannot quiet ourselves. A mark of the emergence of the self is the capacity to be self-soothing (to soothe the destructiveness and make passion safe). In raising my own children, I've been impressed by the extent to which that process is worked on at bedtime, when my wife or I leave the room and my child has to nurse himself or herself to sleep. I've thought that mastering the capacity to be alone in bed, to contain anxiety and put oneself to sleep, is at the heart of beginning to establish a separate self. The child calls on memories of soothing experience with the parents, now being transformed into modes of self-soothing, and imagines a benevolent future in the hours of sleep; you hear me alluding again to the creation of the historical self. The patients I've treated who slept in their parents' bedrooms until they were four, or five, or seven, or fifteen, as adults have either been unable to calm themselves without the help of another, or have led primitively encapsulated lives. (The problem was more complex for those who were exposed to their parents' sex, which of course frightened and enraged them, made them more anxious and harder to calm.)

Both plays I am discussing touch on being unable to fall asleep. As I mentioned earlier, Joe is afraid to close his eyes. And so was Beckett. The same year that Peggy Sinclair passed away, Beckett's father unexpectedly died. Beckett had been quite disabled, unable to work or write, and at war with his mother. His father had been a great support to him, and with his death, Beckett deteriorated further. As Deirdre Bair describes it, "Beckett would awaken in the middle of the night, drenched with perspiration, his heart pounding erratically, unable to breathe or to extricate himself from the blind panic which threatened to suffocate him. He tried to avoid sleeping because he was afraid to dream.... Finally the night terrors became so severe that Beckett could relax only if [his brother] Frank slept in the same bed, to hold and calm him when he was in the grips of nightmarish terror" (174–75). It was this breakdown that prompted his psychoanalytic treatment with Wilfred Bion. (For an interesting account of their relationship, see Simon [1988b]). To free himself from these unremitting passions would require relinquishment and mourning.

Ohio Impromptu was written for a Beckett symposium at Ohio State University in 1981. A Listener and Reader, identical in appearance, sit at a pine-board table, and the Reader reads to the Listener from the last pages of a book. At intervals the Listener directs the Reader to repeat himself by knocking on the table. In brief, this is the story he reads, which is apparently also the story of their relationship: "In a last attempt to obtain relief he moved from where they had been so long together to a single room on the far bank.... Relief he had hoped would flow from unfamiliarity." "In his dreams he had been warned against this change. Seen the dear face and heard the unspoken words, Stay where we were so long alone together, my shade will comfort you." "[But] What he had done alone could not be undone.... In this extremity his old terror of night laid hold on him again.... White nights now against his portion.... No sleep no braving sleep till—(turns page)—dawn of day." One night a man appeared and said that he had been sent by the dear name to comfort him, and he read to him until dawn. This was repeated from time to time until one night the visitor said that he had received word from the dear one that he was not to come again. "So the sad tale a last time told they sat on as though turned to stone. Through the single window dawn shed no light. From the street no sound of reawakening.[... They sat] Buried in who knows what profounds of mind. Of mindlessness. Whither no light can reach. No sound." And at the end: "Nothing is left to tell."

Reading and rereading *Ohio Impromptu,* I find it a moving description of the struggle to mourn, to separate, to join, to become a person. In the theater—and I had the good fortune to see Alan Schneider's production in New York—I found it isolating, even awesomely distancing. I can still vividly remember the staging, but even my wife, who seems to have an infallible memory for narrative, could remember nothing of the story. Beckett brackets the play with disclaimers: it begins "Little is left to tell" and ends with "Nothing is left to tell." In between a great deal is told, especially to one who reads it, more removed from Beckett's theatrical control, freer to use imagination. Maybe that's cheating, but here's what I make of it.

The Listener has suffered the loss of a loved one, a loss so painful that he leaves their home to take up residence in an unfamiliar setting, hoping that he will be able to forget. He spends his days pacing the islet, dwelling on the receding stream, watching "How in joyous eddies its two arms conflowed and flowed united on." A terrible loneliness sets in. In his dreams he regrets the move, but he is determined to stand his ground, as though the only possibility for living requires that he bear being alone. He suffers sleepless nights, "White nights now against his portion," until a reader comes to bring him comfort—

the bedtime stories we read to our children that help them face being alone until they fall asleep. At the end the reader will leave, but they will also join together, joined as one in stone, and perhaps the Reader will read this story to the Listener about the reader and the listener every night forever.

It is possible to read this play as the story of an analysis, even of Beckett's analysis with Bion. (This seems entirely speculative, God knows, but interesting, and has the added lure of narrative closure!) Quite thoroughly done in by his father's death, joined with his father in frightening cardiac symptoms of his own, at his mother's encouragement (and to avoid local embarrassment) Beckett left the family home and went to London to begin his analysis with Bion. Over forty years later, *Ohio Impromptu* was written for the New Land. In a piece he wrote that was attached to the manuscript Beckett expressed his anxiety about the trip to America:

> What am I to say? I said.
> Be yourself, they said, stay
> yourself.
> Myself? I said. What are you insinuating?
> [Yourself before, they said.]
> *Pause.*
> [And after.]
> *Pause.*
> [Not during? I said.]   [Astier 1986, 397]

Those sound to me like the anxieties of a person about to enter analysis—what's going to happen to the me I know? The relationship between Reader and Listener is like that between patient and analyst. The patient tells his story and the analyst calls his attention to thoughts he might skim past; the phrases the reader is asked to repeat focus on his loss. Don't rush past this, the analyst says, let's listen together. In production, the Reader is mechanically impersonal, absolutely distanced from what he is reading; he seems more interested in the construction of the phrases than the meaning they carry (one line he seems to marvel at because it's a perfect iambic hexameter [Astier 1986, 397]). I take this to be Beckett struggling to extend his obsessional control to his analysis—as Deirdre Bair points out, when you think of this man, what could possibly be more threatening than expecting him to tell someone else everything that's on his mind? The double sense in which at the end the Reader and Listener both part and become fused in stone speaks to me of the way in which analyst

and patient part, and yet also in a successful analysis internalize identifications with each other.

I can imagine that Beckett, in writing this, could have been imagining what his analysis might have been, what it might have offered
him, had he stayed with it. Staying with it would have required being
able to mourn, to let go of his entanglement with his mother, to let
Bion replace his father, and he was then unable to do that. Copies of
his earlier drafts of the play are available and I was struck by two
changes in particular that he made (Beja et al. 1983). He changed the
dear face's words from "my ghost will comfort you" to "my shade will
comfort you" (197). This transforms the lost one, perhaps his mother,
from a haunting to a sheltering presence. And near the end, "sound of
renewing toil" became "sound of reawakening" (201). Acceptance and
hope from Beckett—a miracle. Something left to tell after all. It's an
appealing thought that over forty years later, in the writing and rewriting of this piece, Beckett was reworking his analysis, resuming his
story.

It is the freeing of desire and the work of mourning that make possible the assemblage of a life. If desire is felt to be poisonous, and
mourning murderous, then refuge is taken in a schizoid or obsessional
solution. For Beckett, the task seems to be accepting both his hatred
of his mother and his identification with her. That mourning is required for the creation of the historical self is what William James had
in mind when he said that each of us, going through life, leaves behind
a series of murdered alternative selves. In the life passionately lived,
that murder can be borne.

I would like to close by returning to Beckett's third precept for
us—that we be open to experiencing the present moment. We ana-
lysts were told (by Bion) to meet our patients without memory or
desire, without prejudice or need, to be open afresh to the possibilities in each new hour. At the same time, we can only meet our patients
with memory and desire—we are, after all, particular human beings
and we want to open the door. Well, nothing to be done. Maybe I'll
close my garbage can and go rowing on Lake Como.

Notes

1. Biographical information is from Deirdre Bair (1978).

References

Astier, Pierre. "Beckett's 'Ohio Impromptu': A View from the Isle of Swans" (1982). In *On Beckett: Essays and Criticism,* edited by S. E. Gontarski. New York: Grove Press, 1986.

Bair, Deirdre. *Samuel Beckett: A Biography.* New York: Harcourt Brace Jovanovich, 1978.

Beckett, Samuel. *Waiting for Godot: A Tragicomedy in Two Acts.* New York: Grove Press, 1954.

————. *Endgame.* New York: Grove Press, 1958.

————. *Eh Joe* (1967). In *Cascando and Other Short Dramatic Pieces.* New York: Grove Press, 1968.

————. *More Pricks Than Kicks.* New York: Grove Press, 1972.

————. *Ohio Impromptu* (1981). *Rockaby* (1981). In *Rockaby and Other Short Pieces.* New York: Grove Press, 1981.

Beja, Morris, Gontarski, S. E., and Astier, Pierre. *Samuel Beckett: Humanistic Perspectives.* Columbus: Ohio State University Press, 1983.

Loewald, Hans W. "On the Therapeutic Action of Psychoanalysis" (1960). In *Papers on Psychoanalysis.* New Haven: Yale University Press, 1980a.

————. *Papers on Psychoanalysis.* New Haven: Yale University Press, 1980b.

Miller, Walter James, and Nelson, Bonnie E. *Samuel Beckett's "Waiting for Godot" and Other Works.* New York: Monarch Press, 1971.

Schafer, Roy. "Narration in the Psychoanalytic Dialogue." In *On Narrative,* by W. J. T. Mitchell. Chicago: University of Chicago Press, 1980.

Searles, Harold F. "The Function of the Patient's Realistic Perceptions of the Analyst in Delusional Countertransference." *British Journal of Medical Psychology* 45 (1972): 1–18.

Simon, Bennett. *Tragic Drama and the Family: Psychoanalytic Studies from Aeschylus to Beckett.* New Haven: Yale University Press, 1988a.

————. "The Imaginary Twins: The Case of Beckett and Bion." *International Review of Psycho-Analysis* 15 (1988b): 331–52.

Spence, Donald. *Narrative Truth and Historical Truth: Meaning and Interpretation in Psychoanalysis.* New York: W. W. Norton, 1982.

6   "Tender Mercies":
       Subjectivity and Subjection
       in Samuel Beckett's *Not I*

       John H. Lutterbie

F ixed in representation, I seek myself in Beckett's play. In *Not I,* at
his invitation, I seek the outlines of my subjectivity, knowing that my
"self" is always beyond my grasp, revealing itself only in the gaps of
thought, in the intuition of presence. But the dream, the dream of
Artaud, is always to mitigate this distance, to reforge "the chain" between "what is and what is not, between the virtuality of the possible
and what already exists in materialized nature" (Artaud 1958, 27). It
is a wish to transgress the limits of representation, to make manifest
what is beyond consciousness, to know the unknowable. But in this
enunciation I confront another discourse, one that eschews the metaphysics of the immaterial and unveils the imprint of oppression on
"materialized nature."[1] It is the discourse of the "other," the discourse
of the unconscious, that forces me to recognize the subtle slip between "my self" and "itself"—to understand that the desire to know
the other is political. Within the distance that defines the differences
between these two theories of the subject, the conscious subject and
the subject of the unconscious, there is no center in which I can locate myself. Instead, there is the recognition that even if I were to
circumscribe the infinite boundaries of these disparate discourses, I
would not know myself.
    I shall, nevertheless, attempt to define a strategy for talking about
subjectivity, and in the process read Beckett's play. Onstage appears,
in Beckett's writing, a disembodied mouth and a shrouded listener.
The Mouth relates to me, and to the Auditor, a tale about a woman,
"she," who has a catastrophic illness and attempts to recognize what
she knows to be life. In the telling I hear a discourse of the subject

that resonates with certain Freudian concepts of psychic organization, that carries with it a certain existential angst. However, I hear another story as well. It is spoken more quietly, creating a context for the unfolding sonorities of being, providing the landmarks for navigating a world foreign to my perceptual experience. The problem is that those signposts are not innocent. They tell tales of difference, of margins and peripheries, of oppressions that define the "other." My wish is to amplify their voices by turning the play against itself, by using the theory of subjectivity defined in the play to explore the subjective values of the Mouth, the ideology of the speaking subject. The intent is not simply to critique Beckett but to raise questions about strategies used in theories of the subject, and to examine the costs exacted when, inadvertently, ideologies of repression are reenacted.

The surreal staging described by Beckett—the elevated and faintly lit mouth and the lower, shrouded Auditor—is sufficient to support the claim that *Not I* is located in an interior, a psychic landscape. Even if I were to read the speaker and the listener as discrete individuals, any interpretation based in perceptual verisimilitude or describing a system of external relationships would almost immediately be confronted with a host of insurmountable contradictions. The fragmentary, disembodied mouth and the occluded, desexualized body resist reference to a materiality, virtually proclaiming, instead, a metaphysics of alienation. A seemingly untransgressable distance separates the two beings, who attempt communication through gesture and the pause, but who are unable to make contact. They cannot span the gap that marks their existential isolation. A sufficiently desolate picture when conceptualized as pertaining to individuals, it gains in force when conceived of as a metaphor for an intrapersonal dynamic.

Beckett's vision of the subject, within this static staging, is an image of despair. The hopelessness implicit in this construction of the "I" is the effect of an ordering that creates in spatial terms a hierarchy of privilege. Dominant is the mouth, the speaking subject that, in its faltering, streaming insistence, tells of the woman and her catastrophic situation. The Auditor, the obscured hearing subject, can only receive the verbal onslaught and respond weakly with "a gesture of helpless compassion" (Beckett 1984, 215). This vertical relationship within a basically horizontal composition defines a simple modernist model of decentered subjectivity—that is, I seek myself in the imaginary distance between what I say and what I hear myself say.

It is not, however, a matter of splitting that distance, of geometrically bisecting a line constructed between two points. For the question of subjectivity, even within the modernist framework, is not one of symmetry, but of asymmetries. Imbalances continually subvert the reassuring formulation of subjectivity as a cyclical, dialectical unity of mouth and ear. The ear is not simply a conduit for the passive transmission of vibrations but a chamber that can resonate sympathetically. And the authority of the mouth is continually betrayed by the intrusions of its antecedents and the projection of its eloquent self-conceptions. Who is it who interrupts the ellipsis-ridden flow of words? Who challenges the integrity of the voice, repeatedly forcing a denial of subjective complicity: "what?...who?...no!...she!" (217)? Is it the same "I" that demands consideration of all the possibilities? "she did not know...what position she was in [...]whether standing...or sitting...but the brain—...what?...kneeling?...yes...whether standing...or sitting...or kneeling...but the brain—...what?" (217). And are those the same "I"s that laugh at the thought of a merciful God, or scream in the dreaded hope of help? And at the other end of the temporal sequence, who is "she"? Is she, as seems likely, the objectified self? The "I"/"not I"? the self conceptualized as other? The interruptions, on the one hand, and the description of "she," on the other, make a simple conception of the subject untenable. Beckett has effectively undermined the apparent significance of his own powerful stage image—as if in calling into question the "I," he is also challenging the authority and privilege granted to the eye.

Disrupting the dualist concept of subjectivity does not eliminate the question of the subject, however. In naming the play *Not I,* Beckett does not negate the existence of the "I"; he reasserts it. The subjective pronoun functions in the linguistic semiotic as a shifter: a signifier that can be appropriated by any number of signifieds. It can be used by all conscious subjects with equal authority. But every assertion of the shifter has the simultaneous effect of litigating all previous claims, authorizing the "not I." This does not mean that every claim to subjectivity is meaningless. Each articulation of the self constellates particular contents that bear a specific relation to the "I," defining the limits of an affirmation of the self.

In fact, the indeterminacy of the pronoun does not lessen its signifying force; rather it enhances its power. Each content brought into relation with the dominant signifier becomes a sign in its own right, even if it only signifies "not I." The effect is an interrelated field of signs arranged around the "I" or, in the formulations of Deleuze and Guattari, a spiraling chain moving away from the signifier (1987, 113). Although the potential for leaping to any point on the chain exists, the potential for infinite extension is not paralleled by a similar drift toward the center. "The jumps are not made at random, they are not without rules. Not only are they regulated, but some are prohibited: Do not overstep the outermost circle, do not approach the innermost circle" (Deleuze and Guattari 1987, 113). The prohibition does not indicate a void separating the central signifier from subsidiary signs, but the authority of the dominant to determine their position within the chain. A system is established that is determined not by identities or difference, but by similarities, by affinities of *significance*.

Therefore, although I cannot know myself, I can gather indications of subjectivity under the auspices of the "I." This sleight of hand does not limit my self-understanding; instead it provides an environment for the infinite proliferation of self-knowledge, further enhancing the force of the dominant signifier.

> The signifying regime is not simply faced with the task of organizing into circles signs emitted from every direction; it must constantly assure the expansion of the circles of spiral, it must provide the center with more signifiers to overcome the entropy inherent in the system and to make new circles blossom or replenish the old.   [DeLeuze and Guattari 1987, 114]

Therefore, the "I" with which I nominate myself is a symbol not for the network of signs implicated in my experience—which are always insufficient to the task—but for the aggregate of *significance* that links the sign to the dominant signifier. This excess that proclaims similarity nevertheless resists objectification, providing me only with the intuition of a presence beyond knowledge. Ironically, the ever-increasing number of signs I used to define myself fragments myself, indicating the distance I have moved from myself. Far from a stable term through which I can claim identity, this "I" is nothing but an illusory anchor to which I cling while I "sense" my disappearance in the interstices of an ever-fragmenting, ever-disseminating articulation of subjectivity.

As I resist this slippage, I imagine a shrouded Beckett raising his arms "in a gesture of helpless compassion," or perhaps grimly shaking his head and pointing to the Mouth. After all, I am only disappearing in words, in a semiotic of subjectivity. There is still my body, which is here, now, and which I recognize is moving inexorably into a silence greater than that separating the dissipating intonations of thought.

Yet, the semiotic model has helped to define the ground of an argument. The initial concept of a referent, decentered subjectivity is effectively discredited through the absorption of the speaking and hearing subjects into the plane of signification. The Mouth and the Auditor become two signs among many and, within this context, deserve no special privilege. Temporality is introduced as a factor in an otherwise synchronic configuration. The plane of signification, at first glance, appears to describe a spatial relationship in which signs of the greatest intensity occupy positions in the spiral nearest to the dominant sign. But fluctuations within the relationships between associated signs and the dominant adds a diachronic factor that accounts for jumps between signs, the creation of new signs, and the entropy of others. Implicit in this semiotic model is the existence of a force prior to the representation of "being" in language, indicating the need to conceptualize the dynamics of an energetics of presence. However, in seeming contradiction, the emphasis on signification renders considerations of ontology and teleology unimportant to the conceptualization of the subject. Ontological concerns lose relevance because it is not necessary to know the origins of the energetics required to fuel the signifying process—it is sufficient that the force is there. Similarly, subjectivity is defined by the dynamics of the signification process without recourse to an ultimate purpose. It is on this basis that the dynamics of an energetics of presence in the formulation of representations can be investigated.

Embodied Intensities

Presence describes, in the last analysis, not a metaphysics but a materiality: it is only as long as the body is. So when the Auditor raises its arms, I am not seeing an empty signifier, but the evocation of a sonority that resonates beyond the veil of signification. The material mouth of the actor dimly lit upon the stage acknowledges a deeper, unrepresented corporeality: the reality of the body expunged of metaphysics, defining the vehicle that exists prior to, and that makes possible, thought.

Identifying the body in Beckett's work is made difficult by the seemingly conscious effort to erase it from consideration at every conceivable opportunity. The fragmentary mouth and the shrouded figure are the obvious examples, but more significant is "she," the other described in the Mouth's narrative. Walking through a field in April, picking cowslips, she has a catastrophic experience. Her return to consciousness is partial; she is effectively paralyzed, unable to sense her physicality. "she did not know...what position she was in...imagine... what position she was in!...whether standing...or sitting...but the brain" (216). The continually functioning brain and the absence of physical sensation appear to place limits on the field of investigation, but the body refuses exclusion. Its negation becomes the source of its affirmation. Ironically, the mind must affirm the existence of the body—

consider all the possible positions, standing, sitting, kneeling, lying—in order to reaffirm the dominance of thought. The insistence of the physical, its precedence over consciousness, its necessity as the vehicle of thought, make it central to defining the material reality of Beckett's vision. The corporeal debased, reduced to its most fundamental contradictions, allows Beckett to conceive of the body as the indeterminant center of two bipolar oppositions: one temporal, one spatial.

The onset of the catastrophe that leaves the "she" of *Not I* in a state of paralysis is preceded by a description of her movements, which seem, initially to be an ominous forewarning of what is about to occur. "a few steps then stop...stare into space...then on...a few more...stop and stare again...so on...drifting around...when suddenly...gradually...all went out" (216). These phrases evoke the signals sent by the body to announce the onset of disruption, the footfalls of her impending death. But this reading is disputed when her life is described in exactly the same terms. "walking all her days...day after day...a few steps then stop...stare into space...then on...a few more...stop and stare again ...so on...drifting around...day after day" (220). Life becomes a metaphor for death, and death for life. They are commensurate, and Bob Dylan's lyric, "Those not busy being born are busy dying," must be rewritten: "Those busy being born are busy dying."

Nor can solace be found in the cyclical vacillations between the inhalation and exhalation of *Breath,* with its mythical moment of transfer from one action to another. The optimism of life and the pessimism of death create a false dichotomy. Life and death have no turning points; the life of the body is the death of the body. It is a continuum, an unvarying, uninterruptable movement that appears segmentable only in the stolen breath of thought.

> If difference, within its phenomenon, is the sign of theft or of the purloined breath [*souffle*], it is primarily, if not in itself, the total dispossession which constitutes me as the deprivation of myself, the elusion of my existence; and this makes difference the simultaneous theft of both my body and my mind: my flesh. If my speech is not my breath [*souffle*], if my letter is not my speech, this is so because my spirit was already no longer my body, my body no longer my gestures, my gestures no longer my life.   [Derrida 1978, 179]

Nor is it any longer my death, but my death stolen from me at the same moment my life is spirited away. It is the integrity of my body that is subsumed in the optimism of being.

Her state of paralysis not only denies her awareness of physical posture but also negates emotional states. "as she suddenly realized... gradually realized...she was not suffering...imagine!...no suffering!...indeed could not remember...off-hand...when she had suffered less" (217). The fact that I am asked to imagine the absence of suffering indicates, for Beckett, that it is a generalized state of being. Or it at least predominates over the alternative: "just as the odd time...in her life...when clearly intended to be having pleasure...she was in fact... having none...not the slightest" (217). The concepts of pleasure and suffering are used to describe two distinctly opposite physical sensations. They do not describe a continuum, however, in which the absence of pleasure indicates a plenitude of suffering, or vice versa. Rather they are different responses to particular excitations that play across the body, which are not necessary to life but inevitable consequences of it.

My body is, in the last instance, corporeality without differentiated intensities. But it is subject to excitations that result in sensations that I interpret as pleasure or suffering.

> We believe, that is to say, that the course of those events is invariably set in motion by an unpleasurable tension, and that it takes a direction such that its final outcome coincides with a lowering of that tension— that is, with an avoidance of unpleasure or a production of pleasure. [Freud, *S.E.* 18:7]

As Freud implies, not all tensions are necessarily unpleasurable. That the release of certain tensions may cause suffering and that certain tensions may be pleasurable are claims that can be made without assumptions of masochism. Rather, it is the interpretations of the increases and decreases of excitation that define pleasure and suffering: "but the brain still...still sufficiently...oh very much so!...at this stage... in control...under control" (218). This is not to deny the function of the body in conveying shifting intensities or in influencing interpretation, since the sensitivity of the perceptual system to excitations plays an informational role in the interpretative process. Instead, it is to claim that the body relays information in terms of magnitudes, and that the processes of the mind translate them into qualities.

This contextualization of physicality deromanticizes the body as a miracle of nature, an object of divine creation, and refigures it as an imperfect, material object for the conveyance of sensory impulses, reproduction, and life-sustaining functions. Nevertheless, it is the vehicle, the vessel of subjectivity; indeed, it is a necessary condition of consciousness, of the mind's control. The image of a (dys)functional corporeality is a palliative that authorizes metaphysical speculations on the operations of conscious thought. But the body is, to borrow a metaphor from another material discourse, the base on which is built the superstructure of subjectivity. It is the fragile and unstable foundation that makes possible an ideology of the self. I am always and only the body, and in the final analysis, there is nothing else. And yet, the play continues to insist, it is "not I."

Then where am I to find myself? How am I to understand my ability to act upon the world in what is arguably a consistent manner? There must be another movement, process, procedure within the sensate body that makes it possible for me, however feebly and inaccurately, to codify these thoughts—that made it possible for someone named Beckett to write "this" play. "but this other awful thought...oh long after...sudden flash...even more awful if possible...that feeling was coming back...imagine!...feeling coming back!...starting at the top...then working down...the whole machine...but not...spared that...the mouth alone" (219–20). But if I must *imagine* the return of feeling, if I have forgotten how my body feels and yet I am, then subjectivity must be found in what need not be imagined, the machinations of the mouth; and in what is felt, the sense of the voice. I am not conceiving of a cyclical paradox that, ironically, locates subjectivity in the active articulations of the alienated Mouth. Therefore I must shift my focus from the speaking Mouth to the spoken of "she," the voice of the other, to her voices—or more accurately, her sonorities.

Three distinct sonorities are acknowledged in the Mouth's description of her catastrophic experience: the speaking voice, the streaming, and the buzzing. It is in the irreversible movement between them that I can glimpse the outlines of a pragmatic theory of the subject.

She knows she is alive when she regains consciousness because of the buzzing. "found herself in the dark...and if not exactly...insentient ...insentient...for she could still hear the buzzing...so-called...in the ears" (217). The continuation of life is signaled; and the vibrations, Beckett's mental sentience, may affect the ears, but its undefined, uncertain, unimportant origins are within the mind. "in the ears...though of course actually...not in the ears at all...in the skull...dull roar in the skull" (218). The paradoxical description—it is a buzzing, a dull roar—underlines its indefinability and insists upon its metaphorical status. Neither she nor the Mouth know what it is, but they recognize its insistence. "what?...the buzzing?...yes...all silent but for the buzzing ...so called" (218). The relentless buzzing represents the boundary beyond which lies absolute silence, the limit that begins from before birth and finds closure only in death. It connotes the energetics of the body, the determining factor of presence, what Freud identifies as the instinct. "An instinct . . . never operates as a force giving a *momentary* impact but always as a *constant* one. Moreover, since it impinges not from without but from within the organism, no flight can avail against it. A better term for an instinctual stimulus is a 'need'" (*S.E.* 14: 118–19).

The persistence of the demand, in Freud's definition of the instincts, and the inability to construct a line of flight that can escape its continuity establish a sympathetic resonance with the seeming hopelessness of Beckett's work: "in every instance satisfaction, which can only be obtained by removing the state of stimulation at the source of the instinct. But although the ultimate aim of each instinct remains unchangeable, there may yet be different paths leading to the same ultimate aim" (*S.E.* 14:122). The only means of defining an instinct, therefore, is through identifying the object chosen for the release of energy. But the creation of a cathexis is also subject to variations, since "the object . . . is what is most variable about an instinct and is not originally connected with it, but becomes assigned to it only in consequence of being peculiarly fitted to make satisfaction possible" (*S.E.* 14:122). The naming of an instinct, therefore, including Freud's cautious demarcation of the ego and sexual drives (*S.E.* 14:124), is a posteriori and subject to extrinsic systems of valuation. Therefore, the instincts in Freud have, perhaps, more in common with the buzzing, so-called, of Beckett than the teleological image of discrete functions.

Freud's conceptualization of the instinct and its movement within the psyche is of value, in addition to its usefulness in psychoanalytic discourses, to understanding the ordering process that results in consciousness. "Instinct," "need" and "demand" as *concepts* mark the culmination of a movement of energy from the undifferentiated field of force to the surface of language, which for Beckett's "she" is the articulation "God is love...tender mercies...new every morning" (221–22). My knowledge of an instinct is possible only when the object cathected is identified and, through an act of deconstruction, the need hypothesized. The ordering process, therefore, involves the translation of an unknowable quantity (force) into a differentiated quality (the instinct). In *Not I,* the differentiating activity occurs within the remaining two sonorizations.

The smooth surface of the buzzing, disrupted only by the cyclical movements of the sound waves, is distinctly differentiated from the sonority of streaming. The plane of streaming has limits, banks and a bed, and lacks the multidimensional timelessness of presence. It is inflected and bears the traces of language. "words were coming...a voice she did not recognize...at first...so long since it had sounded...

then finally had to admit...could be none other...than her own...certain vowel sounds...she had never heard...elsewhere" (219). Her voice, but not a language she understands. "mouth on fire...stream of words...in her ear...practically in her ear...not catching the half...not the quarter ...no idea what she's saying...imagine!...no idea what she's saying!...and can't stop" (220). She has become possessed by these unfamiliar sounds, the biblical tongues of fire, the syntax of spirit. She hears only vowels, sounds created by the vibrated and distorted but otherwise unrestricted column of air that is her breath. But it lacks the rhythmic pattern of inhalation and exhalation; it is the aspiration of a voice that is unceasing and uncontrollable. "now can't stop...imagine!...can't stop the stream...and the whole brain begging...something begging in the brain...begging the mouth to stop...pause a moment...if only for a moment...and no response" (220). This unceasing, incomprehensible voice, the implacable voice within us, is not the syntax of speech but the current of desire. Desire: the channeled and incomprehensible force that speaks but which I cannot understand.

Freud, as I read him through Derrida, uses the metaphor of breaching to describe the translation of the energy of presence into desire. "Breaching, the tracing of a trail, opens up a conducting path. Which presupposes a certain violence and a certain resistance to effraction" (Derrida 1978, 200). The inhibition, resulting in an incomplete release, will leave an excess that ensures the persistence of the instinct and creates a difference between breaches.

> It is the difference between breaches which is the true origin of memory, and thus of the psyche.... We then must not say that breaching without difference is insufficient for memory; it must be stipulated that there is no pure breaching without difference. Trace as memory is not a pure breaching that might be reappropriated at any time as simple presence; it is rather the ungraspable and invisible difference between breaches. We thus already know that psychic life is neither the transparency of meaning nor the opacity of force but the difference within the exertion of forces.   [Derrida 1978, 201]

Resistances transgressed by the instincts define a motivation determined by the pathway effracted and, implicitly, offer the promise of an object that can be cathected. The teleological aspect projects neither a privileged object nor even the vaguest outlines of what the "other" may be, and it does not guarantee that a suitable object will be found. Rather, the pathway that has been facilitated will admit, by *exclusion,* a range of potential modes of expression. An instinct will also be codified as an intensity, the magnitude of which will depend on the degree of facilitation and, coextensively, by the spacing be-

tween repetitions of the effraction. That repetitions will occur is en-
sured by the inability of the breach to accommodate the full force of
the instinct and the demand of the deferred energy for release. What
was an undifferentiated pressure is thus canalized and spaced—giving
it, metaphorically, a linear trajectory.

This re-presentation of the originary energetics, in "edited" form,
defines for Derrida a "primary" writing that

> cannot be read in terms of any code. It works, no doubt, with a mass of
> elements which have been codified in the course of an individual or
> collective history. But in its operations, lexicon, and syntax a purely
> idiomatic residue is irreducible and is made to bear the burden of
> interpretation in the communication between unconsciousnesses.
> [Derrida 1978, 209]

The idiomatic codification is likened by Derrida, through Warburton
and Freud, to hieroglyphs, "pictographic, ideogrammatic, and pho-
netic elements" (Derrida 1978, 209). This image is principally spatial,
however, and in being static loses the fluid dynamic of shifting forces;
therefore, it does not acknowledge the complex system of relationships established "in the communication between unconscious-
nesses."

Instincts are not univocal. Numerous transgressions, of unequal
force but related to the same need, occur simultaneously along a finite
number of pathways; and the conduits exploited may motivate contradictory responses within the organism. Moreover, effractions of
more than one instinct will occur at the same time, similarly utilizing
a variety of openings, at differing magnitudes, and with the same potential for self-contradiction. These streamings are not autonomous
but flow together, creating dynamic networks based on affinities and
resistances that may result in the linking of contradictory impulses.

The force of the instinct is no longer an amorphous energetics but
an element in the stream of fluctuating intensities that define desire. It
is the unrelenting pressure, of unknowable origin, that refuses to be
silenced and yet is so frustratingly incomprehensible:

> no idea what she's saying...imagine!...no idea what she's saying!...and
> can't stop...no stopping it [...] can't stop the stream...and the whole brain
> begging...something in the brain...begging the mouth to stop...pause a
> moment...if only for a moment...and no response...as if it hadn't
> heard.   [Beckett 1984, 220]

The mouth of desire cannot be responsive to the demands of the
brain—the whole brain or something in it—because the mouth is not
an ear.

There are, nevertheless, moments when it seems possible, if not to know the I, at least to know the desire to know. "straining to hear...the odd word...make some sense of it" (221). She believes that in that word lies the meaning of her struggle. "something that would tell... how it was...how she...what?...had been?...yes...something that would tell how it had been...how she has lived...lived on and on" (221). But to achieve that end she must hear the stream, and glean from it its signification. "so intent one is...on what one is saying...the whole being ...hanging on its words" (219). But she cannot know "something she didn't know herself...wouldn't know if she heard" (221). She cannot know because it is in the wrong language—the glyphics of intensities rather than the syntax of words.

What she can understand, her speaking voice, the third sonority, is heard only three times. When she speaks it is the result of a struggle to organize a coherent statement that will express the turmoil and uncertainty she is experiencing. "or grabbing at straw...the brain... there...on to the next...bad as the voice...worse...as little sense...all that together...can't [...] can't go on...God is love" (221). The three-word phrase, "God is love," is insufficient to the task; it lacks adequate correspondence to the internal movement she is experiencing. "what she was trying...what to try...no matter...keep on [...]hit on it in the end... then back...God is love...tender mercies...new every morning" (223). Three words are expanded to three phrases, which in some labyrinthine way summarize for her the force of her existence—at least insofar as language is able to articulate that force in speech.

A further process of differentiation is required in the movement into speech: an already displaced energetics must seek in language what has been denied it externally, the promised object. The project remains utopian because complete satisfaction lies only in those words that provide absolute proximity between the pure language of desire and the structures of verbal syntax. Desire undergoes another process of translation from the dynamic of hieroglyph, as a fluid totality, into the spaced linearity of language. Implicit in the process are systems of deferral and resistance that impede and frustrate the movement of expression. The inability of language to accommodate the plenitude of desire and its continually shifting intensities disrupts the flow of language—signaling, through the ellipses, the difference between force and release, indicating not a reduction in pressure but a surplus that admits to failure.

In addition to effractions that result in language, there are accompanying breaches that lack the authority of the word but which find expression through pathways incompatible with the privileged sign.

They do not go unheeded, however; they are heard. They surround the word and encase its phonology; they flood the gaps with their complaints. Once in the ear, in the valuation of the word, they trace differences that challenge the integrity of the signifier and the signified appropriated by it. They call into question and critique the system of facilitations and resistances that finds inadequate resolution in a particular word, a particular syntax. And so the process continues.

Subjectivity, as imagined through the metaphor of sonorities, resists concretization because it is inscribed within the dynamic movement of fluctuating intensities. Nevertheless, the outlines of a subject position are engraved in the system of resisted and encouraged pathways that permit, for the moment, the use of specific modes of expression. Insofar as I can know myself, it is through the object, the words, used to express my self; but these representations of desire lack consistency and will be altered in response to fluctuating intensities, the availability of desired objects, and the interpretation of the response to my actions. Implicit in this formulation is the idea that permutations in external and internal circumstances can alter, if only to a degree, the practices in which I engage. But in order to understand my potential for change, I must explore how patterns of repression and facilitation are constituted.

Material Conditions of Subjectivity

Insofar as there are innate resistances to the expression of the energetics of desire, they must function by gross generalization. They can define neither a motive nor an object but exclude paths that are detrimental to the survival of the preconscious being. Learned inhibitions, and the consequent displacements and condensations, are specifically related to the determination of motives and objects, if only in terms of categories. The selection of the object is not made autonomously, however. Desire is polyvocal and the expenditure of energy occurs continuously through a multiplicity of cathexes. The dominant expenditure and return will be determined by the magnitude of the force required to effect the effraction. Simultaneous but subsidiary expressions (those necessitating lesser intensities) will interweave a context within which the primary return is valued. Moreover, the privileged discharge will not necessarily determine the outcome of the evaluation. Although secondary breaches require less energy to *effect* discharge, this does not mean that less energy is expressed. A facilitated path, with its virtual guarantee of release and promise of "easy" repetition, may provide greater, though less noticeable, releases of energy. Breaches, however pleasurable, that threaten such a habitual path with inhibition may be interpreted negatively—as painful—and repetitions of the effraction more forcibly resisted. Moreover, shifts in external circumstances can result in very different interpretations of an event, giving rise to inconsistent behavior or behavioral relativity.

At the core of this inconsistency, however, are habitual practices, defined both as strongly facilitated modes of expression that promise regular releases of excitation and as strongly held resistances to specific effractions. Consistent behavior evolves through patterns of return that define an action as, most simply, pleasure or pain. Knowledge of myself is founded on the resulting pattern—that is, the regular repetition of specific facilitations and resistances. Indeed, the ordering process that allows me to perceive this organization is the effect of such repetitions. Another determining factor in habitual practices is the evaluation of responses to the expression in a variety of contexts. Limits placed on my subjectivity result from successful and unsuccessful interactions with specific objects of desire. These interactions occur in circumstances organized according to reinforced patterns of expression; these facilitated avenues are established through the interpretation of responses received from external, material contexts.

It is the same for her. "so no love...spared that...no love such as normally vented on the...speechless infant...in the home...no...nor indeed for that matter any of any kind...no love of any kind...at any subsequent stage" (216). Repeated absence of an object of desire, and the attendant pleasurable return, creates a negative expectation—that is, the intensification of resistance, signaling a limit on consciousness. Acceptable modes of social behavior, for her and the society that repeatedly proffers a negative return, will be defined by these limits. Outcast at birth, she remains outcast and the conditions of her existential solitude are defined; but simultaneously boundaries are established that indicate the limits of the community.

Social systems require a periphery, margins of opposition that reinforce an ideological hegemony, that conserve structures of power within the community. She is, for the community, a passive reminder of the threat posed by antisocial elements—her humiliation becoming a reification of the limits on acceptable behavior. It falls to her (though it only seems to be her fate) to live on the margins, at the negative limits of society; and there she must try, and largely fails, to construct her subjectivity. However, it is a symbiotic rather than parasitic relationship. She is defined by her placement in circumstances that encourage negative behavior; but these imposed limits provide positive canalizations of desire as well. Unable to defend herself when accused of committing a crime, she satisfies the social need to reinforce moral behavior, "that time in court...what had she to say for herself...guilty or not guilty...stand up woman...speak up woman...stood there staring into space" (221), and her need for human contact, "glad of the hand on her arm" (221). Her inability to communicate in banal, everyday situations describes a negative image of social propriety, while freeing her from experiencing the rejection of interpersonal contact.

> even shopping...out shopping...busy shopping centre...supermart...just hand in the list...with the bag...old black shopping bag...then stand there waiting...any length of time...middle of the throng...motionless...staring into space...mouth half open as usual...then pay and go...not as much as good-bye. [219]

Inscribed as society's "other," she embodies the inverse of the dominant ideology.

Margins are marked by patterns of inclusion as well as exclusion. Her complicity with the ideological system that marks her oppression is affirmed by the significant investment she makes in religion. "she fixing with her eye...a distant bell...as she hastened towards it...fixing it with her eye...lest it elude her" (218). Her fixation on the bell, her fear of losing it, acknowledges its status as an object of desire that implicitly promises expenditure. The connection between faith in God and the return of love was made at the same time, and in the same circumstances, that cathexes with other people as positive objects of desire were repressed. "brought up as she had been to believe ...with the other waifs...in a merciful [...] God" (217). The displacement, encouraged in childhood, offers up the promise of nothing less than salvation—not as a metaphysical potential but as a very real and physical liberation. "God is love...tender mercies...new every morning" (221–22). Implicit in the promise is renewal, a rebirth distanced from the frustration and suffering imposed on her by a callous and indifferent society.

But the "tender mercies," the privileged release, come at a cost. To be saved she must willingly embrace a further system of resistances that places strict limitations on her behavior. "The individual *is interpellated as a (free) subject in order that* [she] *shall submit freely to the commandments of the Subject, i.e., in order that* [she] *shall (freely) accept* [her] *subjection.... There are no subjects except by and for their subjection*" (Althusser 1971, 182; emphasis in original). Explicit within the ideology of salvation is the codification of the law that makes the satisfactory release of desire contingent upon the valuation of certain modes of behavior. Acquired resistance to the selection of certain objects of desire is a condition that must be met if she can hope to find ultimate release. Failure to make the correct choices threatens the loss of the Subject, forcing her to interpret negatively otherwise positive effractions, causing an inversion of what may be pleasurable into what *is* painful. "that notion of punishment...for some sin or other...or for the lot...or no particular reasons...for its own sake ...thing she understood perfectly...that notion of punishment" (217). Suffering as a way of life, as the appropriate definition of her "lot in life," perpetually postpones the expenditure, or allows its release only through the anticipation of a future satisfaction. The pathways effracted that lead her to move toward the bell—the fetishized substitute for the promised-but-never-present object of desire—activate an expression of energy of such magnitude that it is equaled only by the dread that an inhibition will be imposed, that the metonymic symbol will be spirited away, that punishment for some sin—real or imaginary—will be exacted.

The resistances that constrict her social behavior also place limits on her ability to experience herself. She is able neither to experience pleasure nor to find release through tears.

> one evening on the way home [...] sitting staring at her hand...there in her lap...palm upward...suddenly saw it wet...the palm...tears presumably ...hers presumably...no one else for miles...no sound...just the tears...sat and watched them dry...all over in a second.   [220–21]

The uncertainty she experiences when confronted with tears—her insensate body and the detachment with which she observes the event—serves Beckett's seeming desire to negate the body, but it also describes the effects on subjectivity of social patterns that define marginality. But the excess of frustration resulting from the extreme repression of desire eventually creates a force of such magnitude that normal patterns of resistance are disrupted. "sudden urge to...tell... then rush out stop the first she saw...nearest lavatory...start pouring it out...steady stream...mad stuff...half the vowels wrong...no one could follow" (222). The intensity of her frustration forces a breach—a defecation of desire—in a language known only to herself but understood by no one. The experience becomes excruciatingly painful after the release of effraction, with the return of the prohibition. "till she saw the stare she was getting...then die of shame...crawl back in" (222). Violation of the resistance to interpersonal communication, expended on an unsympathetic object, strengthens the repression and reinforces the belief that life is suffering. The restoration of the inhibition produces a pain far more acute than the emotional discomfort of embarrassment because it cannot be localized. It can only be conceived of as an intensification of the buzzing, the streaming that cannot be stopped.

Further articulations of desire are impossible, in part because of the paucity of language, but also because forms of signification are always secondary modes of release. That which makes known the objects of desire and their opposites, that which allows us to speak of desire and its repression, has already been denied more immediate and satisfactory expression. Yet even this mode of displacement is denied her; but it is not refused the Mouth, or me. It is through language that I construct a narrative for *her*, that I understand the poignancy of *her* situation, acknowledge *her* as an object of *my* desire. Through her I recognize the manifestations of my subjectivity. But I am not alone in constructing her. As you are creating her in terms of my discourse, so I create her through the discourse of the Mouth. Therefore, to understand the Mouth as an ideological subject, I must return to its language, its description of her, recognizing I cannot know the intensities of desire but can only know contaminated representations.

Subjection

The Mouth does not name her but generalizes her identity through the use of the pronomial shifter, "she." An ambiguous dichotomy is established between the "I" of the Mouth and the third-person pronoun. On the one hand, the difference initiates a play of meaning between the two terms: "I" am not "she"; therefore, "she" is "not I." This tautology is destabilized, ironically, by the insistence on separation: "what?...who?...no!...she!" (220). The emphatic denial and its repetition can be read as a resistance to acknowledging identity, making the inverse tautology equally possible: "I" am "she"; "she" is "I." The play becomes more dangerous as a result of the denial because a new configuration arises: I am not I. Metaphysically there is no problem because the configuration supports the analytic of the sonorities: I am what I cannot know; therefore, what I know is not I. But that is only part of the difficulty, because it does not confront the processes that deny self-knowledge, that determine how the self is experienced. It is the discourse of the body, scarred by the imprint of power, of force and resistance, that disrupts the eloquent simplicity of the metaphysical assertion. The shift in focus does not invalidate the metaphysical model, but it dislodges from the background adjacent discourses that frame the representation of the unknowable. It is through an examination of this context, of the "she," that the outlines of the Mouth as subject begin to appear.

She is someone who picks flowers and goes shopping, who follows the sound of a bell, who speaks uncontrollably, who is accused of committing crimes, who is unable to feel pleasure, and who finds it difficult to cry. She is a victim, deserted by her parents, unloved in the home, imprisoned for a crime she may not have committed. She is irrational, breaking into incomprehensible diatribes in front of strangers. She is frigid, unable to feel pleasure or pain. She is passive, needing to be aroused to experience pleasure, following the object of her desire rather than seeking it out. She is the "other" who is acted upon but is not an agent on her own behalf. She is what the Mouth needs her to be, an object on which it can release the intensities of its desire.

A satisfactory conclusion to the Mouth's cathexis can be guaranteed because the "other" is not an object but an object in language. The attributes selected, the signs activated to specify the "she," create a narrative that defines her. This context indicates patterns of facilitation within the speaking subject that ensure minimal resistance, habits of consciousness that privilege particular scenarios. In fact, the actual, material existence of the "she" is inconsequential because the image is sufficiently vivid to satisfy the requirements for effraction.

The privilege granted her is, however, a ruse, because the Mouth does not need her for herself: the dialectic, in the final analysis, is not between "I" and "she," but between "I" and "not I." The context she creates vouchsafes the solipsistic cathexis between the I and the not I. She is the landscape on which the analytic of sonorities is played out, in which the struggle for subjectivity takes place. Like the body and material reality in *Not I,* she is negated, relegated to the peripheries of the discourse, subjected but not subject.

She is the key to unraveling a mystery, to locating a missing person: the I. Or those aspects of the self that I cannot know. This reading echoes the tendency in postmodern thought from Nietzsche onward to feminize the unknowable in subjectivity.

> Right across the spectrum of contemporary Continental and especially French philosophy the "feminine" functions as a powerful vehicle to convey the critical attempts to redefine human subjectivity. . . . the feminization of thought seems to be prescribed as a fundamental step in the general programme of anti-humanism which marks our era. [Braidotti 1987, 236]

The appropriation of the female to represent the other-that-is-I parallels the use of "she" as a landscape against which the problem of the subject is argued. She is an image that is defined only to be absorbed as the background. The face, critiqued by Deleuze and Guattari as the despotic construction of *signifiance* and subjectivity, is transcribed within all landscapes.

> All faces envelop an unknown, unexplored landscape; all landscapes are populated by a loved or dreamed-of face, develop a face to come or already past. What face has not called upon the landscapes it amalgamated, sea and hill; what landscape has not evoked the face that would have completed it, providing an unexpected complement for its lines and traits?   [Deleuze and Guattari 1987, 172–73]

As the "other," "she" does not define the limits of subjectivity but inscribes the parameters, the closure of representation within which the subject must be conceived. She is the mirror in which I seek my lost self.

My desire to return to undifferentiated being is, necessarily, enwrapped in representation, in images of differentiation. In defining the goal I become entrapped in a spatial topography of here and there, in the trope of the "other." To describe myself I must create a mystery that embodies that which I have lost and wish to repossess. And I name it the "other." In so nominating it, I invoke another chain of signifiers, and in *Not I* I name it "she." I invest her with the mystery, and through her hope to possess myself. But in the feminization of the other, I engage another discourse, embrace another ideology. The virtue of the dream is compromised by an investment in sexual differentiation.

I am not the landscape "she" is; I do not lack a body. I can act through my agency, or the illusion of it, which mitigates the impact of the despair I encounter in Beckett, though it also defines it. This position is not available to her, nor to the female reader. In the definition of the subject, "she" is equated with both the "I" and the "not I," without difference or distinction. She represents but is neither the mystery I cannot unravel nor the material body. There is no room for her within this configuration to define a subject position, since she is merely a figure in the discourse of the self. "The enigma that *is* woman will therefore constitute the *target*, the *object*, the *stake*, of a masculine discourse, of a debate among men, which would not consult her, would not concern her. Which, ultimately, she is not supposed to know anything about" (Irigaray 1985, 13).

For me it is different because I constitute a fourth term in the process: "he." Instead of being ensnared in the triadic equation I = she = not I, I can construct a line of flight through the masculine shifter

and, with the knowledge gained, assess my own subjectivity as a response to the existential dilemma posited by Beckett. I am the autho-
rized reader, spectator, because, and only because, I am "he," "having
vanished...thin air...no sooner buttoned up his breeches" (Beckett
1984, 216). She is not so fortunate; she is trapped within the text
without the right of refusal. "A reserve supply of negativity sustaining
the articulation of their moves, or refusals to move, in a partly fictional
progress toward the mastery of power. Of knowledge. In which she
will have no part. Off-stage, off-side, beyond selfhood" (Irigaray
1985, 22).

If the pain I feel in *Not I* is real, then so is the pleasure I receive,
which arises, at least in part, from the images of an abused woman
used to evoke my despair. But my pleasure lies not in her violation but
in her marginalization. It is acceptable to me because it defines a community of subjects from which she is excluded, and I am not. It limits
a discourse in which she appears but in which she cannot participate.
It reinforces my belief that I can exercise the power of agency within
a dominant, if not hegemonic, male structure.

Is there a way in which I can represent myself to myself, talk about
my subjectivity without the objectification of the "other"? I see no
easy answer. It is not simply a question of sensitizing Beckett to the
problem, or rewriting or deconstructing *Not I* as a text, in performance—though it would be a step. Rather the tendency to oppress the
other in the process of defining the self questions the systems of
power and representation within a partriarchal society: calling into
question practices, making manifest practices that reinforce limits on
community, that guarantee limited distribution of power. It cannot be
simply a negative project, however, but must be one that alters the
construction of environments, that creates circumstances that facilitate, rather than resist, patterns of behavior conducive to the self-
determination of identity. As a very first step, this project requires the
initial recognition that "she" is not the other-that-I-speak, but that she
is a subject to whom I must listen.

Note

1. The desire to transgress implies a boundary between the knowable self
and the unknowable other, with the latter figured, from Nietzsche onward, as
the mystery, the feminine. Luce Irigaray, among others, quite rightly asserts
that these metaphors are not innocent but represent real practices, that they
validate ideologies of rape and violation. This paper is, in part, an investigation

of the effects of feminized images on the subjective and material existence of those appropriated by the metaphor.

References

Althusser, Louis. *Lenin and Philosophy and Other Essays.* Translated by Ben Brewster. New York: Monthly Review Press, 1971.

Artaud, Antonin. *The Theater and Its Double.* New York: Grove Press, 1958.

Beckett, Samuel. *Not I* (1973). In *The Collected Shorter Plays of Samuel Beckett.* New York: Grove Press, 1984.

Braidotti, Rosi. "Envy: or With My Brains and Your Looks." In *Men in Feminism,* edited by Alice Jardine and Paul Smith. New York: Methuen, 1987.

Deleuze, Gilles, and Guattari, Félix. *A Thousand Plateaus: Capitalism and Schizophrenia.* Translated by Brian Massumi. Minneapolis: University of Minnesota Press, 1987.

Derrida, Jacques. *Writing and Difference.* Translated by Alan Bass. Chicago: University of Chicago Press, 1978.

Freud, Sigmund. *The Standard Edition of the Complete Psychological Works of Sigmund Freud.* Edited and translated by James Strachey. 24 vols. London: Hogarth Press 1953–74.

    "Instincts and Their Vicissitudes" (1915), vol. 14.

    Beyond the Pleasure Principle (1920), vol. 18.

Irigaray, Luce. *Speculum of the Other Woman.* Translated by Gillian C. Gill. Ithaca: Cornell University Press, 1985.

7 Post Apocalypse with Out
Figures: The Trauma of Theater
in Samuel Beckett

Anthony Kubiak

*B*reath. Each inspiration different and each the same. The illumination rising and falling, appearing and disappearing like clockwork ("3 to 6 and back"). An alien and familiar condensation collects at the edges like the "miscellaneous rubbish" barely visible in the faint stage light. The silence evokes phantom whispers and mute reflections broken by the sudden intake of breath and the cry, and the seemingly empty stage replicates the spectral eyes watching beyond the pit. It is as if nobody were here, as if nobody were watching the ceremony. It is as if nothing were present *but* the cry ("instant of recorded vagitus") and the breath ("Amplified recording"), not yet verbal or nominal, still disembodied and abstracted, lacking any quality that consensus might declare "real" performance—devoid of actors, speech, and plot. Seemingly devoid of the very theater that gives it birth.

Breath invokes an imaginary theatrical apocalypse, the final movement of the performative erased of everything but its own scene. Even the bare text suggests a ruin, the riddling fragments of a dying theater, a theater destroyed, perhaps, through a prolonged epoch of repressive control and ideological instruction by which the very *idea* of theater is scoured from public memory. Or conversely, perhaps, the piece suggests a different kind of finish, in which the *phenomenon of theater* (what I will hereafter simply call "theater") is not condemned, but apotheosized and consequently disintegrated in a kind of naive monomania, the very separations and conventions that held it before the public eye dissolved in an ethos of communality and shared experience—perhaps some participatory ideal has finally emptied theater entirely of the possibility of its otherness, its reason for being.

But this is surely absurd, a *dying* theater ("expiration and, decrease"). A marginal and nearly nonexistent theater ("Silence and hold about five seconds. Curtain"). How can there be such a thing when performance has "always already" reformulated itself in the imagination, when theater "always already" *re*appears in the mind that *is* the *mise-en-scène*, in the very *Breath* that comes before the "instant of recorded vagitus"?

By postulating a theater that is at the edge of appearance and disappearance, Beckett brings us to the most fundamental moment of theatrical perception—the moment in which one asks what it is that makes "it" theater, the moment in which the mind's eye perceives itself seeing, and thinks itself thinking the *mise-en-scène*. Certainly the entire Beckettian project impels us at times to perceive the dissolution of boundaries between mind and stage, impels us to see the profound scenic qualities of consciousness itself.

The psychoanalyst J.-B. Pontalis hints at the scenic agency of consciousness when he writes that, just as "there can be no film without a screen, no play without a stage, be it just one imaginary line," there can likewise be no dream or memory without a theater to receive it (1981, 30). In fact, while describing dream reality and, by extension, memory reality, Pontalis casts that reality exclusively in terms of a theater that moves between dreamed consciousness and a "real" stage:

> When a conflict is ceaselessly *enacted* on the stage of the world, we are refused entry in to the stage of the dream. "Real" space takes up all of the room. Our objects of cathexis catch the ego's interests and the sexual instincts, confusing them, and mobilize all of our energy.   [37]

Now several theories of mind or unconscious as *mise-en-scène* have been developed in recent years, most notably in the work of Herbert Blau, but also in the writings of Jean-François Lyotard, Michel Foucault, Gilles Deleuze, and Jacques Derrida. (Derrida's essay "Freud and the Scene of Writing" serves, in fact, as the necessary background to the present work. What Derrida submits as "writing" I would identify as theater.)[1]

These theorists have with varying degrees of success postulated philosophical theaters, theaters of mind, or stagings of consciousness preceding and melding seamlessly into the "real" theater. But while this medium, the medium of thought itself, could easily be described in other than theatrical terms (as "writing" for example), one still wonders at the significance of the almost reflexive tendency to describe mind in theatrical metaphors. Why is the phenomenal moment of perception, the "instant of recorded vagitus," so easily identified with theatrical performance?

Moreover, if "the mind" is identified as *mise-en-scène,* then what are we to make of the arcane and gratuitous *activity* called performance, the impulse that immediately insists on exteriorization, reenactment, and embodiment? What is the relationship between that *state* of perception that is theater, and the *activity* of performance itself, a relation that Deleuze (1983a, 147–95) might characterize as a "dialectical/antidialectical" opposition? How to move from one to the other, from mind to production, from the dialectic to the "flow"? And how to begin? How to *think* about beginning? Where to go from here?

Beckett tells us, of course; it begins, he says, with the *Breath,* with the remnant, the shred, the *ghost.* The circularity of theatrical perception finds a kind of phantom completion in the circulation of breath itself: postapocalypse becomes prehistory, *Breath*'s end, like breath, becomes its beginning, and the cycle, for good or bad, is forever renewed, forever concealed in its renewal.

Yet while the *Breath* fantasia suggests these things, it also suggests none of them. *Breath* is a mere shell, after all, an *essentially* empty space—the scene of theater's immanent disappearance darkening into ghostly afterimage; even as the blackout comes, I begin to discern in the gloom an other outline, the residual and troubling presence of a different sort of theater suggested not only by my very participation in the fantasy, but more perceptibly in the faint presence of certain "paralinguistic" tracings (the stage read left to right), certain linear striations ("No verticals") which have initiated the fantasy, half-eradicated relics just beyond apprehension ("Curtain 1 . . . 2 . . . 3 . . . Curtain").

Breath's theater in fact gives birth to writing as much as it is determined by it: is "stage read left to right" a reading effect, or is the appearance of the written page and the "dream rebus" a metaphor of the performative space? Certainly, when I speak of "another kind of theater," I am not alluding to the mere presence of those "texts" littering the landscape like "miscellaneous rubbish," "all scattered and lying." I am not suggesting that theater represents a mere variation on Derridean inscription; the designs I see in the gloom are disturbing, seemingly more elemental—the material tracings of a still indecipherable *history* read in the landfill of some future civilization.

Breath suggests, alongside its other psychic broodings, an Imaginary origin and end, the dawn and closure of the modern age, or, indeed, the dawn and closure of history and consciousness itself read regressively and catastrophically in the modern age—an age characterized, in part, by its suspicion that theater is no longer possible, that theater has disappeared, been usurped by its "double," by a "dinner theater," by mere archival "texts" or various kinds of bastardizations and corruptions. The very emptiness of *Breath* suggests a desire to cleanse or be cleansed by a troubled catharsis, a purgation that signals a need to return, somehow, to a "purer" theater, a theater of element, primal substance, and impulse—a theater that would represent a paradoxical return both to its origin and to its apocalyptic disappearance, and thus to the disappearance/apparition of history and consciousness itself. This, as Artaud realized, has always been theater's dream—a world rid of theater, and so a world of *pure* theater, a theater of pure consciousness, a stage rid of everything but its own absolute and objectless presence.

The dream of presence, theater's *eternal* dream, has been the special fantasia of theater in the modern period. From the psychodrama of Strindberg, through the dreamwork of Artaud, radically rearticulating itself in Piscator and Brecht, foregrounding itself in Genet and the performance movements of the sixties and seventies, exemplifying itself most acutely, perhaps, in Beckett, the dream of arriving, somehow, at theater's originary impulse and its annihilating limn has haunted the modern stage as no other theater before it. The critical obsession of the modernist stage is the stage itself: "Faint light on [empty] stage. . . . Hold about five seconds. Curtain."

So while the concealed compulsion to ends and origins is not unique, then, in theater history, its modern obsessiveness and intensity is. What is the meaning of this necessity to retrace theater's origins in the modern period? Is the desire to "go back" to some aboriginal theater, even unconsciously, not an attempt to further mystify theater through its apparent demystification? What is the mechanism that generates the cathexis of theater by theater? If mind *is mise-en-scène* and *mise-en-scène* mind, how is this cathexis *performed* in the modern period? How might the stage be read as its own commentary on the romance of origins, especially in the modern/postmodern period, the romance of what has come before, and what will come after?

In part, the modernist fantasia of origins and ends represents, as I have already suggested, the compulsion to repeat without end the Imaginary moment of theater's birth and death in the endlessly reproduced schizogenesis of modern and postmodern consciousness. This schizogenesis describes one of the most painful conditions of modern, postindustrial capitalism—the final inability of a reified consciousness to fulfill its own self-generating need. The modernist fantasia of theatrical origins and ends, then, attempts to objectify and exteriorize some holistic or Imaginary "first moment" of perception and desire—a "scopic drive" that seems, paradoxically, to contain both our phallocular doom as well as our politicocultural origins. As Mouth says in *Not I:* "...but the brain—...what?...lying?...yes...whether standing...or sitting...or kneeling...or lying...but the brain still...still...in a way...for her first thought was...oh long after...sudden flash" (1984, 217).

In the "sudden flash" of that "lying brain" one can glimpse a psychic reality that has always been pained and painful. But while its paratheatrical fantasias have been revisited in different theatrical forms in each age, it is the modern realization of a failed, *empirical* rationality, the "sudden flash" gone dark, that has perhaps exacerbated the psychic wound that is perception beyond tolerance, and driven consciousness to find its first cause and insight, its "first principle": "first thought was...oh long after...sudden flash...she was being punished...for her sins...a number of which then...further proof if proof were needed ...flashed through her mind" (217). The desire for an *empirical proof* and cause of consciousness' pain, and the experience of that pain as guilt or *punishment,* are perhaps the most powerful forces behind the modernist obsession with the theater of ends and origins, an obsession often expressed, ironically, as negation—the almost self-conscious attempts to suppress and repress pain and punishment in postmodern art, for example, or the complementary "repressive desublimation" of body art that formalizes pain while emptying it of its content.

One can read the fixation with ends and origins in the postmodern period as a fetishization of form to the exclusion of content. In recent years the formalization of consciousness/perception in the work of artists like Robert Wilson or Richard Foreman, for example, suggests a *hyperreification* of consciousness reflected in the hyperrational and paradoxically *antirational* focus of much postmodern theory and criticism (see, for example, the work of Deleuze and Guattari).

It does not require a great leap of intuition or insight, then, to imagine that the very reification of consciousness that has allowed such inquiries to formulate themselves in the modern and postmodern period—plus the apparent tendency of a reified consciousness to reconstruct itself dialectically according to the very historical constraints and conditions that define it (the production of "history" itself in the nineteenth and twentieth centuries, according to Foucault, and "history"'s intrinsic concern with origins and teleologic ends)[2]—would produce an especially acute and absurd desire to bring to consciousness some "first moment" of consciousness; the moment such a reification becomes conscious, in other words, one wants to assign it an origin.

Yet the very phenomenon of reification suggests that all such origins are illusory and are mere by-products of reification itself. Thus the circular or spiraling effect of such plays as *Not I* or *Krapp's Last Tape*—plays that begin, in a certain sense, where they end—emerges as a kind of critique of origins and their illusory nature.

Ultimately, in the modern theater, the circular and contradictory tendency of reification both to produce and conceal its origins leads to the reproduction of that contradiction in the inquiry itself: thus while the modernist theater manifests a consciousness of its own reification as a compulsion to drive theater to its seeming ends and origins "beyond reification," that same theater, as a consequence, seems to exhibit a fundamental desire to *rid itself of (reified) theater* and thus "purify" itself. In the midst of theaters that may ostensibly reject originary concepts, we seem to be faced, in plays like *Breath,* with the apparent "death" of theater in modernism occurring *as* its very origin—literally nothing comes before, and nothing comes after. Or again, the remembrance of theatrical death in the modern period, its wake as it were, becomes the very moment of its birth. The romance of ends and origins seemingly critiqued in *Breath* is parallel to theater's obsession with its own reification, its sense of absence and presence, its life and death *as* theater.

This Eros/Thanatos obsession suggests an earlier theatrical tradition (the very thematic that haunts Freud himself after *Beyond the Pleasure Principle,* the thematic in which the subject is continuously articulated and menaced "in the locus of the Other"—Life sentenced to Death, Death sentenced to Life) and is, in late modernism, seemingly transferred to a structural metaphysics of theater itself, a metaphysics that displaces birth and death as ontological principles with appearances and disappearance, the *phanisis* and the *aphanisis* of origins and ends, presence and absence.

And death or disappearance is not simply the death or disappearance of the subject, as *Breath* shows.[3] Indeed, here is a death that, as Jean Laplanche says, "in the unconscious ... would be always the death of the other, a destruction or loss we provoke" (1976, 6). This alien death is, in other words, an *intentional* construct that emerges in the very Lacanian "locus of the Other" in which I formulate my "self." But while "I" am formed in the locus of the Other and subsequently experience my own life as a seeming disappearance, and while the Other may be "always already" there to receive me—while the Other represents an unrecoverable origin, in other words—the Other, *through the image of the other's death,* also represents the enormity of Death as absolute catastrophe, apocalypse, or holocaust: the impossible death of the Other itself. The imaginary or threatened death of the Other—a death that would seem contradictory and unthinkable—would thus appear as the locus of the Law of (that is) Death. The Other would represent not only seeming origins, but unthinkable ends as well.

This double (or multiple) face of the Other—the unrecoverable origin that gives birth to an unthinkable death, a consummately Beckettian image—comes to represent the doubleness or *alienated moment* of theater/consciousness itself: "...out...into this world...tiny little thing...before its time," says Mouth in *Not I,* unsure if the "little thing" is subject or object of performance, spoken in any case "out into this world," the world that is, quite literally, theater—but a theater whose final moment of articulation is always the curtain, the blackout, the evacuation and silencing of the performative space.

Theater—continuously recalling and threatening us with death and birth, in and out of the "godforsaken hole"—is, like the economized arena of pleasure/pain that Nietzsche postulates in *Genealogy of Morals,* the site of a specific coercion, a particular and subtle ideological production ("brought up as she had been to believe...in a merciful [*Brief laugh.*]...God") that constructs "history" and "memory" from the outside in, after the fact, *as performance.* Theater accordingly introjects itself into culture as something like an Althusserian "omnihistory"—a "history" (or memory) that has no real history behind it (Althusser 1971). This "omni-history" operates, according to Althusser, precisely *as* ideology. Theater, in fact, obtains its cultural force through this very ability to exteriorize and deploy the problematic of an alienated consciousness or primal repression *as* ideology in the production of "history," while, at the same time, concealing that alienated consciousness through the fantasy of a unified audience-as-community.

So while seeming to celebrate a *shared* experience of history and self-consciousness, this theater is in fact the site in which the fragmentation of the self and its "community" is preserved. These operations are at once unconscious and theatrical: "notion of punishment...for some sin or other...or for the lot...or no particular reason...for its own sake." The ideology of theater may not so much, as a consequence, teach us what to think as keep us from thinking: while deploying pain and the fear of pain for its own unconscious ideological ends, ideology in the theater would thus conceal the indeterminate nature of that pain in various "stories," "histories," and rememorations; it would conceal pain's indeterminate moment in specific, constructed stages of trauma, reproducing itself in them as the apparent site of communal reaffirmation through pain and its catharses, the scene of the ritual by which the community receives and affirms its repressive myth-histories (this repressive tragic function was, in part, the reason Brecht took such a dim view of tragedy). Thus the *mise-en-scène* as unconscious that Lyotard identifies as the primary theatrical scene is the same *mise-en-scène* as Jameson's "political unconscious."

But while it is relatively easy to imagine how this repressed production might appear in the "institutional" theater, how and *why* it is produced in the individual *mise-en-scène* of mind is much more problematic, and is bound up in the experience of the ego or *self* as the indeterminate source of psychic pain or trauma. When the self/ego represses or forecloses[4] its pain—the pain of primal repression—it reappears as what might be called "history" or "memory," differentiated from the actual history that Fredric Jameson equates with the Lacanian Real and its pain. This actual history, however, can never be apprehended as some reified force, but can only be known through its effects, according to Jameson, through its necessary repression into discourse, "history," analysis, or theater (1981, 102). "History," according to this formula, appears in the theater/*mise-en-scène* either as a kind of narrative symptom or as effective hallucination generated by some *real,* and necessarily misunderstood, historical pain.

The "problematic" of theatrical origins is not merely structural or formal, then, but is a consequence of the experience of real pain or trauma generated by the fundamental breach of being born in the locus of the Other—what Lacan identifies as "the locus of the Law," or culture and its theater ("theater's double" in Artaud's phrase). Thus the birth or emergence of the subject in the Other—the subject articulated by the symbolic as embodied in a particular culture—reconstitutes political culture in and as self; the pain/trauma that is history is thus "always already" reconstructed or re-presented by theater seemingly *for the first time* as "history" or "traumatic memory" in the alien landscape of consciousness—more simply stated, theater is historically determined and determining and is, especially in the period of the postmodern, bound to confront this fact, another result and predicament of reified consciousness.

Although one may wish to differentiate "consciousness trauma" from a more seemingly specific *historical* pain like sexual trauma, this, as Brecht himself understood, is not so easily accomplished. In fact, the never-ending struggle of politics in the theater is characterized in

part by the very impasse that demands a confrontation with a historical pain that is, in the theater at least, often impossible to locate or
articulate as anything but pure illusion. This impasse is amplified by
Freudian theory's insistence that while the "original" trauma (either
personal or social) may be generated by an actual and discrete experience in an individual's past, the *locatability* of this moment is
deeply problematic. And yet it is the very unlocatability of the moment that indicates its historicity and its pain: the alienation of
thought in the unlocatable is precisely what hurts (and "what hurts"
is what Jameson calls history).

The revelatory processes of psychoanalysis and theater are, I would
insist, necessarily fictional and repressive, more a process of rehears-
ing and reenacting a *constructed* trauma *in the present* than of finding
and recuperating the "real" moment of the actual trauma. In analysis
(and theater), for example, the construction of the trauma is enacted,
as Freud suggests, *retrogressively* as remembrance. Remembrance is
felt at the individual level as a seeming recuperation of the actual
trauma *as* trauma (which it may not have been originally), and at the
social level as the pain of "historical" trauma "represented for the first
time." Thus traumatic pain, experienced either as "memory" or "history," does not *necessarily* originate in some past historical trauma
reenacted, however, but is, rather, the pain that is its own presentation
as history—the pain that constitutes and is constituted by theater.

One often does not remember this traumatic pain, Freud suggests,
because the traumatic incident with which it is associated is quite
possibly without realized pain; rather one creates the pain of the
trauma (and assumes the guilt of the incident) for the first time in the
future, and this pain is then "read back" to the original incident; psychoanalytic theory does not claim, however, that no pain is "really"
suffered but holds that the origin of trauma's pain is radically indeterminate; moreover, the mechanism *through* which—and not "in
which"—this rehearsal of the indeterminate (what we might also call
primal repression) occurs is scenic, in Pontalis's terms, or *theatrical*
in my own.

This paradoxical cross-penetration—trauma generating theater,
theater as the generational principle of trauma—is central to Freudian
theories of trauma, memory, and consciousness. Although many writers like Pontalis have recognized an essentially theatrical contextualization by which Freud dramatizes certain "primal" moments of psy-
chosexual development (the "primal scene," "the seduction scene,"
"screen memories," the very spatial and theatrically bound idea of the
represented), these moments are often assumed to have taken on the-

atricality *after the fact* so to speak: Freud merely uses the theater as a preexisting metaphor for certain psychic mechanisms, or he assumes that both psyche and theater emerge from some common perceptual apparatus that inflects each with the peculiar sense of spatiality, separation, and rememoration that somehow characterizes basic psychic operations as theatrical production.

But if one looks at any of these Freudian "performance metaphors" from the standpoint of theater *or* trauma theory, one comes to realize that there is nothing, that there can *be* nothing, preceding these Freudian mechanisms but theater itself (what Derrida would call "writing"): the fascinated, but ultimately alienating, *aphanic* moment of perception by which the self emerges as an object of consciousness in the displacing movements of the "mirror stage" *is* the moment of theater's perception, and it is the psyche itself, emerging as dream, memory, ego, that occurs after the theatrical fact. It is fruitless, then, to argue for this theatricality simply as a ground upon which the figuration of perception appears, just as it would be absurd to call *Breath* "pure" theater because of the absence of actors.

It is illusory, therefore, to think of dream or memory and their associated traumas as phenomena that occur "within" a performative context. Rather the performative itself is the necessity through which something like the seduction scene and its delayed trauma come into being. Freud seems, at some subliminal level at least, to presuppose such a necessity; although he never belabors (as I am afraid I have) the paradigm of the theatrical, he develops his theory of sexual trauma along essentially theatrical lines when he "metaphorically" places such phenomena as memory or dream within a preexisting and essentially performative context—a *theater* that is "always already" there to receive it.

Thus when the phobic Emma, whom Freud discusses in the "Project for a Scientific Psychology," *re*-presents a childhood sexual assault through the process of analysis that she undergoes as an adult, she represents it through a kind of theatrical rehearsal. In Freud's writing Emma's trauma "scene" (like any such scene in analysis) is presented regressively—the usual sequence of psychoanalytic discovery of trauma—and begins with a *memory* (a false memory, as it turns out) that Emma associates with the origin of her phobia. In this memory, she goes into a shop to buy something and sees two shop assistants who are laughing together, perhaps at the way she is dressed, and she runs out of the store in a fright. This memory informs her phobia. She becomes, as an adult, terrified to enter a store.

As it turns out, the memory is associated with a childhood sexual assault, in which Emma, then eight, had gone into a shop to buy some candy. The shopkeeper grabs her genitals through her clothes, and Emma flees, but returns later to the same scene and another assault. What is fascinating and most germane to the discussion here is the manner in which the original incident is created or "represented for the first time" by a theatrical lie that is then, through analysis, reformulated again as the "truth." This incident—the rememoration of trauma and its analysis, a "true scene borne of a false spectacle," as Genet says in *The Balcony*—finds its essential generative principle in repetition, specifically in a rehearsal through which the trauma of "the original memory" is created.

Here is how Freud and his interpolator Jean Laplanche (whose comments are within the brackets) articulate this incident:

> Here we have an instance of a memory exciting an affect which it had not excited as an experience, because in the meantime the changes produced by puberty had made possible a new understanding of what was remembered. Now this case is typical of repression in hysteria. We invariably find that a memory is repressed which has become a trauma *after the event* [here is the heart of the argument: we try to track down the trauma, but the traumatic memory was only secondarily traumatic: we never manage to fix the traumatic event historically. This fact might be illustrated by the image of a Heisenberg-like "relation of indeterminacy": in situating the trauma, one cannot appreciate its traumatic impact and *vice-versa*.] The reason for this state of things is the retardation of puberty as compared with the remainder of the individual's development.   [Laplanche 1976, 41]

The "retardation of puberty" that Freud sees as the cause of this retrograde traumatic event underscores Freud's conviction that this mode of trauma creation—the mode in which the actual traumatic event is indeterminately situated *both* in the past and in the future— was necessarily linked to the sexual aura that surrounds such assaults. Setting aside for the moment the dubious notion of the assault originating in a "seduction by the child," we are still faced with Freud's conviction that this particular trauma mechanism is bound up inextricably with the "dawning" of sexuality in puberty, or with sexuality in general. Nonsexual traumas, in other words, would presumably be exempt from such a process.

But the problem of sexuality in Freud is obviously quite complex— Laplanche, for example, describes how Freud theorizes the moment of sexuality as arising only in its cleavage from the "vital order," from something like a "mating instinct." It is, in other words, only after sexuality splits from instinct that it becomes what it is, a constructed "drive" that is *in every case* a "turning away from" or perversion of the "vital order." Thus even though one may identify the "sexual function" as the impetus behind the formation of the sex drive, the cleavage that occurs marks a radical discontinuity between function and drive—in the theater of the psyche, literally nothing "precedes" the drive and nothing comes after the function: both sexuality and its traumas are born in a cleavage, in the almost infinitesimal breach of the "anaclisis" or "propping" by which the sexual and its traumas are born.

But even though the very moment of sexuality is the moment of its cleavage, its trauma, what does this mean when sexuality begins at once to sublimate and disperse itself? At what point, in other words, is sexuality sufficiently attenuated so that this model of trauma formation is no longer valid? When is sexuality sufficiently displaced from its original production so that it is no longer "sexual"? How, finally, can trauma be separated from sexuality—to what degree is sexuality inherently traumatic, and to what degree is trauma inherently sexual?

Although the questions seem to point up the difficulty of determining the limits either of sexuality or of the nonsexual, this indeterminacy also allows for the development of the regressive sexual trauma theory as a general model of trauma formation—a general theory of dream, "memory," and "history," all of which are *to some degree* capable of taking on the retrograde and repressive guilt that Freud associates with the sexual trauma or the trauma of the sexual, the event that occurs in the "scene," on the stage. The centrality of the remembered sexual tryst of *Krapp's Last Tape,* for example, operates as a kind of psychic spindle around which the play turns. This tryst was apparently the source of pleasure in the past and trauma in the present/ future but is an incident whose sexual nature is finally quite irrelevant to Krapp's pain. The memory of the tryst is the stage within the stage upon which a different and essentially indeterminate trauma is articulated.

In Krapp, then, it is not so much sexuality but rather the spiraling movement of memory itself that seems to generate his pain. This movement seems (initially at least) quite simple but is really maddeningly elliptical. The perversion of time and its productions that begins with *Krapp's* opening line-direction—"A late evening in the future," written in the past, performed in the present as future—immediately reinverts itself as Krapp takes out his recording spools one at a time and rehearses his past as present *and* his present as past, and does this on that one paradoxical "late evening in the future."

While recovering from this temporal vertigo, one begins to see how

Krapp's trauma is seemingly composed in the present, and how it (re)generates the past as pain. One then begins to suspect that this pain may or may not have existed during the original recorded incident. This retroactive memory shows in Krapp's reminiscences of his "happy" youth; these are reminiscences presently (but also "in the future") filled with disgust and intolerable shame, a shame suggested in Krapp's voice, already once removed from him as a recording, that "Sneers at what he calls his youth and thanks to God that it's over" (1984, 58).

These taped recollections deal with a past that never existed as Krapp now experiences it. This "past" instead reemerges in the present only as an absence: "Perhaps my best years are gone. When there was a chance of happiness. But I wouldn't want them back. Not with the fire that is in me now" (63). In the tape within the play the pain of the past is generated in the present only to be thrust toward some future time—now past, of course—when the "fire that is in me now" will somehow bear fruit, a fruit that we, the audience of the future, already know is shriveled on the vine. The locus in which pain production "originally" occurred or occurs can not be located—the "original" moment of the trauma is absolutely indeterminate.

While one might shrug and accept the indeterminacy of Krapp's "present-creating-past" as the simple functioning of an old man's memory—burdened with its inevitable injuries, the "vicissitudes of life"— one also realizes that Krapp's mind is a *theater* that is casting reality and history at once into the future toward performance, and into the past toward an imagined origin.

Consequently, the stage becomes the *doubled* site in which the indeterminate nature of trauma articulates itself in multiple directions at once. And yet for all of its self-conscious theatricality, this Beckettian articulation is, in fact, a theatrical countereffect: while the theater is by definition an agency for the ideologic production of "memory" and "history," *Krapp* subverts that production by presenting memory and history as radically unknowable. This unknowability is embodied in Krapp himself, who occupies at once the site of both old and new trauma; Krapp *is himself* the site of age, pain, and death as it exists in the present as remnant of the past: "a wearish old man...Rusty black narrow trousers too short...White face. Purple nose...Cracked voice... Laborious walk."

Krapp's final stage, then, is the site of history's ruin, and the site of the ruin is a staged event: like the theater in *Breath,* Krapp's archive is filled with the miscellaneous decrepitude of time past. Also, as in *Breath,* the rubbish is unidentifiable: the wearish old man and his

boxes of indecipherable spools suggest an accumulation of anonymous waste, boxed exhibits from an archaeological dig, the leavings
of some now-extinct consciousness "being or remaining," but a consciousness that, like its "history," is elevated to some seemingly higher,
absurdly transcendent, level of significance.

The artifacts that compose this "history" are in fact themselves decomposed. The archival spool itself suggests the impacted spoor of
memories waiting to be unwound and dispelled in the "laxation" of an
alimentary performance. But the dead, retentive historiography of
Krapp's hebephrenic mind will not let that history dispel itself. Instead, Krapp latches on to "history" with a psychotic fascination and
revulsion by fixating on the anal association between "stool" ("crap"/
"Krapp") and "spool" (the archive/memory): "The sour cud and iron
stool. [*Pause*] Revelled in the word spool [*With relish*] Spooool! Hap-
piest moment of the past half million." The entire movement of Krapp,
so to speak, represents something like the alimentary movement of
"history" as crap itself, beginning with the ingested banana and tape
feed, and ending with the discarded peel and the empty spool, the
evacuation of a memory that is at once desired and foreclosed:
"*Strokes banana, peels it, tosses skin into pit*...I wouldn't want them
back...No, I wouldn't want them back...*The tape runs on in silence*."

But the bleak temporal disorientation serves to highlight something even more troubling and regressive about Krapp's predicament:
not only is the most basic organization of the individual terribly confused (emblematized in the object that is at once phallic and fecal—
the banana—which plugs up the oral agency of Krapp's mouth), but
as the play itself moves continuously from future to past, the past/
present becomes saturated with the vision of an unbearable and alien
future (which is, of course, our present). The tape, recounting the
past, runs on in silence toward death. Thus even as the play subverts
the tyranny of an Imaginary, ideologically constructed sense of "history" and "memory," it succumbs to this constructed determinacy by
capitulating to the romance of ends and origins.

This is not merely an ideological criticism of Beckett's play, however: rather we might suppose that the play's "message" represents a
particularly bleak assessment of the possibility of authentic historical
change in the face of death—a death that has in many ways become a
culturally exaggerated emblem of enforced hopelessness, of inefficacy
as ideology.

And yet before criticizing Krapp's pain and hopelessness as "false
consciousness," one ought to recognize this hopelessness as universally (at least in the West) theatrical—indeed, we might have replaced

the word "death" with the word "theater" in the preceding paragraph. Krapp's trauma is ghosted by all of the permutations of pain/trauma that have come to us through theater history as tragedy: from the playback of life's deeds in *Everyman,* to the obsessive recounting of failed personal histories in Ibsen and Chekhov in the modern period and beyond, the corpus of Western drama seems obsessively trapped in the grinding cycle of history as pain, failure, and hopelessness.

What *is* this theater that "turns around" on trauma as a misremembered event, an event that appears as the ideologically constructed "history" created *through* a remembering theater? And what is that ideological construct? A *hallucination* that seemingly precedes perception—something like Genet's "true scene born of a false spectacle"—or the performative tendency of consciousness to reconstruct trauma dialectically "for the first time" after the perceptual fact, suppressing the original and *real* historical trauma as a mere *seeming* effect of that consciousness? Is theater, in other words, more like foreclosure or more like repression? More like Krapp's indeterminate "spiralling time" or more like *Breath*'s linear "ends and origins"?

But these two concepts align and oppose themselves perhaps a bit too neatly, especially in light of what I have already said about theater's other indeterminacies. Thus, whereas theater-as-foreclosure tends to suggest a more or less "schizoanalytic" approach to "reality testing"— that representations such as theater are hallucinatory realities based on radical displacements, displacements in which the arbitrary relation between sign and thing is completely unrecoverable or nonexistent—theater-as-repression suggests something more like the repressive nature of theatrical representation in which sign and thing relations (symptoms and their traumas) *are to some degree* linked and recoverable.

But clearly the trauma theory of Freud, and correspondingly the theater of Beckett, show not only that such oppositions (between metaphor and metonymy, between psychosis and neurosis, between foreclosure and repression, between the theater of "ends and origins" and the theater of "spirals," between, finally, mind as *mise-en-scène* and theater production) are theoretically suspect, but that they are, as Derrida demonstrates, epistemologically questionable as well. Indeed, these oppositions may be operating as a kind of foreclosure of the foreclosed, to twist Laplanche's terms, because in either case (foreclosure or repression), the original trauma is not necessarily linked to its recovery or its symptom in any interpretable way by the individual suffering it. So while psychoanalysis might provide a specific meaning to a symptom, and while it may identify as hallucinatory the "symptom" that has no necessary meaning or origin, such identities are imposed to some degree *from the "outside"*: but where is the "outside" of theater? Where is the sociocultural vantage point from which we can name the identity of theater either as the return of the repressed, or as some grand sociopolitical hallucination?

The repressed and the foreclosed, then, are not so easily separable according to notions of neurosis or psychosis, especially if one wishes to cast them (repression and foreclosure) as sociopolitical symptomatologies, as Jameson might. For if one looks at theater in a Jamesonian way as the social manifestations of what at the individual level emerges either as dream/symptom or hallucination, one begins to suspect that what the theater is is precisely *the trauma that is unrecoverable*, "the hallucinated remains of a denied enormity, cast back into the world" (Kubiak 1989, 20). Thus while the appearance of the trauma *in* the theater may appear as the return of the repressed, the theater itself appears as a kind of cultural hallucination, the phenomenon that proclaims its truth to be the truth of illusion, the "true scene borne of a false spectacle."

Conversely, as theater begins, again and again, trying to understand its pain, and attempts to resolve it *outside of itself* "in the world," it fails because theater—the schism of thought "released into structure," in the words of Herbert Blau—is itself the generating principle of the trauma and its "history." Theater, like the recurring traumatic dream, perpetuates its own disease *as itself*: it is itself the very trauma that it unconsciously tries to heal; it is itself the crime it attempts to solve; it is itself the generating principle of the pain around which it forms its obsession—the pain of a consciousness that is theatrical. Theater, then, born of itself, is the very thing that theater must "cure," and perhaps only theater is capable of accomplishing this productively in the world. The problem of history and the consciousness that is its trauma is, finally, the problem of the "pure" theater and its dream. It is, finally, the problem of theater itself.

Notes

1. In *Of Grammatology*, for example, Derrida reverses the usual (as evidenced in the work of Rousseau) binary opposition between speech and writing by placing "writing" anterior to speech. In doing so, he is able to foreground and deconstruct a previously repressed metaphysics of presence. This metaphysics in fact dialectically constructs the categories of being and identity through the presumed necessity of an authorial presence or "origin" that

gives birth to utterance and writing (thus the primacy given to the Author-as-origin in any act of writing). Through his deconstruction of speech/writing, or presence/absence, Derrida shows that we are born into *writing*, into a space of inscription that always precedes us—we are not the origin of our utterances, rather writing articulates us. This, needless to say, marks the crucial intersection of Derridean philosophy with the work of Freud and his notion of primary repression, and with Artaud, who postulated a theater that "preceded" theater's double in much the same way that Derridean writing precedes utterance.

2. Henceforth, what I will write as "history" (in quotes) represents something like the weak sense of history that we find elucidated by Nietzsche in *On the Advantage and Disadvantage of History for Life*—history as a fiction that comforts and paralyzes us.

3. I would ask a certain tolerance for an inexact terminology in what follows: I am undoubtedly reifying terms and categories that Lacan clearly did not. I would present these reifications, however, as theoretical moments in themselves.

4. A Lacanian term that designates, in psychosis, the mechanism by which a traumatic incident is absolutely excluded entry into either Imaginary or Symbolic orders, and is therefore cast back into the Real, from whence it emerges *as* reality to the person experiencing it, albeit a *hallucinatory* reality. The term corresponds to Freud's *repudiation* in describing certain psychotic mechanisms of reality refusal, but it is less problematic than Freud's term because Lacan uses it only in relation to psychosis. Lacan's term is correspondingly more radical in that it represents not the mere repression of a traumatic incident but the rejection of the entire signifying order of reality, the refusal of the Name-of-the-Father (Laplanche and Pontalis 1973, 166–69).

References

Althusser, Louis. "Ideology and Ideological State Apparatuses." In *Lenin and Philosophy and Other Essays*, translated by Ben Brewster. New York: Monthly Review Press, 1971.

Beckett, Samuel. *Breath. Krapp's Last Tape. Not I.* In *The Collected Shorter Plays of Samuel Beckett.* New York: Grove Press, 1984.

Blau, Herbert. *Blooded Thought: Occasions of Theater.* New York: Performing Arts Journal Press, 1982.

Deleuze, Gilles. *Nietzsche and Philosophy.* Translated by Hugh Tomlinson. New York: Columbia University Press, 1983a.

———. "Plato and the Simulacrum." *October* 27 (1983b): 44–56.

Deleuze, Gilles, and Guattari, Felix. *Anti-Oedipus: Capitalism and Schizophrenia.* Translated by Robert Hurley et al. Minneapolis: University of Minnesota Press, 1983.

Derrida, Jacques. *Of Grammatology.* Baltimore: Johns Hopkins University Press, 1976.

————. "Freud and the Scene of Writing." In *Writing and Difference,* translated by Alan Bass. Chicago: University of Chicago Press, 1978.

Foucault, Michel. "Theatrum Philosophicum." In *Language, counter-memory, practice,* translated by Donald F. Bouchard. Ithaca: Cornell University Press, 1977.

Freud, Sigmund. *The Standard Edition of the Complete Psychological Works of Sigmund Freud.* Edited and translated by James Strachey. 24 vols. London: Hogarth Press, 1953–74.

  "Project for a Scientific Psychology" (1950 [1895]), vol. 1.
  The Interpretation of Dreams (1900–1901), vols. 4, 5.
  Three Essays on the Theory of Sexuality (1905), vol. 7.
  "Repression" (1915), vol. 14.
  "The Unconscious" (1915), vol. 14.
  Beyond the Pleasure Principle (1920), vol. 18.

Jameson, Fredric. *The Political Unconscious: Narrative as a Socially Symbolic Act.* Ithaca: Cornell University Press, 1981.

Kubiak, Anthony. "Stages of Terror." *Journal of Dramatic Theory and Criticism* 4, no. 1 (1989): 3–30.

Laplanche, Jean. *Life and Death in Psychoanalysis.* Translated by Jeffrey Mehlman. Minneapolis: University of Minnesota Press, 1976.

Laplanche, Jean, and Pontalis, J.-B. *The Language of Psychoanalysis.* Translated by Donald Nicholson-Smith. New York: W. W. Norton, 1973.

Lyotard, Jean-François. "The Unconscious as *Mise-en-scène.*" In *Performance in Postmodern Culture,* edited by Michel Benamou and Charles Caramello. Madison, Wis.: Coda Press, 1977.

Nietzsche, Friedrich. *On the Advantage and Disadvantage of History for Life.* Translated by Peter Preuss. Indianapolis: Hackett, 1980.

Pontalis, J.-B. *Frontiers in Psychoanalysis: Between the Dream and Psychic Pain.* Translated by Catherine Cullen and Phillip Cullen. London: Hogarth Press, 1981.

8 Recovering the *Néant:* Language and the Unconscious in Beckett

Stephen Barker

> *Toward a characterization of* "modernity."—*Overabundant development of intermediary forms; atrophy of types; traditions break off, schools; the overlordship of the instincts (prepared philosophically: the unconscious worth more)* after the will to power, the willing of the ends *and* means, has been weakened.   —Friedrich Nietzsche, *The Will to Power* (1968b, 74)

> *The unconscious is that chapter of my history which is marked by a blank or occupied by a falsehood: it is the censored chapter.*   —Jacques Lacan, *The Language of the Self* (1968, 21)

> *I have to speak, whatever that means. Having nothing to say, no words but the words of others, I have to speak. No one compels me to, there is no one, it's an accident, a fact. Nothing can ever exempt me from it, there is nothing, nothing to discover, nothing to recover, nothing that can lessen what remains to say.*   —Samuel Beckett, *The Unnamable* (1965, 314)

I want to gather here, as Beckett consistently does, a constellation of voices forming a *pensum.* In doing so, my aim is to think about what cannot be thought; that is, it is not only thinking the *néant*[1] that concerns us in Beckett but thinking and *enacting* it. In the dialectic of the *pensum* and the unconscious we discover and recover Beckett's autoaesthetic strategy, the crisis of etiolated meaning infusing the particular postmodernity, despite and as a result of its parodic armor. This dialectic-beyond-dialectic crystallizes in the course of Beckett's writ-

125

ing. In increasingly condensed fashion, page by page he sculpts his "mud," the metonymic siglum for the "ground" (/*abgrund*) of meaningful action through which imagery reveals itself. Beckett's versions of the postmodern are always subversions, to borrow Herbert Blau's words; his intense investigations isolate and explore the nature of human action as it does and does not constitute meaning and value, and as it transforms itself *into* language-as-ground. In *The Unnamable,* as the quintessential text of the unconscious's centrality, Beckett explores the conundrum of the written unconscious.

Beckett's critique of action in *The Unnamable* focuses on four central forces, to which he alerts the reader:

1. the nothing or *néant*

2. the unconscious

3. language

4. recovery

In analyzing Beckett, the reader must do what he need not: separate and isolate; in so doing, we may attempt to decipher the web of associations in which Beckett immerses his words, finally becoming aware of Beckett's layered complexity in using these forces to constitute a problematic sense of action, derived from the unconscious.

The Néant

> *About myself I need know nothing.*
> —*The Unnamable* (1965, 294)

From Gogo's first words in *Waiting for Godot* ("Nothing to be done") to the opening of the last section of *The Lost Ones* ("There is nothing at first to distinguish him from the others dead still where they stand or sit in abandonment beyond recall"), Beckett confesses his concern with the nothing. This ontological puzzle has troubled us since Parmenides declared the impossibility of speaking of what is not, breaking his own law in the process of stating it and thereby throwing all that *can* be declared into question.[2] In fact, as Plato inadvertently demonstrated, the nothing is indeed the ground of being. Plato's refutation of Parmenides, in the *Republic,* states that whatever the philosopher thinks about *is;* in this gesture toward what we now call the Cartesian, Plato fuses imagination, rhetorical power, and inner psychological process (which were all, according to him, highly subversive) into a sublimated version of the unconscious, the "state" underlying consciousness and therefore "reality." Like all thinkers who have toyed with the *néant,* Plato must pay the price: he subverts the very *paideia* he wishes to validate and support. The nothing simply will not stand still for analysis.

And yet the *néant* always offers a fair exchange. At the beginning of *Molloy,* the first in the trilogy of novels concluded by *The Unnamable,* the narrator tells a story of writing what we are reading: as he is writing the novel, "someone" takes the pages away. "So many pages, so much money," he tells us. In this narrative economy, the writer recounts that "when I've done nothing, he gives me nothing" (1965, 7), and that when pages are returned, "they are marked with signs I don't understand, Anyway, I don't read them." The condition in which the writer writes is one pervaded by the unknown, the nothing, a *paideia* that teaches nothing and cannot be understood. Beckett's first postmodern subversion, even though he must speak, is that he does so with "nothing to say."

As Heidegger shows in "What Is Metaphysics?" there are two ways to look at this "nothing to say." Either we can see it as a negation, a "not saying anything," or as a constitutive statement, a "saying (the) nothing." The effect of Beckett's words is to engage both meanings simultaneously, as in the quotation from *The Unnamable* cited in the epigraph; the passage is essential to understanding both the novel and Beckett's use of the *néant* as unconscious. The speaker declares that he has to speak, "whatever that means." Then he makes a curiously conditional statement, which comments on this imperative: "Having nothing to say, *no words but the words of others,* I have to speak." Beckett's implication is that *because* he has (the) nothing to say (in a positive sense), *because* he has no words but the words of others (which can also be *his* words—that is, collective words), he is compelled to speak. Yet lest we think this the uncomplicated truth, he states immediately that "no one compels me to," indeed that "there is no one" (again a potentially positive statement, in the sense that someone exists, and that someone is "no one").

Having burrowed like a worm[3] into the thought of (the) nothing, Beckett/narrator rhapsodizes on it, inscribing a string of poetic references repeating the keyword: "nothing can ever exempt me from it, there is nothing, nothing to discover, nothing to recover, nothing that can lessen what remains to say." This series of appositive phrases, additive but disjunctive, begins to break up as it is read. "There is nothing," he says, then qualifies it to state that (there is) "nothing to discover," an additive that radically alters the meaning of the initial phrase (for instance, it seems to add a subject). Then "nothing to recover," a most enigmatic use of what seems to be an oppositional appositive (but which will turn out to be much more), again changing direction. The final phrase, "nothing that can lessen what remains to say" is an alluvial fan of meanings, reopening all possibilities. Indeed, Beckett's text here declares that it is itself precisely the nothing that can lessen what remains to say, in its saying lessening that remainder, which seems to be reduced to *nothing* by the end of *The Unnamable*[4]—to silence (which denies the opening statement of this passage, that the narrator "has to speak"). What seems at first to be a series of laconically nihilistic phrases opens out into a *pensum* on the nature of the *néant*. Beckett here expresses the Heideggerian "negation of the totality of beings" (1976, 100) and initiates the intertextual tension ("anxiety") of which the passage and the narrator are composed.[5] Like Nietzsche's "modernity," Beckett's is an "overabundant development of intermediate forms" that declare the *néant*—and deny nihilism. Beckett heeds the Nietzschean warning to beware at all costs the enervation of the nihilistic urge, that "hatred of the human," the animal, and the material, "this horror of the senses" and "longing to get away from all appearance, change, becoming, death, wishing, from longing itself" (1969, III, 28); Beckett's poetic prose tumbles toward these catalysts. Nietzsche's complex sense of appearance or change, for example, is that they incorporate a positive dis-ease, which Beckett infuses into his prose: "In a word, no change apparently since I have been here, disorder of the lights perhaps an illusion, all change to be feared, incomprehensible uneasiness" (1965, 295).

We must remember as we analyze passages from *The Unnamable*, "all this noise about nothing" (376), that Beckett has provided us a *conceit* and an appendix for that nothing: in *Texts for Nothing* he compiles, just at the end of the period in which he wrote the trilogy of novels, a series of thirteen sketches that begin where *The Unnamable* concludes. The English text of the novel concludes "I can't go on, I'll go on," which is echoed in the opening words of the stories: "Suddenly, no, at last, long last, I couldn't any more, I couldn't go on" (1967, 75). The narrator resumes his struggle with the *néant,* only to find at the conclusion of his efforts that he has arrived in the same place, the place at which he concluded before, though in *different words:*

> And were there one day to be here, where there are no days, which is no place, born of the impossible voice the unmakable being, and a gleam of light, still all would be silent and empty and dark, as now, as soon now, when all will be ended, all said, it says, it murmurs. [1967, 140]

Beckett has made no "progress" in the interval since *The Unnamable,* yet still finds himself unexempted from the effort to constitute action, still declaring the "nothing that can lessen what remains to say."

Beckett, however, in working through the *néant* as a function of action, is not satisfied with it as part of a topological model. Nothing in Beckett is more difficult to isolate or more important to understand. He does not see the nothing as a place or condition from which or toward which to write; rather, he is concerned with transcending the dialectics of "nothing" and "something" to isolate the threshold of the nothing's appearance, the undisclosable "moment" of deferral and distance, that force Derrida has called *"différance."*[6] Beckett's words more and more energetically attempt to focus on this "moment of appearance," out of the nothing, of words and their structural interactions. This (impossible) threshold of the *néant* is the emergent energy of the nameless and unnameable beginning, the origin of being and of action, the desired *topos,* and the goal of Beckett's writing. Beckett always seeks what Derrida calls, in "Freud and the Scene of Writing," the "archi-trace," the mark of the beginning, but as we read in Derrida, the archi-trace is always a repression; or, to Derrida,

> the erasure of selfhood, of one's own presence, and is constituted by the threat or anguish of its irremediable disappearance, of the disappearance of its disappearance.[7] An erasable trace is not a trace, it is a full presence, an immobile and incorruptible substance....
>
> This erasure is death itself.... It is the very structure which makes possible, as the movement of temporalization and pure *auto-affection,* something that can be called repression in general, the original synthesis of original repression and secondary repression, repression "itself." [1978, 230]

Beckett's palimpsestic "system" of writing affords this invitation to the erasure of the archi-trace. The reversals and qualifications one finds so pervasive in Beckett's texts have their roots in this strategy of erasure since, as Derrida claims, "writing is unthinkable without repression" (1978, 226). In courting the death of erasure, Beckett builds the structure that self-destructs—indeed, there is "nothing that can lessen what remains to say." The voice of the Unnamable informs us of this intermediary role:

> I shall transmit the words as received, by the ear, or roared through a trumpet into the arsehole, in all their purity, and in the same order, as far as possible. This infinitesimal lag, between arrival and departure, this trifling delay in evacuation, is all I have to worry about. [1967, 349]

The "lag" Beckett's narrator must worry about, here stated as the crisis of corporeal metaphoricity, is the deferral of all textuality—that is, its relation to the threshold of the *néant.*

Beckett's immense satisfaction ("long may it last"), which consists of the perpetual acknowledgment of suffering, is to be found in knowing that this threshold is a function of the scene and the moment of writing's emergence. In the sixth "text for nothing" Beckett describes this shadowy *seuil* remarkably:

> Ah to know for sure, to know that this thing has no end, this thing, this thing, this farrago of silence and words, of silence that is not silence and barely murmured words. Or to know it's life still, a form of life, ordained to end, as others ended and will end, till life ends, in all its forms. Words, mine was never more than that, than this pell-mell babel of silence and words, my viewless form described as ended, or to come, or still in progress, depending on the words, the moments, long may it last in that singular way.   [1967, 104]

The sense of eager, open-ended finality here is delicately balanced with the perpetual reemergence of the energy not only to go on but to celebrate that reopening: "long may it last." If this at first seems unlike Beckett, I am suggesting precisely that: in Beckett one is not dealing with a nihilist but with a kind of tightrope walker, poised between ecstasy and oblivion. The image of the tightrope walker comes, of course, from the preface to *Thus Spoke Zarathustra,* where Nietzsche describes the scene of a remarkable event in Zarathustra's first journey. Encountering a town square crowded with people looking up toward a performer about to cross the square on a rope, Nietzsche/Zarathustra takes advantage of the crowd's attention and cries out:

> Man is a rope, tied between beast and overman—a rope over an abyss. A dangerous across, a dangerous on-the-way, a dangerous looking-back, a dangerous shuttering and stopping.
>
> What is great in man is that he is a bridge and not an end: what can be loved in man is that he is an *overture* and a *going under.*   [1966, 4]

The richness of this description of man poised "in-between" (the tightrope walker eventually falls to his death) haunts all of Nietzsche's subsequent images and may give rise to many such images in modern literature—for example, in *Waiting for Godot,*[8] the two tramps "caught-between" or the "slave/performer" at the end of a rope (Lucky) who cannot "bridge the gap" to human discourse, who cannot tell his story.

Nietzsche's image here is a vitally important one to an understanding of Beckett's scene.[9] Beckett's sense of the "moments" through which this emergence occurs is an energizing and, to use Sartre's word, a nauseating one, nowhere more forcefully expressed than by the Unnamable:

> perhaps that's what I am, the thing that divides the world in two, on the one side the outside, on the other the inside, that can be as thin as foil, I'm neither one side nor the other, I'm in the middle, I'm the partition, I've two surfaces and no thickness. . . . I alone am immortal. [1965, 383]

Beckett's play with the *néant* in his sense of "moment" is much like that ascribed to Cézanne by Merleau-Ponty: "What I am trying to translate to you," Cézanne says, "is entwined in the very roots of being, in the impalpable source of sensations" (1964, 159). Beckett's images hover over the abyss from which they confess themselves to have come, always ready to sink back into the silence of the *néant:* "the image involves a certain nothingness," says Sartre in *Being and Nothingness* (1956, 18). Through the course of the trilogy, Beckett moves further and further from images as such and toward a kind of pure narration of narration; gradually locatable physical existence is replaced by floating references to the narrative itself. In *The Unnamable,* gone are Molloy's mother, his clothes, his journeys through a countryside; gone are Malone's stories and Moran's son and household. In *The Unnamable* one confronts the most elemental advances and reversals, beginning with the detached but poignant "Where now? Who now? When now? Unquestioning. I, say I" (1965, 291), which, as bleak as it seems and is, also recapitulates the emergence to himself of the narrative voice. As Heidegger tells us, "in the clear night of the nothing of anxiety the original openness of beings as such arises" (1976, 105); the Unnamable seems to declare his first, raw opening out of the nothing, and exhaustingly to sustain it:

> I'm all these words, all these strangers, this dust of words. . . . I am they, all of them, those that merge, those that part, those that never meet, and nothing else, yes, something else, that I'm something quite different, a quite different thing, a wordless thing in an empty place, a hard shut dry cold black place, where nothing stirs, nothing speaks. [386]

The merging of all narrators into one voice, a structural and fictional internalization of Otherness, in the multiplicitous Unnamable, is the culmination of Beckett's obsession with the *personal* in the written or spoken voice. Throughout the trilogy, Beckett moves closer and closer to this "ideal" voice, poised on its tightrope between nothing and something. For the voice of the Unnamable, Beckett's "last," having developed out of the voices of Murphy, Watt, Mercier, Molloy, Malone, and so forth,[10] and then having evolved into the incorporeal syntax of speech/writing itself, *nothing changes,* and as it changes, the Unnamable comes into being, across the threshold of the *néant.*[11]

This is precisely the developmental movement through which Nietzsche had gone in depicting the Dionysian. At first, it occupies a dialectical space "beside" the Apollonian, as in *The Birth of Tragedy,* in which the two forces vie and balance with each other, standing metaphorically for opposites eternally in conflict. By the time of *The Gay Science,* Nietzsche has collapsed the two together into something else, the fusion of the ecstasy of Dionysus with the ordering dream of Apollo—into the philosopher/poet or tragic poet; needless to say, both Nietzsche and Beckett fit the description of this self-overcoming figure, insofar as this can occur. This "new" Dionysian poet is identified by "the desire for *destruction,* change, and becoming" as "the expression of an overflowing energy that is pregnant with future" (1974, 370). Beckett echoes this development. Until *How It Is,* he had been concerned chiefly with mind/body dualism, so evident in his early poetry and prose, from *Whoroscope* to *Murphy;* after *How It Is,* he concentrates increasingly on the inner workings of the imagination and on the writing/telling process itself, as Dearlove suggests (1982, 86). Although Beckett claims that his chief subject is "impotence," clearly it is a certain kind of impotence—one that continues to generate remarkable energy and power. This combinative Dionysian process reaches its culmination in the Unnamable's claim that "I am he who will never be caught, never delivered, who crawls between the thwarts, towards the new day that promises to be glorious, festooned with lifebelts" (339). Both Beckett's and Nietzsche's attempt at self-overcoming is always a failure, by definition, an "intermediate form" that never lessens what remains to say. In Beckett one sees this from the earliest poetry at least to the French conclusion of *The Unnamable:* "là où je suis, je ne sais pas, je ne le saurai jamais, dans le silence on ne sait pas, il faut continuer, je vais continuer" (1953, 262), which reads in translation "there where I am, I don't know, I'll never know it, in the silence you don't know, one must go on, I'll go on" (1965, 414).[12] This (Nietzschean) affirmation of life, so unexpected in Beckett, even at its blackest and most taxing is a self-realization emanating from a view of becoming that Nietzsche calls "joy in destruction" in "What I Owe the Ancients" (1978, 5). In this collapsing together of opposing forces into one "internalized" or imaginative force,

Nietzsche sets the scene for the emergence of the (Dionysian) unconscious.

The (Dionysian) Unconscious

> *There I am back at my old aporetics.*
> —*Malone Dies* (1965, 181)

In the "pure aporia" declared by the Unnamable on the first page of its text (1965, 291), in that "raw" and enigmatic voice, Beckett poses his greatest challenge to the reader: he writes the unconscious. The Unnamable is that disembodied voice that incorporates itself in order to live out, fictionally, the crisis of action the unconscious represents. Beckett's statements about this crisis are clear and unequivocal: "I think," he says, "any one nowadays who pays the slightest attention to his own experience finds it is the experience of a non-knower, a non-can-er. The other type of artist—the Apollonian—is absolutely foreign to me" (Dearlove 1982, 6). Beckett characterizes this *étrangeté* as impotence and ignorance, unexplored artistic phenomena; clearly, however much Beckett may claim that the Unnamable's is a "voice which has denatured me" (1965, 351), his is a perpetual crisis of action, read as psychological impotence. That no serenely detached abstract concept, even that of the *néant,* exists outside the aegis of psychology has become a cultural commonplace. Richard Rorty declares that since Nietzsche, indeed, no possibility of philosophy as such exists, but *only* psychology, since all abstraction comes pragmatically from discourse of, in, and on the mind (1982, 151ff.). In this light, the connections between the *néant* and the mental and physiological phenomena we now call the unconscious begin to emerge forcefully and clearly. This has been the case for twentieth-century philosophy and literature, as one can see for example throughout *Being and Nothingness;* instead of asking the question of being, Sartre asks "What must be the nature of consciousness in order that man in consciousness and in terms of consciousness should arise in the world as the being who is his own nothingness and by whom nothingness comes into the world?" (1956, 45).[13] The nature of the consciousness capable of posing such a question is clearly the Dionysian one, which relates itself to the *néant,* as the unconscious, in Beckett's play of the nothing and the unconscious from his earliest writing: in *Proust* (written in 1930, when Beckett was twenty-four and working on his M.A. in Dublin), which analyzes the nature of Proust's involuntary memory, Beckett makes his first case for the *inner* nature of that nothing from which his own writing will emanate. His analysis of Proust is so heavily laden with his own (Nietzschean) concerns that it sometimes looks less like criticism than a poetic disquisition on the psychology of the Dionysian unconscious:

> We can only remember what has been registered by our extreme inattention and stored in that ultimate if inaccessible dungeon of our being to which Habit does not possess the key, and does not need to, because it contains none of the hideous and useful paraphernalia of war. But here, in that "gouffre interdit à nos sondes," is stored the essence of ourselves, the best of our many selves and their concretions that simplists call the world.   [1957, 18]

Here Beckett initializes the "gulf" or "abyss" from which his dark characterizations will flow. In that "gouffre interdit à nos sondes," the "abyss forbidden to our soundings," the *néant* emerges as the unconscious. This abyss, Beckett subsequently tells us, stores the best of our *many* selves—all the selves that can be uttered are indeed what Nietzsche calls "abysmal" selves.

When we dive (Beckett's image) into that abyss, what do we find? In one of his richest and most enigmatic passages, Beckett tells us that within that black and unknown otherness we perceive "the fine essence of a smothered divinity whose whispered '*disfazione*' is drowned in the healthy bawling of an all-embracing appetite, the pearl that may give the lie to our carapace of paste and pewter" (1957, 19). Concealed, then, in the censored depths *forbidden* to our soundings is not just a "divinity" who whispers a tortured, pseudo-Italian *word,* "*disfazione*" ("disfaction," or, implicitly, "antidisorder"), a word that whispers at the Dionysian union Nietzsche and Beckett say we wish for but never achieve; this "divinity"'s whisper is "drowned" in an "appetite" anthropomorphized into, in rapid succession, a newborn infant whose first cries are for satisfaction, and then (beyond the corporeal into the metaphoric) into the perfect spherical object of desire, the pearl whose authenticity "gives the lie" to our "carapace," our outer shell of (false) protection/censorship. The complexity of the imagery to which this diving into the gulf gives rise points to that even greater complexity of the states or forces to which the images refer.

The Return of the Repressed

> *To make me believe I have an ego all my own, and can speak*
> *of it. . . . Another trap to snap me up among the living.*
> —*The Unnamable* (1965, 345)

Beckett's Unnamable thus sets the stage for the return of the repressed; the sublimated name of Freud[14] must now appear. And just as
Freud had to suppress Nietzsche in order to think his own thoughts,
only to find those abysmal thoughts returning pervasively in his
work,[15] Beckett suppresses his concerns with the unconscious into
the succession of fictional voices out of which it nonetheless shows
itself. This concealment/revelation follows precisely the pathway of
Freudian process. David Hesla points out that *The Unnamable* goes
through "Something in order to arrive at Nothing"—Mercier's words
about his own novel—but that perhaps it "goes through Something
and demolishes it on the way in order to get to Something . . . unap-
proachable by any way other than this version of the *Via Negativa*"
(1971, 115). For Nietzsche the unconscious is an arena of confused
emotions, thoughts, and forces that reenact the past stages of development of the individual and the species (Beckett concurs: "I am the
ancestor of whom nothing can be said" [1965, 352]), but which "remembers" what the conscious mind covers over with its activity of
repression; similarly, for Freud the unconscious is inferred in its symp-
tomatic otherness, as a complex, dense, sexually charged, and troubling web of urges.[16] For both Nietzsche and Freud the unconscious
is, at base, *metaphoric;* that is, it grounds itself in transference.[17] What
is too painful for consciousness to hold in view is concealed (repression) or rechanneled (sublimation) in a censorship that "deserves to
be recognized and respected as the watchman of our mental health"
(*The Interpretation of Dreams, S.E.* 5:567); in the characteristic
double bind of repression, however, we know about these data *and
this censorship* only through inference, since data in the unconscious
are neutralized while concealed and the process of censorship denies
itself.

This is one of the most fascinating aspects of the apparatus of the
mind: the most complicated of thoughts can take place without arous-
ing consciousness (see *S.E.* 5:612ff.). When these unconscious activities show themselves, it may be in completely altered form. Nonetheless, as Freud points out in a note of 1912, "every psychical act begins
as an unconscious one" (*S.E.* 12:264). Freud's revolution in the creation of dynamic psychoanalysis can be seen, among many other things,

as the declaration of the unconscious as the basis of "psychic occur-
rences" (subjected to Nietzsche's "unmasking"):[18]

> the unconscious must be assumed to be the general basis of psychical
> life. The unconscious is the larger sphere, which includes within it the
> smaller sphere of the conscious. Everything conscious has an uncon-
> scious preliminary stage; whereas what is unconscious may remain at
> that stage and nevertheless claim to be regarded as having the full value
> of a psychical process. The unconscious is the true psychical reality; *in
> its innermost nature it is as much unknown to us as the reality of the
> external world, and it is as incompletely presented by the data of
> consciousness as is the external world by the communications of our
> sense organs.* [*S.E.* 5:612–13; emphasis in original]

Here Freud states the double bind of which psychoanalysis and Beckettian prose are constructed: the unconscious is at once the nexus of
potential meaning and action and at the same time purely chimerical,
bound by this split identity in a condition of absolute otherness. Like
Emerson's concentric circles of experience, Freud's topography of the
consciousness suggests a hierarchical model—which privileges the
unconscious. In this model, consciousness is a palimpsest "over"
the unconscious, a superstructure built on the substructure of unconscious forces.

Ideally, the conscious mind translates the demands of the unconscious into terms in which those demands are no longer "the 'daemonic' power which produces the dream-wish" (*S.E.* 5: 614), but
these indwelling spirits are obviously the source of anxiety and fear,
since what is concealed remains concealed, never to be disclosed except by proxy. The Unnamable's voice divulges this unexpected part
of itself in language well predicted by Freud (and the Dionysian), asserting that it manifests itself "like a caged beast born of caged beasts
born of caged beasts born of caged beasts born in a cage and dead in
a cage, born and then dead, born in a cage and then dead in a cage, in
a word like a beast, in one of their words, like such a beast" (1965,
387). The "beast" can be "freed" only at the threshold of the unconscious, and so it is "always seeking something," which because of the
double bind in which the threshold of the unconscious is always
caught remains the same: "I seek nothing, nothing" (387). Given that
for Freud the existence of the unconscious denotes goal orientation,
unconscious motives (vital to Freud) are a kind of *cause* of behavior,
and therefore in themselves a kind of elemental[19] action of originary
(*daemonic*) significance. In this *daemonic* guise, the unconscious represses the beast/body according to the laws of transformation to
which the unconscious is subjected. The speaker may have no sense

of a body at all, or may have a distorted self-image.

The transformations occurring to and within the bodies of the narrators of Beckett's *Stories and Texts for Nothing*, for example, are good examples of the sort of transformations that occur. In "The Expelled," the narrator is thrown out of "his" house and finds himself, at the story's opening, looking up the front stoop of the house *at himself* in the doorway. As the story progresses, the narrator's shape becomes increasingly grotesque, his movements increasingly tortured. He becomes the beastly narrator of the unconscious, haunting himself and his own story: "I had the deplorable habit, having pissed in my trousers, or shat there, which I did fairly regularly early in the morning, about ten or half past ten, of persisting in going on and finishing my day as if nothing had happened" (1967, 14). The implication that nothing *has happened,* inside the monstrous trousers of the protagonist, brings up the most Dionysian of thoughts in the reader. As the Expelled becomes the narrator of "The Calmative," physical ailments give way to a general anxiety that will not permit him to function, his mind "panting after this and that and always flung back to where there was nothing" (44). The "cyst" about which the narrator of the third and last story of the sequence is concerned is only one of many mental and physical ailments from which he suffers. These later stories lack the balance of ailments Beckett explores in *Waiting for Godot,* for example, in which the pairs of characters suffer from complementary complaints.

Increasingly, Beckett's characters do not represent a schematic depiction of illness or incompleteness or the suffering of life, but rather experience states of removal or anxiety in which they alone suffer and which they suffer alone. Beckett's sense of human community, the notion of shared conscious existence interwoven with others, gradually vanishes in the face of his concentration on the unconscious. Although it is structured and obeys its own laws (which cannot be known to the intellect and are not susceptible to analysis), concentration on the unconscious produces a radical solipsism. Beckett's solitary characters are dramatic demonstrations of this, searching their memories and the woeful "facts" of an apocryphal past and present world for a solace that can only come through renewed concentration on reaching the vanishing point of the Dionysian threshold. As we have seen, the unconscious seeks simultaneously to conceal and reveal its contents and forces, existing like Proust's diver in the memory trace (*S.E.* 5:539–40, 540n.).[20] As Derrida has shown, what Freud calls the memory trace is itself an instance of repression and reassertion, another locus of the threshold of meaning for which Beckett always seeks. It is in this light that Freud's first statement about the unconscious (to the London Society for Physical Research in 1912 [*S.E.* 12], that we obtain our concept of the unconscious from the theory of repression) appears in its full meaning. Freud's assertion contains its own negation—it others itself in its utterance.

Language and the Unconscious

First I'll say what I'm not.   —The Unnamable (1965, 326)

If the concept of the unconscious comes from another theory (repression), the theorizer remains thereby quite separate from the unconscious "itself"; further, if repression informs us initially of the existence of the unconscious, are we not subject, from that inception forward, to the *étrangeté* of which all our information about the unconscious will be constructed? How are we to approach the unconscious on these terms, except in treating it "after the fact," as a "memory trace"? This question underlies Jacques Lacan's reformulation of Freud's structural analysis of the unconscious. Lacan's answer brings us face to face with the most uncanny truth about the unconscious, and at the same time establishes finally the problematic identity of Beckett's evolving narrator. Inherent in Freud's unconscious is the primordial *étrangeté* of its inaccessibility to direct analysis or access of any kind. For Lacan, and finally for Beckett, Freud's essential discovery is the radical *otherness* of the discourse we call the unconscious. In Freud's claims that consciousness "rests" on the unconscious and that it can only be known to exist through the theory of repression, he provides the guarantee Lacan needs to proceed: that *all* thinking is "thinking other," that there is no stability, no coming to rest, and, most important, no supreme system that can be known.

This guarantee is inherent in the Nietzschean view of the Dionysian force, which is itself a metaphorical transference, a discourse of the other. Nietzsche saw this from the outset; "What then is truth?" he wrote in 1871, but "a moveable host of metaphors, metonymies, and anthropomorphisms, which have been poetically and rhetorically intensified, transferred, and embellished, and which, after long usage, seem to a people to be fixed, canonized, and binding. Truths are illusions which we have forgotten are illusions" (1979, 84). His contention that all we can know is the *residue of a metaphor* causes Nietzsche to declare the basic human drive: metaphor formation. That is, language makes us human and, concurrently, *other.* This declaration lies behind Freud's systematically combinatory psychic levels, and behind Lacan's treatment of Freudian theory. This theory, in turn, capitalizes on the Saussurean linguistics developed at the same time psychoanalysis was being formulated, combining it with the subsequent history of the centrality of transference Freud learned from Nietzsche (which informs contemporary literary theory and philosophy, as well as much of psychology). From this combinatory strategy Lacan produces a primary key to Beckett's poetic strategy, in the "speaking unconscious" (Bowie 1979, 152). For Lacan, the otherness inherent in the Freudian model of layered mental interactions transmutes into a structure of incompleteness, in which the unfulfillable desire to speak Lacan's "Full Word"—the desire itself—is what one *can know*. Just as the Unnamable discovers, as do all of Beckett's later narrative voices, that it is impossible to *say nothing* and impossible to stop trying, Lacan makes this discovery of the unconscious: it is constructed in and on grammar.

Lacan himself repeatedly declared that he did *no more* than read Freud afresh, and the roots of Lacanian (linguistic) psychoanalysis are indeed inherent in Freudian theory. For Freud, as we have seen, the consciousness is a "ciphered formula," "a more or less fantastic commentary on an unconscious, perhaps unknowable, but felt text" (Ellenberger 1970, 273). From the beginning of his specific writings on the unconscious, Freud recognized the "word-presentation" that becomes conscious speech ("The Unconscious," *S.E.* 14:203). Working toward "regaining the lost object" of repression, the patient and the analyst must follow the "verbal part of it," always to content themselves with words in the place of things (*S.E.* 14:204). Lacan sees that Freud had been quite explicit about this linguistic association: in the censorship between the unconscious and the preconscious, for example, we are "safe" from the unconscious because "no matter what impulses from the normally inhibited *Ucs.* may prance upon the stage, we need feel no concern; they remain harmless, since they are unable to set in motion the motor apparatus by which alone they might modify the external world" (*S.E.* 5:568). Only in "translation" into language or imitation by language can this intractability of the unconscious be altered, and then only in the form of a transference. Beckett's voice of the unconscious states this precisely when he/it declares that

> it's of me now I must speak, even if I have to do it with their language, it will be a start, a step towards silence and the end of madness, the madness of having to speak and not being able to, except of things that don't concern me, that don't count, that I don't believe, that they have crammed me full of to prevent me from saying who I am, where I am,

> and from doing what I have to do in the only way that can put an end
> to it.   [1965, 324]

For Freud and Lacan, this censorship is a function of the unconscious's
voice, itself always *l'Autre.* The analyst/reader must face the constant
danger of forgetting what Beckett, in his fiction, always remembers:
abstract thinking threatens to force us to neglect—to repress—the
connection between words and the "concrete ideas" (laws) of the unconscious (Freud, *S.E.* 14:136). In order not to forget this, Lacan asserts that the unconscious is *"structured like a language"* (1981,
20),[21] that it is the "discourse of the other" (1968, 27).[22] Lacan's notion of Otherness—the *étrangeté* that simultaneously identifies, alien-
ates, and stimulates—is itself a double bind. On the one hand it is
"transindividual" (Wilden 1968, 264), a collectivity (revealing its already problematic status as a tool for self-examination), and on the
other it deflects itself in its own declaration; as Malone reports, "my
notes have a curious tendency ... to annihilate all they purport to
record" (Beckett 1965, 259). In Lacan and Beckett, as in Freud, the
discovery and declaration of the unconscious are themselves subject
to dispersion and displacement in the repression that *remains* present
in its constitution as discourse.

In other words, narration for Beckett is an active renaming of the
néant. The Unnamable states it flatly: "where I am there is no one but
me, who am not" (1965, 355).[23] Beckett's narrator reflects back on
the project of the nothing, uncannily echoing the antiname of the
narrator he has always been:

> As if I didn't know, as if there were two things, some other thing besides
> this thing, what it is, this unnamable thing that I name and name and
> never wear out, and I call that words. It's because I haven't hit on the
> right ones, the killers, haven't yet heaved them up from that heart-
> burning glut of words, with what words shall I name the unnamable
> words?[24]   [1967, 105]

Beckett knows that the action of naming (*as*) the unconscious constitutes whatever meaning action may have (see Genesis 2.19–20). In
this respect, according to Lacan's use of the term, Beckett is the ultimate realist, since the order of the "Real" is the "primordial chaos
upon which language operates" (Bowie 1979, 133). The world of
words creates the world of things, including experience of (and the
telling of) the self. The unconscious is "this other to whom I am more
attached than to myself since, at the heart of my assent to my own
identity it is still he who agitates me?"[25] (Lacan 1977, 172). Lacan's
psychoanalysis and Beckett's fiction assert positively that language

consists of irony and contradiction, that to enter discourse is "to enter the realm of the senseless" (Bowie 1979, 145), always to write the censored chapter of one's history.

Recovery in Style

> And yet I have high hopes, I give you my word, high hopes, that one day I may tell a story. —*Texts for Nothing* (1967, 105)

Thus, decidedly on a note of recovery, Beckett continues immediately following the section from *Texts for Nothing* quoted in the preceding paragraph. In light of Lacan's latent *Verbe,* the potential Full Word of self-declaration, and in light of this sort of statement from Beckett, his "running down to nothing" must be rethought. The nihilistic emptiness or verbal enervation Beckett's writing initially suggests is activated, metamorphosed into a vital (even obsessive) desire for articulation of the elemental action of the linguistic unconscious. Beckett's stories *return* to us from the unconscious, as in posthypnotic suggestion or the return of the repressed in sublimation or surrogation, heralding an *action* that while seemingly motiveless is in fact "aporia, pure and simple," not revealed to consciousness.[26] As Lacan has told us and Beckett has shown us, this action requires *écriture.* But since all narration is an actively metaphoric simulation of that *other* action, specifically of the unconscious action it represents, no action could be more meaningful than the attempt to return to the nexus of language/action itself, the chimerical "moment of writing out of the unconscious."

Thus the *néant,* like the "nonsense" Lacan investigates in *Écrits,* becomes a plenitude rather than an absence of sense, precisely because it cannot be said. The very words "the unnamable" are a plausible translation of "absurd," through its Latin roots (Hesla 1971, 7). This reversal of sense is the first of the reversals by which we are constantly surprised in Lacan and in Beckett, but by no means the last. As we read a novel like *The Unnamable,* we must strive to keep on seeing Beckett's sense of his project anew, as he renders it in passages like the one to which we return:

> I have to speak, whatever that means. Having nothing to say, no words but the words of others, I have to speak. No one compels me to, there is no one, it's an accident, a fact. Nothing can ever exempt me from it, there is nothing, nothing to discover, nothing to recover, nothing that can lessen what remains to say.   [1965, 314]

Indeed, there is *precisely* "nothing to recover." Beckett's dis-covery of the *néant* takes place where "something stumbles" on itself in a sentence, exactly where Freud dis-covers the unconscious—that is, at the moment of "impediment, failure, split," according to Lacan (1981, 25). This is a regression and a progression, working both ways at once, the last doorway the Unnamable must face:

> nothing left but the core of murmurs, distant cries, quick now and try again, with the words that remain, try what, I don't know, I've forgotten, it doesn't matter, I never knew, to have them carry me into my story, the words that remain, my old story, which I've forgotten, far from here, through the noise, through the door, into the silence ... now it's I at the door, what door, what's a door doing here, it's the last words, the true last, or it's the murmurs.   [413–14]

Beckett always reopens himself to those words that remain and that propel him toward the doorway of *the last words*. Remembering Nietzsche's Gateway, which as the portal of Zarathustran "moment" is itself grammatical, we must also remember Derrida's *pharmakon*, the grammatological doorway, which is coequally remedy and disease.[27] In the institution of the *pharmakon*, we "repeat without knowing that writing consists of repeating without knowing" ("Plato's Pharmacy," in Derrida 1981, 75), never able to come to rest (which is Beckett's desired *remedy*), or to desire to continue *not* to (which is his *disease*).

How, then, is this strategy of reopening a recovery—even of nothing? As Beckett uses it, the word "recovery" is itself a *pharmakon*, a double-bind word that displays its own reversal. To recover is to convalesce, heal, improve, recuperate, rejuvenate, rescue, relieve; but it is also to cover again, to relapse, lose, regress, revert, forget, elude, evade. In both senses, Beckett has "nothing to recover."

This reversal is inherent in Freud's unconscious as well as Lacan's and Beckett's. In his determination that contraries are an archaic, inherent trait of human thinking, Freud drew heavily on Karl Abel's *The Antithetical Meaning of Primal Words* (Bowie 1979, 125), which although later discredited had tremendous influence on Freud's view of the impossibly dichotomous nature of language.[28] Lacan, in much more Beckettian fashion, formulates the *pharmakon* as a narrative, altering the Cartesian *cogito ergo sum* to the protracted, insecure "je ne suis pas, là où je suis le jouet de ma pensée; je pense à ce que je suis, là où je pense pas penser [I am not there where I am the plaything of my thought; I think about what I am, there where I do not think that I am thinking]" (1957, 70). This Beckettian sentence moves across Beckett's changing ground, from Descartes to Derrida. Lacan's "I," like Beckett's, is always "not there" in its narrative, as Beckett's unnamable punctuates itself with "a story": "now I've told another little story, about me, about the life that might have been mine for all the difference it would have made" (1965, 398). The perpetual crisis of action, in the accruing of words, occurs in its own declaration.

Beckett's crisis of action in the search for the moment of the *pharmakon* evinces itself most subtly in Beckett's style. As words gather, each one its own problematic reopening, that gathering itself is disclosed as a repression. But because "repression" is also subject to the *pharmakon,* Beckett subverts the additive effect of syntax and leaves the reader with the impression that the gathering is "an accident, a fact." Typical of this accumulation of language is the "dog story" at the opening of *Godot*'s second act, echoed in *The Unnamable:* "a dog crawled into the kitchen and stole a crust of bread . . . ," a story concluding with the inscription of the tombstone on which the dog's endless story is inscribed—and so on. Verses gather into endless piles, repeating without reiterating the problem of errant meaning. Beckett provides the key to this stylistic strategy at the opening of *Endgame:*

> CLOV: It's finished, nearly finished, it must be nearly finished.
> (*Pause.*)
> Grain upon grain, one by one, and one day, suddenly, there's a heap, a little heap, the impossible heap.

Each part of this speech contributes to the accumulative effect of the whole. Clov's first utterance (the play's first line) finishes as it begins: "It's finished." This gives way to the qualified "nearly finished," which, although it "heaps" the word "finished," means in everyday speech something utterly different. This is followed by the anxious ignorance of "it must be nearly finished," which although it continues toward a heap moves the listener/reader another quantum leap from the certitude with which he began. At the same time that we heap, we remove. Beckett's trilogy of novels is an effort toward that potential, sudden, magical heap of stories that will always behave in the same way: their style is itself the chimerical heap that approaches the *néant.* Beckett's accumulative style, as though he were a common magnet for words, plays with the sudden formation of the magical heap, the inception of meaningful action in narration. From Beckett's first use of the "heaping" image in the trilogy, in *Molloy* ("If all muck is the same muck that doesn't matter, it's good to have a change of muck, to move from one heap to another a little further on" [1965, 41]), to its repressed last usage in *The Unnamable* ("I see nothing else for the moment, yes I do, I conclude, . . . to pass the time . . . why it piles up all about you, instant on instant, on all sides, deeper and deeper, thicker and thicker,

... why it buries you grain by grain neither dead nor alive" [1965, 389]), narrative piling and compiling produce the "wordy-gurdy" (399) on which Beckett plays. And yet the heap, the impossible heap, is itself a recovery of the *pharmakon.* The heap seems to accumulate, but still, according to the Unnamable, "I have dwindled—I dwindle" (331). The heap of words simultaneously subverts and re-covers its subject.

And the subject of Beckett's discourse is always, as we have seen in the discussion of the *néant,* at the vanishing point "into" the Other. The subject of discourse, as Nietzsche told us as early as 1873, "is not something given, it is something added and invented and projected behind what there is.—Finally, is it necessary to posit an interpreter behind the interpretation? Even this is invention" (1968b, 481). The style of the Unnamable, as the language of the unconscious, is a style of borrowed voices, the culmination of a history of borrowing in Beckett's writing that goes back to the voice of Descartes in *Whoroscope;* Beckett introduces into the Unnamable's attempt at a heap the voices of all his previous narrators, "all these Murphys, Molloys, and Malones," but "they do not fool me. They have made me waste my time, suffer for nothing" (1965, 303). When the subject, in a clinical as well as a grammatical sense, is the unconscious, its interpretive invention (that is, its narration or inscription) marks out the point of emergence of the *pharmakon* as concealment/repression and as declaration, without ever being that point.

The voice of the unconscious is the voice of desire for recovery that can never be recovered; as the Unnamable, the articulation of the unconscious, the voice is that of "the World in full flight," since "the word includes the discourse of the other in the secret of its cipher" (Lacan 1968, 44). Working through this strategy of the "cipher"/mark, the Unnamable/unconscious *must* declare "First I'll say what I'm not, that's how they taught me to proceed, then what I am, it's already under way, I have only to resume at the point where I let myself be cowed" (1965, 326). The Unnamable asserts that it is *not* those former narrative voices, but finally, "the ancestor of whom nothing can be said" (352). As it approaches the vanishing point, the Unnamable begins to be able to deny any connection to specific narrators whatsoever, in a gathering set of gestures toward acknowledging itself as *not* subject:

> But enough of this cursed first person, it is really too red a herring, I'll get out of my depth if I'm not careful. But what then is the subject? Mahood? No, not yet. Worm? Even less. Bah, any old pronoun will

do, provided one sees through it. Matter of habit, To be adjusted later. [343]

Habit, we must remember, is what Beckett has told us (in *Proust*) prevents our exercise of the involuntary memory, which is revealed as the *name* of the first step toward the articulation of the unconscious; *The Unnamable* is the last.

Beckett does not advance beyond the extraordinary sophistication of elemental narration he achieves in the conclusive novel of the trilogy, but in subsequent works strives to recover that same microscopic energy of attention. As his style strives to name him, Beckett's narrative voice goes through increasing compaction, from the fulsome Molloy to Worm, and beyond.[29] Worm, as the most elemental of narrators, is the metaphor for those fetal corpses emerging from Beckett's writing. He/it is for the Unnamable not in the first person but in the third, found "huddled in a heap" (359). Worm is the final metaphoric guise of a narrative voice at the threshold of the *pharmakon,* the name of life and death: "he knows it is a voice, how is not known, nothing is known, it's inexplicable. . . . the end is in sight" (359).

But Beckett so relentlessly explores the moment of writing at the threshold of the unconscious that he suspends even the *last* heap of words at the conclusion of the novel, the end that is in sight for narrator and reader, in an impossible heap of references to Freud, Nietzsche, and his own past work, which need to be read carefully (they appear unabridged in the appendix) for the effect of the recovery of and in style: "that's all words, never wake" he/it declares

> all words, there's nothing else...until they say me...perhaps they have said me already, perhaps they have carried me to the threshold of my story, before the door that opens on my story...I'll never know, in the silence you don't know...you must go on...I can't go on, I'll go on.   [414]

The ironic "period" with which the novel concludes is the final *néant,* a disorienting mark of closure on what the narrator has asserted, reopening in the whiteness of the remainder of the page on which it is printed the question of action. For Beckett's unconscious, that reopening, its recovery in both senses, is the instigation and the conclusion of all action, the alpha and the omega of all our energy. Thus Beckett's question about the nature and location, indeed the very existence, of any meaningful action remains as open, subversive, creative, and disruptive as the unconscious itself.

Appendix

Beckett's trilogy of novels, among many other things, is an expansive treatment of the *néant* and its relation to the psychic and linguistic forces of the unconscious. Here follows a series of passages from the three novels, some of which appear in the preceding essay and some of which do not; they may be read as distillation of the theme of the nothing, relative to Beckett's working out of character within the aegis of the unconscious. It is important to remember that the *néant* is always to be read in its "positive" or assertive guise, as the something that is nothing. Novel by novel, character by character in the trilogy, Beckett rigorously explores the *u-topos.*

MOLLOY

And once again I am I will not say alone, no, that's not like me, but how shall I say, I don't know, restored to myself, no, I never left myself, free, yes, I don't know what that means but it's the word I mean to use, free to do what, to do nothing, to know, but what, the laws of the mind perhaps. [1965, 13]

Not to want to say, not to know what you want to say, not to be able to say what you think you want to say, and never to stop saying, or hardly ever, that is the thing to keep in mind, even in the heat of composition. [28]

In reality I said nothing at all, but I heard a murmur, something gone wrong with the silence, and I pricked up my ears, like an animal I imagine, which gives a start and pretends to be dead. And then something arose within me, confusedly, a kind of consciousness, which I express by saying, I said, etc. [88]

It seemed to me that all language was an excess of language. [116]

What a rabble in my head, what a gallery of moribunds. Murphy, Watt, Yerk, Mercier, and all the others. I would never have believed that—yes, I believe it willingly. Stories, stories. I have not been able to tell them. I shall not be able to tell this one. [137]

I have spoken of a voice telling me things. I was getting to know it better now, to understand what it wanted. It did not use the words that Moran had been taught when he was little and that he in his turn had taught to his little one. So that at first I did not know what it wanted. But in the end I understood this language. I understood it, I understood it, all wrong perhaps. That is not what matters. It told me to write the report. Does this mean I am freer now than I was? I do not know. I shall learn. Then I went back into the house and wrote, It is midnight. The rain is beating on the windows. It was not midnight. It was not raining.   [(conclusion), 176]

MALONE DIES

Yes. It is quite dark. I can see nothing. I can scarcely even see the windowpane, or the wall forming with it so sharp a contrast that it often looks like the edge of an abyss. I hear the noise of my little finger as it glides over the paper and then that so different of the pencil following after.   [1965, 208]

That is not what I said. I could swear to it, that is what I wrote. This last phrase seems familiar, suddenly I seem to have written it some-where before, or spoken it, word for word. Yes, I shall soon be, etc., that is what I wrote when I realized I did not know what I had said, at the beginning of my say.   [209]

But my fingers too write in other latitudes and the air that breathes through my pages and turns them without my knowing, when I doze off, so that the subject falls far from the verb and the object lands somewhere in the void, is not the air of this second-last abode, and a mercy it is.   [234]

And if I ever stop talking it will be because there is nothing more to be said, even though all has not been said, even though nothing has been said. But let us leave these morbid matters and get on with that of my demise, in two or three days if I remember rightly. Then it will be all over with the Murphys, Merciers, Molloys, Morans and Malones, unless it goes on beyond the grave.   [236]

I am lost. Not a word.   [263]

he will not touch anyone any more, either with it or with it or with it or with or
or with it or with his hammer or with his stick or with his fist or in thought in dream I mean never he will never
or with his pencil or with his stick or
or light light I mean

never there he will never
there
any more   [(conclusion), 288]

THE UNNAMABLE

Where now? Who now? When now? Unquestioning. I, say I. Unbelieving. Questions, hypotheses, call them that. Keep going, going on, call
that going, call that on.   [1965 (opening), 291]

Nothing ever troubles me. And yet I am troubled. Nothing has ever
changed since I have been here. But I dare not infer from this that
nothing ever will change. Let us try and see where these considerations lead.   [293]

For even should I hit upon the right pensum, somewhere in this
churn of words at last, I would still have to reconstitute the right lesson, unless of course the two are one and the same, which obviously
is not impossible either.   [311]

I am he who will never be caught, never delivered, who crawls
between the thwarts, towards the new day that promises to be glorious, festooned with lifebelts, praying for rack and ruin. . . . There at
least is a first affirmation, I mean negation, on which to build.   [339]

I'm ready to be whatever they want, I'm tired of being matter, matter, pawed and pummelled endlessly in vain. Or give me up and leave
lying in a heap, in such a heap that none would ever be found again to
try and fashion it. . . . It isn't silence, it's pitfalls, into which nothing
would please me better than to fall, with the little cry that might be
taken for human, like a wounded wistiti, the first and last, and vanish
for good and all, having squeaked.   [348]

I who am on my way, words bellying out my sails, am also that
unthinkable ancestor of whom nothing can be said. But perhaps I shall
speak of him some day, and of the impenetrable age when I was he,
some day when they fall silent, convinced at last shall never get born,
having failed to be conceived. Yes, perhaps I shall speak of him, for an
instant, like the echo that mocks, before being restored to him, the
one they could not part me from.   [352–53]

thinking I know, that nothing has befallen me, nothing will befall
me, nothing good, nothing, bad, nothing to be the death of me, noth-

ing to be the life of me, it would be premature. I see me, I see my place, there is nothing to show it, nothing to distinguish it, from all the other places, they are mine, all mine, if I wish, I wish none but mine, there is nothing to mark it. . . . it enfolds me, it covers me, if only this voice would stop, for a second, it would seem long to me, a second of silence.   [363–64]

Perhaps I've missed the keyword to the whole business.   [368]

that's all words, never wake, all words, there's nothing else, you must go on, that's all I know, they're going to stop, I know that well, I can feel it, they're going to abandon me, it will be the silence, for a moment, a good few moments, or it will be mine, the lasting one, that didn't last, that still lasts, it will be I, you must go on, I can't go on, you must go on, I'll go on, you must say words, as long as there are any, until they find me, until they say me, strange pain, strange sin, you must go on, perhaps it's done already, perhaps they have said me already, perhaps they have carried me to the threshold of my story, before the door that opens on my story, that would surprise me, if it opens, it will be I, it will be the silence, where I am, I don't know, I'll never know, in the silence you don't know, you must go on, I can't go on, I'll go on.   [(conclusion), 414]

Notes

1. The effect of the *néant,* as opposed to the nothing, is itself mildly alienating and, like Nietzsche's perennially untranslated *ressentiment,* provides the momentary otherness he, Beckett, and I sometimes wish to evoke. It is to be hoped that when the *néant* appears, it brings a good deal of Nietzschean, Sartrean, and Beckettian baggage with it.

2. See Nietzsche's *Philosophy in the Tragic Age of the Greeks,* 69–95, for a discussion of Parmenides in response to Heraclitus. (All references to works by Nietzsche cite section number; all citations of other sources, unless otherwise indicated, are of page numbers.) Fortunately, Beckett did not take Parmenides' advice any more than Nietzsche did; without this breaking off of the Parmenidean tradition, contemporary philosophy, psychology, linguistics, semiotics, science, and literature would not exist.

3. "Worm" is one of the Unnamable's two guises/disguises; the worm occupies the *topos* balanced between life and death (the worm lives, but lives on death), beginning and end (the worm is the nascent phase of many insects, but also the image of decay). The action of the worm is to promote life and to speed death.

It is also interesting to remember that the "worm" is a snake, in terms of the biblical overtones always present in Beckett. The Edenic serpent uses words to produce disorder where there has been order, again demonstrating that caught-between-ness in which Beckett writes.

4. In book 4 of Nietzsche's *Thus Spoke Zarathustra* ("The Magician"), the prophet encounters by chance a man uttering cries of distress, "a trembling old man with vacant eyes," who cannot stand up, and who moans

Unnamable, shrouded, terrible one!
Thou hunter behind clouds!
Struck down by thy lightning bolt,
Thou mocking eye that stares at me from the dark:
Thus I lie
Writing, twisting, tormented
With all eternal tortures.
Hit
By thee, cruelest hunter,
Thou unknown *god!*

I will suggest how indeed the Unnamable, in Beckett, can be seen as a kind of god: the force and energy of the nothing, the unconscious.

This theme is taken up in a different but closely related context by Juliet Mitchell and Jacqueline Rose in their study of Lacan, Freud, and feminine sexuality; in place of a "belief" in "God," Lacan declares "I believe in the *jouissance* of the woman in so far as it is something more. . . . Might not this *jouissance* which one experiences and knows nothing of, be that which puts us on the path of ex-istence? And why not interpret one face of the Other, the God face, as supported by feminine *jouissance*" (1982, 147). Lacan's notion of "one face of the Other, the God face," is derived precisely from Nietzsche, through Freud, out of this sensing of the unknown and its naming ("God").

5. The repetition of the word *nothing* in Beckett has a haunted quality much like the one Sartre suggests when he declares that the "necessary condition" for the *néant* is that "non-being be a perpetual presence in us and outside of us, that nothingness haunt being" (1956, 11).

Obvious reflections of the Heideggerian and Freudian *unheimlich* resonate here as well. In Beckett's narrator's list of "nothings," the reversals that constantly reorient us are at once uncanny and soothing, a grounding instance of Beckett's "autoaesthetics."

6. See Derrida's discussion of *différance* in *Writing and Difference,* particularly the chapter "Freud and the Scene of Writing," and in the essay entitled "*Différance*" in *Margins of Philosophy.*

7. Just as in Freud, the repression is itself always repressed.

8. *Godot* itself must be seen as caught between *Malone Dies* and *The Unnamable;* the similarities between the play and the last novel of the trilogy are so striking that they bear only biographical interest; *except* that in the present context, *Godot* appears as the conscious, characterized, "worlded"

version of *The Unnamable*. I will call attention to a few salient textual similarities later in the paper.

9. See also *Zarathustra*, book 3, "On the Vision and the Riddle," for Zarathustra's encounter with the "Gate of Moment," which has "two faces; two paths meet here; no one has yet followed either to its end." This section lays out Nietzsche's parable of the moment of emergence, so similar to Beckett's.

10. These voices become what Lacan calls the *epos* (1968, 17).

11. Having developed in some slight detail the connection between the Nietzschean gateway and the threshold of emergence, I must mention briefly that this gateway is closely associated with the Derridean "fold," which comes out of Mallarmé's concept of the *hymen* (Derrida develops this idea in his discussion of Mallarmé in the "Double Session," in *Dissemination*). For Derrida, this "folding" of discourse comes, as it does in *Dissemination*, out of the *pharmakon* (see 1981, 95–117), the potential of inward reversal in all language, which constitutes the recovery out of which this paper comes.

12. In literally thousands of places in the text of *L'Innommable*/*The Unnamable* matters of translation could and should be discussed in terms of the *néant* and the unconscious; another time.

13. Ruby Cohn's short discussion of Sartre and Beckett (1973), concerned with *The Unnamable*, is characteristically interesting, particularly in terms of the association between Beckett's "Worm" and Sartre's. As always, one wants Professor Cohn to push her thoughts further into a theoretical context; as always, she declines.

14. Another repressed must also surface. Deirdre Bair associates the Unnamable with the "complete disintegration" discussed by Jung in the third Tavistock lecture: "The fascination of the unconscious contents gradually grows stronger and conscious control vanishes in proportion until finally the patient sinks into the unconscious and becomes completely victimized by it" (1978, 400). However, Beckett's obsession with the continuation of the *possibility* of action, in language, precludes this complete victimization, as strongly suggested in David Hesla's interpretation of *The Unnamable* (1971, 86–128), and in my own.

15. It is impossible to overestimate Nietzsche's direct and indirect effect on Freud, as Henri Ellenberger points out in *The Discovery of the Unconscious*, and as Derrida discusses frequently, as in "Freud and the Scene of Writing." Freud himself, according to Ernest Jones, "several times said of Nietzsche that he had a more penetrating knowledge of himself than any other man who ever lived or was ever likely to live. From the first explorer of the unconscious this is a handsome compliment" (1955, 344). In *The Interpretation of Dreams*, Freud states, "We can guess how much to the point is Nietzsche's assertion that in dreams 'some primaeval relic of humanity is at work which we can now scarcely reach any longer by a direct path'" (*S.E.* 5:548–49). This inception of his thoughts on the unconscious is not the only direct debt Freud owed to Nietzsche; among the most dramatic of the others is the "id" (*das Es*), the name and idea of which Freud borrowed from *Thus Spoke Zarathustra* ("On the Despisers of the Body").

16. See Joseph Smith's discussion of the theme of inferred otherness and the unconscious in *Psychoanalysis and Language* (Psychiatry and the Humanities, vol. 3). See his comment (xiii) on Freud's claim that "reality will always remain 'unknowable'" (*S.E.* 23:196–97), and Smith's statement (xvii) that for Freud "unconscious" came to be a "quality that could pertain to aspects of id, ego, or superego phenomena"—that is, it has not erupted into awareness. A number of the essays in that volume relate to this hiddenness and otherness of the unconscious.

17. Recent research has shown a much stronger case for the existence of the unconscious than Freud could demonstrate. Work by John Kihlstrom at the University of Arizona, Elizabeth Spelke at Cornell, Kenneth Bowers at the University of Waterloo in Toronto, Ernest Hilgard at Stanford, and others has built a strong case not only for the existence of the unconscious but for its great complexity—greater than the Freudian model would indicate. It seems that the unconscious is a much more sophisticated mechanism than previously believed, capable of genuine "thought" and of performing complex operations unavailable to the conscious mind. This new view of the unconscious makes Beckett's view and use of it all the more accurate and provocative.

18. According to Freud, "there are two kinds of unconscious, which have not yet been distinguished by psychologists. Both of them are unconscious in the sense used by psychology" (*S.E.* 5:614), but they can be meaningfully differentiated. These are the unconscious "*inadmissible to consciousness,*" which we call the unconscious, and that "able to reach consciousness," which we call the preconscious (*S.E.* 5:615). This differentiation serves to strengthen the view that the psychic process is characterized by combination and transference.

The psychodynamic model of the "mind" has all sorts of challenges, of course. As more and more is known about the central nervous system, for example, it is becoming increasingly clear that retention of past experiences appears to depend on levels of ribonucleic acid (RNA) in the brain. In addition, bringing preconscious and even unconscious data to consciousness can be clinically enhanced by direct electrical stimulation of the reticular activating system. The future of psychoanalysis may well become more a function of chemistry and physics than psychology. Beckett has taken these possibilities into account also: see the conclusion of "The End" in *Stories and Texts for Nothing.*

19. I have discussed what I call the "elemental" style in Beckett elsewhere ("Conspicuous Absence: *Tracé* and Power in Beckett" in *Rethinking Beckett: Poststructuralist, Philosophical, and Linguistic Approaches,* ed. Lance St. John Butler [1990]. "Lecture and *Lecture:* Teaching Beckett's *Waiting for Godot,*" in *Approaches to the Teaching of Beckett's Waiting for Godot,*" ed. June Schlueter and Enoch Brater [1990]). I mean elemental in a "chemical" sense, as a matter of fundamental building blocks, in opposition to claims that Beckett's style is "minimalist," with its insinuation of the nihilistic.

20. Freud's discussion of the memory trace, with its clear links to Derrida and Beckett, occupies this section of *Dreams* and continues in the "Mystic

Writing-Pad" (1925) and *Beyond the Pleasure Principle* (1920); clearly, the idea of the tracing of memory (that is, its suppression) occupied Freud centrally. The Brill translation of the footnote quoted here has Freud claiming that he "thought that consciousness occurs actually *in the locality* of the memory-trace" (1978, 396), a formulation even closer to the Beckett-Derrida line I am taking here.

21. Even in the *most* fundamental Lacanian concept, the metaphoric arises: Lacan's declaration mimics what he calls the central problem of the unconscious, its displacement into an unconscious discourse that always interferes with and rivals the conscious one. In an extraordinarily Nietzschean strategy, playing through just the sort of association Lacan claims the unconscious has with conscious discourses, he restates, by imitation, the otherness he wishes to overcome. The entire essay in which this monumental statement occurs ("The Freudian Unconscious and Ours") is vital to an understanding of Beckett.

22. The quotation is from Lacan's *Discours de Rome,* delivered in 1953.

23. See David Hesla's discussion of voice and identity in *The Unnamable,* in *The Shape of Chaos* (1971, 111–25).

24. Lacan declares that Freud "found his inspiration" for the unconscious in 2 Corinthians 3.6: "the letter killeth while the spirit giveth life." Lacan says that "the pretensions of the spirit would remain unassailable if the letter had not shown us that it produces all the effects of truth in man without involving the spirit at all. It is none other than Freud who had this revelation, and he called his discovery the unconscious" (1977, 159). Lacan's comment in conclusion: "The spirit is always somewhere else" (1968, 34).

25. Lacan goes on in this passage to provide insight into Beckett's narrative strategy: the presence of this Other

> can be understood only at a second degree of otherness, which already places him in the position of mediating between me and the double of myself, as it were of my counterpart.
>
> If I have said that the unconscious is the discourse of the Other, it is in order to indicate the beyond in which the recognition of desire is bound up with the desire for recognition.
>
> In other words, this other is the Other that even my lie invokes as a guarantor of the truth in which it subsists.   [1977, 172]

This is the "aporia, pure and simple," in which the Unnamable begins his story, literally lost in rhetoric (291).

26. We have seen Freud's topographic model of the conscious/unconscious, the circle in the circle; Lacan translates this into a complex linguistic and semiological model whose basic question is now: "Is the place that I occupy as the subject of a signifier concentric or excentric, in relation to the place I occupy as subject of the signified?" (1977, 165). One must see Lucky's monologue from act one of *Godot* in these terms, as remnants of a forgotten, unconscious discourse.

27. Derrida's discussion of the *pharmakon,* in *Dissemination,* is a critique

of Plato's condemnation of writing: "Plato decides in favor of a logic that does not tolerate such passages between opposing senses of the same word, all the more so since such a passage would reveal itself to be something quite different from simple confusion, alteration, or the dialectic of opposites" (1981, 98–99). Plato "dreams," according to Derrida, of a "memory without a sign" (109). Derrida's claim is not only that this dream is an impossible one (surely a sign of repression) but that in the reversal of *all* grammatology is to be found the "dangerous supplement" by which language recovers its tracks.

28. Bowie points out how fascinating it is that Freud thus based "a characteristic wishful fantasy," of an uncontradictory dreaming mind that knows no contradiction, upon "a piece of fairy-tale philology" (1979, 124–25). Freud himself had been, however, indisputably influenced by this fairy tale, as his 1910 review of Abel's book shows ("The Antithetical Meaning of Primal Words," *S.E.* 11:155–61); this review is reproduced in *On Creativity and the Unconscious* (1958).

29. Beckett emulates the Nietzschean strategy of *Zarathustra* here: in Nietzsche's work, the narrator adopts the same position of "inner distance" as does Beckett's; in *Zarathustra,* the "narrator" turns out to be Zarathustra's "shadow," and not the prophet at all. In the same way that the Beckett narrators are transcended by the voice articulating them, so is Zarathustra passed by. This is true in Freud's treatment of the dream story, as well, and in Lacan's consideration of the attempt to *say* the "*je.*"

References

Bair, Deirdre. *Samuel Beckett.* New York: Harcourt Brace Jovanovich, 1978.

Beckett, Samuel. *En attendant Godot.* Paris: Les Éditions de Minuit, 1952.

———. *L'Innommable.* Paris: Les Éditions de Minuit, 1953.

———. *Waiting for Godot.* New York: Grove Press, 1954.

———. *Proust* (1931). New York: Grove Press, 1957.

———. *Three Novels (Molloy, Malone Dies, The Unnamable).* New York: Grove Press, 1965.

———. *Stories and Texts for Nothing.* New York: Grove Press, 1967.

———. *The Lost Ones.* New York: Grove Press, 1972.

———. *Collected Poems in English and French.* New York: Grove Press, 1977.

———. *Endgame.* New York: Grove Press, 1980.

Blau, Herbert. *The Eye of Prey: Subversions of the Postmodern.* Bloomington: Indiana University Press, 1987.

Bowie, Malcolm. "Jacques Lacan." In *Structuralism and Since: From Lévi-Strauss to Derrida,* edited by John Sturrock. New York: Oxford University Press, 1979.

Cohn, Ruby. *Back to Beckett.* Princeton: Princeton University Press, 1973.

Dearlove, J. E. *Accommodating the Chaos: Samuel Beckett's Nonrelational Art.* Durham, N.C.: Duke University Press, 1982.

Derrida, Jacques. *Margins of Philosophy*. Translated by Alan Bass. Chicago: University of Chicago Press, 1972.

———. "Freud and the Scene of Writing." In *Writing and Difference,* translated by Alan Bass. Chicago: University of Chicago Press, 1978.

———. *Dissemination.* Translated by Barbara Johnson. Chicago: University of Chicago Press, 1981.

Ellenberger, Henri F. *The Discovery of the Unconscious: The History and Evolution of Dynamic Psychiatry.* New York: Basic Books, 1970.

Federman, Raymond. *Journey to Chaos: Samuel Beckett's Early Fiction.* Berkeley and Los Angeles: University of California Press, 1965.

Freud, Sigmund. *The Standard Edition of the Complete Psychological Works.* Edited and translated by James Strachey. 24 vols. London: Hogarth Press, 1953–74.

   The Interpretation of Dreams (1900–1901), vols. 4, 5.

   "A Note on the Unconscious in Psycho-Analysis" (1912), vol. 12.

   "The Unconscious" (1915), vol. 14.

———. *On Creativity and the Unconscious.* Edited by Benjamin Nelson. New York: Harper and Row, 1958.

———. *The Interpretation of Dreams.* Translated by A. A. Brill. New York: Modern Library, 1978.

Heidegger, Martin. *Being and Time.* Translated by John Macquarrie and Edward Robinson. New York: Harper and Row, 1962.

———. "What Is Metaphysics?" In *Basic Writings.* Edited and translated by Farrell Krell. New York: Harper and Row, 1976.

Hesla, David H. *The Shape of Chaos: An Interpretation of the Art of Samuel Beckett.* Minneapolis: University of Minnesota Press, 1971.

Jones, Ernest. *The Life and Work of Sigmund Freud.* Vol. 2. New York: Basic Books, 1955.

Lacan, Jacques. "L'Instance de la lettre dans l'inconscient ou La Raison depuis Freud." *La Psychanalyse* 3 (1957): 47–81.

———. *The Language of the Self: The Function of Language in Psychoanalysis.* Translated by Anthony Wilden. New York: Dell Publishing (Delta), 1968.

———. *Écrits: Selections.* Translated by Alan Sheridan. New York: W. W. Norton, 1977.

———. *The Four Fundamental Concepts of Psycho-Analysis.* Edited by Jacques-Alain Miller. Translated by Alan Sheridan New York: W. W. Norton, 1981.

Merleau-Ponty, Maurice. "Eye and Mind." In *The Primacy of Perception,* edited by James M. Edie. Evanston, Ill.: Northwestern University Press, 1964.

Mitchell, Juliet, and Rose, Jacqueline. *Feminine Sexuality.* Translated by Jacqueline Rose. London: Macmillan, 1982.

Nietzsche, Friedrich. *Philosophy in the Tragic Age of the Greeks.* Translated by Marianne Cowan. Chicago: Regnery Gateway, 1962.

———. *Thus Spoke Zarathustra.* Translated by Walter Kaufmann. New York: Viking Press, 1966.

————. *The Birth of Tragedy.* In *Basic Writings,* translated by Walter Kaufmann. New York: Random House (Vintage), 1968a.

————. *The Will to Power.* Edited by Walter Kaufmann. Translated by Walter Kaufmann and R. J. Hollingdale. New York: Random House (Vintage), 1968b.

————. *On the Genealogy of Morals.* Translated by Walter Kaufmann. New York: Random House (Vintage), 1969.

————. *The Gay Science.* Translated by Walter Kaufmann. New York: Random House (Vintage), 1974.

————. *Twilight of the Idols.* Translated by R. J. Hollingdale. New York: Penguin Books, 1978.

————. "On Truth and Lies in a Nonmoral Sense." In *Philosophy and Truth: Selections from Nietzsche's Notebooks of the Early 1870's,* edited and translated by Daniel Breazeale. Atlantic Highlands, N.J.: Humanities Press, 1979.

Rorty, Richard. *Consequences of Pragmatism.* Minneapolis: University of Minnesota Press, 1982.

Sartre, Jean-Paul. *Being and Nothingness: An essay on Phenomenological Ontology.* Translated by Hazel Barnes. New York: Philosophical Library, 1956.

Smith, Joseph H. "Introduction." In *Psychoanalysis and Language,* edited by Joseph H. Smith. Psychiatry and the Humanities, vol. 3. New Haven: Yale University Press, 1978.

Wilden, Anthony. "Lacan and the Discourse of the Other." In Lacan, *The Language of the Self* (1968).

9   The Fragmented Self,
         the Reproduction of the Self,
         and Reproduction in Beckett
         and in the Theater of the Absurd

Bennett Simon

The "self" is in terrible trouble in the twentieth century. The term *modern,* as in "modern art," "modernist," and "postmodern," broadly speaking connotes portrayal of the self that is different from the "classical" (classical ancient, and classical eighteenth century) and the "romantic" visions of the self.[1]

There was trouble enough in the literature of the later nineteenth and early twentieth centuries, when the self was "doubled," as in Conrad, Dostoevski, and others. But in the twentieth century, the century of "The Hollow Men," the self is disintegrated, deconstructed, shadowed, fragmented, submerged, unstable, and scarcely able to tell a coherent story.

In much of modern art, self as body has become decomposed into multiple perspectives, multiple geometric forms, hidden, taken apart and reassembled in weird ways, and been rendered exceedingly abstract. Through a convergence of attempts to express and solve problems of composition, perspective, and radical new psychological perceptions of the body and of the person, "modern art" has evolved to a point where we almost take for granted the portrayal of bodies and objects in cubist art, in much of the work of Picasso, spanning many decades, and in artists such as Paul Klee. World wars and the attendant persecutions and terrors have added more fuel to the "deconstruction" and dismembering of the body in art.

In psychology and especially in psychoanalysis, "disorders of the self" have somehow or other gained a toehold in theory, perhaps even

Based on a talk given at the Smithsonian Beckett Symposium in Washington, D.C., on 3 March 1989.

157

in life, and "self-psychology," for better and for worse, is definitely "in." "Fragmented selves," schizoid selves, selves that are incomplete or multiple or hiding out, as if in a subterranean bomb shelter, false selves providing the "cover story," as it were, for "true selves" that are too fragile or too awful to let on that they exist—all these and more populate the world of contemporary psychoanalysis, clinical psychiatry, and, in various forms, the world of pop psychology, as in "the me generation." Life, unfortunately, has not been too kind to "selves" in this century either—selves and persons have been literally fragmented, lives torn apart, people torn apart by torture, numbed by various forms of "brainwashing" and terror, abused physically and sexually as small children, and finally threatened with ultimate extinction by nuclear war or environmental disaster.

My argument is that the modern problematic of the self goes hand in glove with a set of modern concerns and anxieties about conception and contraception, about the quest for and possibilities of reproduction by technological means. These modern concerns entail an eschewing and a deep dread of the personal and sexual intercourse, the intercourse between man and woman that leads to procreation and necessitates child rearing. The problematic of the self that is expressed in so much of modernist literature is entwined with the problem—both the threat and the promise—of the discontinuity of generations and the discontinuation of generation.

In Beckett and, more generally, in the theater of the absurd, splitting, cloning, xeroxing—any method other than standard heterosexual intercourse—is the key to reproduction. I will pose a "chicken-and-egg" question: does a faulty self lead to a lack of will for and lack of faith in procreation and in progeny, or do disturbances in the will for, capacity for, and faith in procreation and in progeny "beget" disturbances of the self?

The Self in Beckett

Any reader of Beckett's works, or viewer or auditor of his plays, quickly concludes that there is something amiss with the "selfhood" of his characters. At the level of audience response, there is the common feeling that the characters are "two-dimensional" or that they lack a kind of nucleus of self-activating and self-generating modes of operating in the world. They do not seem to grow or change much— except to wind up, or wind down; they lie in bed, and what movement there is consists of going around and around in ever-decreasing concentric circles (see the "Dog" song in *Waiting for Godot* [1954, 37–38]) or rocking, as Murphy does in *Murphy*. Characters within Beckett's works frequently complain about themselves in ways analogous to audiences' complaints about the characters.

One critic of Beckett, Linda Ben-Zvi, a Beckett scholar, has admirably cataloged and summarized the problems of "self" in Beckett's work. Time and place are never clearly defined, and hence the continuity of the self in time and the fixity of the person in place are problematic. *Krapp's Last Tape* takes place in Krapp's den (a rather specific but nonspecific place) at "a late evening in the future." And Krapp is one of the more continuous and stable of Beckett's characters! Beckett's narrators, in general, are among the more problematic of narrators in modern literature, a literature that abounds in, and indeed prides itself on, problematic, incompetent, and "unreliable" narrators.

To quote from Ben-Zvi:

> Further complicating the quest for self, Beckett also indicates that at any given moment the self exists as two separate entities: an outer I, alive in the macrocosm, commingling with the physical world, and an inner me, unseen, unheard, alive only to the I. This microcosmic aspect of the self has no means of communication and is able to talk only through the I, constantly monitoring the physical external self, offering, as it were, a running commentary heard by the I alone. Its very existence causes the disjunction and schism that all Beckett figures experience. Because of this other self, characters are never able to use the singular pronoun; the other voice, alive in the head, disavows the limiting appellation: "did you ever say I to yourself in your life come on now . . . could you ever say I to yourself in your life," the inner voice in *That Time* asks. In particular works the focus may shift, sometimes on the external self, sometimes on the inner me. "It was he, I was inside," the speaker in *Fizzles* says. "My brother inside me, my old twin," the voice in *Radio II* claims. The question of pronoun juggling becomes more than a verbal game; it becomes a sign of the impossibility of ever uniting the parts of the self. Because of this disjunction, all of Beckett's people have the continual sense that they are being watched, if only by themselves. [1986, 5–6]

This hypertrophied self-awareness has been noted by many critics both as a feature of Beckett's work and as a characteristic of "modernist" literature (Sass 1985)—or, according to some, of "postmodernist" literature.

In addition to the split between an outer and inner self, there are splits between mental self and bodily self, and a weirdness and instability in the conception of the body. Drawing on the work of Albright (1981), in an earlier publication (1988a) I wrote about the self in Beckett:

> Particularly in the later plays, there are parts of the self, loosely or poorly integrated, organs with autonomy, or aspects of the self, different ages and stages, that do not convey a coherent, agent-centered sense of self. The instability of the image of the self is epitomized in *The Unnamable* (pp. 305–06) where the hero describes himself with a ceaseless abundance of images—a talking ball, a hairless wedgehead, a skull made of solid bone, a tympanum, a red-mouthed half-wit; his genitals, hair and nose have fallen off. No single image is held longer than an instant; each image drives out the image before it, as if the imagination's perfection consisted not in creating images but in extinguishing them.   [346]

I have also discussed the importance of twinning and replication of self (selves) in Beckett. In *Endgame,* Hamm, terrified and increasingly desperate that his audience is leaving or dying or disappearing through indifference, soliloquizes.

> All kinds of fantasies! That I'm being watched! A rat! Steps! Breath held and then...
> (*He breathes out*)
> Then babble, babble, words, like the solitary child who turns himself into children, two, three, so as to be together, and whisper together, in the dark.   [1958, 70]

Molloy provides examples of the most elaborate multiplication of selves, or as one critic puts it, in describing Moran's pursuit of Molloy, "Molloys multiply dizzyingly in his presence" (Albright 1981, 178).

> Between the Molloy I stalked within me thus and the true Molloy, after whom I was so soon to be in full cry, over hill and dale, the resemblance cannot have been great...The fact was there were three, no four Molloys. He that inhabited me, my caricature of same, Gaber's and the man of flesh and blood somewhere awaiting me...I will therefore add a fifth Molloy, that of Youdi...But let us leave it at that, if you don't mind, the party is big enough.   [115]

The self portrayed in Beckett is at once punning, clever, recondimently erudite, and stupid, retarded, virtually incapable of connected logical and symbolic thought. The narrator in *The Unnamable* talks of the jumble of meaningless words and images he knows.

> I must have forgotten them, I must have mixed them up, these nameless images I have, these imageless names, these windows I should perhaps rather call doors, at least by some other name, and this word man which

is perhaps not the right one for the thing I see when I hear it...I call that the dark, perhaps it's azure, blank words, but I use them, they keep coming back, all those they showed me...it's a lie, a score would be plenty, tried and trusty, unforgettable, nicely varied, that would be palette enough...that's how it will end, in heartrending cries, inarticulate murmurs, to be invented as I go along, improvised, as I groan along. I'll laugh, that's how it will end, in a chucke, chuck, chuck, ow, ha, pa, I'll practice nym, hoo, plop, psss, nothing but emotion, bing gang, that's blows, ugh, pooh, what else, oooh, aaah, that's love, enough, it's tiring. [1958, 407–8]

The self that is portrayed may not be able to tolerate even the "heartrending cries, inarticulate murmurs" and try to protect itself and make itself cohere with mechanized, arithmetic modes of experiencing and relating.

> Passion and human preference threaten the "system" of permutations and combinations. In the first part of *Molloy,* there are sixteen sucking stones—they must be arranged in the right order. In *Murphy,* the hero becomes aware of the fact that he could eat his five different biscuits in one hundred and twenty different orders, if only he were not bothered by his preferences! [Simon 1988a]

At the opening of *Endgame,* a *mise-en-scène* of the end of the world, of the cumulation of immense amounts of suffering, Clov is piling up (literally or figuratively) "grain upon grain,...a little heap, the impossible heap." He continues, "I can't be punished any more. (*Pause*) I'll go to my kitchen, ten feet by ten feet, and wait for him to whistle me...Nice dimensions, nice proportions" (1–2).

An extension of the mechanized mode of operating of some of the characters is the "mathematization" or "geometrization" of pain and suffering that is reflected particularly in later Beckett compositions, such as *Lessness* (1970) and *Imagination Dead Imagine* (1965), which opens with:

> No trace anywhere of life, you say, pah, no difficulty there, imagination not dead yet, yes dead, good, imagination dead imagine. Islands, waters, azure, verdure, one glimpse and vanished, endlessly, omit . . . No way in, go in, measure. Diameter three feet, three feet from ground to summit of the vault. Two diameters at right angles AB CD divide the white ground into two semicircles ACB BDA. Lying on the ground two white bodies, each in its semicircle.

Both the characters and the settings are contained by precise numbers, angles and boundaries, not just defensively against enormous pain and loss, but almost as if their "selves" were reduced merely to measurements and proportions.

Another important and recurrent feature of the Beckett characters, and of their sense of self, is that there is no "sense," no meaning. The self is not experienced as a center and generator of meaning but rather as an entity that has to make the best it can of living in an absolutely senseless world. Both Beckett himself and his characters repeatedly deride the effort to discern meaning, let alone *the* meaning, of a gesture, a life, or a play.

Central to the argument I am going to present is that the "self" of the characters in Beckett is not embedded in a coherent narrative, in a coherent story. Many critics have commented on the plight and blight of storytelling in Beckett, and I have found Kristin Morrison's *Canters and Chronicles* especially illuminating in this regard. Again, I quote from my earlier work:

> Storytelling is repeatedly mocked, undermined, made more and more involuted; when not mocked, the act of storytelling appears as an impossible task, for which there is no incentive and no energy. In many different contexts, for Beckett's characters, the fundamental linking entailed in one person telling a story to another, in one person linking events together in meaningful sequence—that activity is derided.   [1988a, 347]

The self is scarcely embedded in a chain of generations, scarcely linked to one's own parents, and almost never existing by extension through children, and there are fewer and fewer stories to tell about ancestors and no children left to whom to tell those stories. *Endgame* is the work par excellence about the end of storytelling and the end of the self having a meaningful connection with another.

Finally, the most devastating aspect of the self in Beckett is that having been born is itself a terrible mistake, perhaps even a crime. "His birth was the death of him...At suck first fiasco" (*A Piece of Monologue*). Or, from an early novel (and a very funny one), *Murphy,* comes this comic version of Job's tortured lament: "Neary leaned against the Pillar railings and cursed, first the day in which he was born, then—in a bold flash-back—the night in which he was conceived" (46).

This last feature of the self—"best is never to have been born" (Sophocles)—leads back to my main argument, namely, that the problematic self and the denigration of birth (and intercourse) are closely connected in Beckett and, more generally, in the theater of the absurd.

Beckett on Birth—Blighted Eggs and Blighted Selves

Beckett's penchant for his characters' attacking or denigrating birth, as well as his personal statements bemoaning the fact and the method of his own conception and birth, is apparent in almost all of his oeuvre, though especially in his plays. Starting with some of his earliest works, one can now see in Beckett how pervasive are the themes of the problems inherent in conception and birth, the inherent problematic of male and female getting together. Failures of the process— sterility, abortion, stillbirth, and the death of young children, including death by neglect or murder—litter the Beckettian landscape. The urge to get "unborn," to shrink back to nonexistence, also pervades his oeuvre. This urge is apparent not only within the works but in the author's attitude toward his own work. Everything must be shrunk back and at least partially "unborn." Beckett is reported to have said that he regretted writing *Waiting for Godot* in two acts—it should have been one; *Endgame* was shortened as it went through drafts into only one act, and it was shortened again as Beckett translated it from French into English. The minimalist artistry of Beckett, in contrast to the proliferative and polyphiloprogenitive artistry of James Joyce, is illustrated in cartoons by Guy Davenport, from Hugh Kenner's *The Stoic Comedians: Flaubert, Joyce and Beckett.*

These observations have been brought into focus by Deirdre Bair's biography of Beckett, where she assembled material relevant to Beckett's "insight" about how he had been "incompletely born." This "realization" was achieved during the course of his two years of psychotherapy-psychoanalysis with W. R. Bion (1933–35). Beckett and Bion, at an impasse in the therapy, at Bion's suggestion went to hear a lecture by Jung at the Tavistock Clinic. Bair tells this fascinating story and thereby has helped Beckett readers to appreciate the centrality of the theme of blighted birth, of the blight *of* birth, in Beckett's work. Bair and others have also highlighted the recurrence in Beckett's work of attacks on, or dread of, female sexuality, especially in relation to the problematic of birth.[2]

Insofar as critics have thought about the sources of Beckett's attitudes, preoccupations and fears regarding all aspects of conception and birth, explanations have tended in the direction of looking at Beckett's personal psychology. This is an entirely appropriate line of speculation, though speculation it must largely remain. I have written on aspects of Beckett's dread of birth, and I have suggested some possible meanings accruing to his attitude, as well as some relationship to the preoccupations of Bion (Simon 1988b). I have elaborated how Beckett and Bion, who had no contact with each other after therapy ended, nevertheless profoundly influenced each other. Bion was later to become one of the important figures in the "British object-relations school" of psychoanalysis, although by temperament he eschewed any and all such prepackaging and labeling. His clinical work concentrated heavily on patients with blighted defective sense of self, and his theoretical and literary-imagistic works also dealt with the problem of the birth and development of the self in all of us. In various interesting and at times convoluted ways, Bion too was preoccupied with both defective selves and the problematic of birth. Among his works are a loosely connected series of imagistic autobiographical memoirs, featuring dialogues between various stages of the embryo and various postnatal stages of the self, of himself.

I would like to expand my previous argument about the role of personal and experiential factors in the life of Beckett the man, and argue that in regard to preoccupation with the processes of reproduction and the nature of the self, it is useful to view Beckett the writer within a larger context. My working hypothesis is that something in Beckett's personal inner dramas resonated with and in fact amplified currents in the twentieth-century literary, social, and political realms. These currents include a preoccupation with issues of conception and contraception, which are subtly or not so subtly represented in that mix of plays and playwrights that Martin Esslin first called the theater of the absurd.

Elsewhere I have argued that tragic drama, from its beginning in fifth-century Athens down to the present day, has included as one of its preoccupations an attack on birth, especially the birth of man from woman (Simon 1988a). Aeschylus's *Oresteia* has as its dramatic resolution the assertion of a fantasy/theory that the woman is strictly incidental in the birth process, that the father is the only true parent, and cites as witness Pallas Athene, begotten from her father's head. "Best is never to have been born," proclaims the chorus in Sophocles' *Oedipus at Colonus,* and that chorus continues through Shakespeare as Lear curses the very process of conception and gestation, as well as the reeking, sulfurous female needed for that process. *Macbeth* presents the vision of a man not of woman born, re-presenting the recurrent wish in Greek tragedy, especially Euripides, that men could beget children without women. Therefore, I argue, Beckett, as part of the tradition of Western drama—in fact, as a kind of commentator on that tradition—extends and deepens the presentation of the problematic of birth depending on a relationship and connection between a man and a woman (Simon 1988a, 249).[3]

But now I shall review some instances of Beckett on birth, beginning with an analysis of an early work, *Whoroscope,* his first published poem, written in 1930.

Whoroscope was written quickly for a contest on the subject of "Descartes and Time," but there is ample evidence that Beckett had been immersed in Descartes's life and writings well before this contest appeared.[4] In the title, Beckett condenses the themes of time (hor-), Descartes's attacks on astrology (horoscope), and women as problematic or betrayers and slayers (whores). The entire poem is filled with recondite details and allusions, and the few notes that Beckett added at the insistence of the publisher make it only marginally intelligible to readers not deeply steeped in the life and lore of Descartes.

He takes up allusively Descartes's idiosyncrasies regarding eggs. Beckett introduces his laconic notes thus:

> René Descartes...liked his omelette made of eggs hatched from eight to ten days; shorter or longer under the hen and the result, he says, is disgusting.
>
> He kept his own birthday to himself so that no astrologer could cast his nativity.
>
> The shuttle of a ripening egg combs the warp of his days.

The narrator moves from eggs to ovaries to dead child.

> What's that?
> A little green fry or a mushroomy one?
> Two lashed ovaries with prostisciutto?
> How long did she womb it, the feathery one?
> Three days and four nights?

The theme of eggs, incubation, and hatching is coupled with a glancing sideswipe at female sexuality—ovaries "lashed" with prostitution. Beckett then takes up the death of a child, alluding to the death by an overwhelming infection, of Descartes's six-year-old illegitimate but much-beloved daughter.

> And Francine my precious fruit of a house-and-parlour foetus!
> What an exfoliation!
> Her grey flayed epidermis and scarlet tonsils!
> My one child
> scourged by a fever to stagnant murky blood—

Thus, even the allusions to Descartes's "love child," Francine, are associated with rotting and decay. The themes of eggs, decay, blighted birth, and woman as dangerous prostitute are echoed in the last part of the poem:

> Are you ripe at last, my slim pale double-breasted turd?
> How rich she smells,
> this abortion of a fledgling!
> I will eat it with a fish fork.
> White and yolk and feathers.
> Then I will rise and move moving
> toward Rahab[5] of the snows,
> the murdering matinal pope-confessed amazon,
> Christina the ripper.[6]

It is noteworthy that in a poem about the philosopher, who par excellence took up questions about whether we exist and how we know we exist, Beckett at once goes to the representation of Descartes's mind suffering from painful issues about conception, female sexuality, genealogy, birth, and survival of children in the world. He also includes, manifestly alluding to a childhood playmate of Descartes's, a little cross-eyed girl, the lines:

> My squinty doaty!
> I hid and you sook.

This last line has been cited as equivalent to Beckett's motto in relation to the question of where the meanings of his works are, and I would add that the line also captures something essential as to Beckett's version of the self—if it exists, it is in hiding.

Lines 45ff. allude to Descartes's famous dreams, dreams that supposedly led to his realizations about the relationship between thinking and existence, and the problem of doubt and deception about one's own senses. These dreams, as pointed out by the psychoanalyst Bertram Lewin many years ago, are also marked by the replication of *splits within the self,* between the mind and the body, the observing ego and the observed person, and other splits.

> A wind of evil flung my despair of ease
> against the sharp spires of the one lady:
> not once or twice but . . .

(A character who is "flung," rather than engaging in self-generating movement, is a recurrent feature of the Beckett landscape—for example, Watt in his walking, and most prominently the lone character in *Act without Words.*)

Thus, we find that in his very earliest writings he seizes upon a model, or a subject at least, Descartes, who combined a passion for understanding the possibilities of existence and knowing about existence, a zeal to understand birth (inter alia, he wrote a treatise on the fetus),[7] and deep doubts and anxieties about himself in relation to woman. These concerns are coupled with a deep anxiety about variety of splits and oppositions within the psyche and between the psyche and the body.

The preoccupation with birth and with birth as a dire event persists until the present, or near present, in Beckett's works. The overlap between birth and death, both numbing and joyless states, is also recurrent.

In *Not I* (1972), a stage play, relating the lonely death of a lonely old woman, Beckett's "Mouth" begins:

> Out...into this world...this world...tiny little thing...before its time...in a godfor-...what?...girl?...yes...tiny little girl...into this...out into this...before her time...godforsaken hole called...no matter...parents unknown...unheard of...he having vanished...thin air...no sooner buttoned up his breeches...she similarly...eight months later...almost to the tick...so no love...spared that...no love such as normally vented on the...speechless infant...in the home...no.

Endgame, of course, is the work that is most explicit in its horror of the process of reproduction and of its results, and it is the most "obliterative" of Beckett's works. It is the end of the world, some sort of postnuclear holocaust setting, some variant of Noah-in-the-ark— but perhaps with the flood waters never receding. The play is replete with attacks on birth and procreation. Hamm denounces his father: "accursed progenitor," and "scoundrel, why did you engender me?" References to birth are hardly kind or loving, such as Clov's "I'm trying ...Ever since I was whelped," or the punning allusions to female genitalia and female procreation, "where did he come from? He named the hole" (52), or "If he was laying we'd be bitched" (34). There are efforts to stamp out all potential generative life, be it a boy or a flea or a rat.

I have cited already Hamm's speech comparing his mental state with that of a terrified child, "like the solitary child who turns himself into children, two, three, so as to be together, and whisper together, in the dark."

Thus, in the play that works toward the elimination of all reproduction, we still see the urge and the need, however conflicted, to have other beings around.[8] The "method," after all sexual reproduction is denounced and eliminated, is a psychic equivalent of asexual splitting, bacterial division, a kind of cloning.

Another instance of how the lonely self is "reproduced" in Beckett is seen in *Krapp's Last Tape.* There Krapp, lonely by virtue of his abandoning and being abandoned, having foresworn what we might call "fructifying intercourse" with others (several young women, his dead mother), is left evoking past "tapes" of the self, keeping company and making company by creating personages out of his own previous life stages and life scenes. And in *Molloy,* we also find the most striking examples of reproduction by replication of the self.

This means of replication seems to be splitting, fragmenting, cloning; the motives seem to be loneliness and the dread of the entanglement between two people, especially that between a man and a woman that could produce a child, with all the real and imagined dangers inherent in that prospect. More of that at the end.

Reproduction in the Theater of the Absurd

Esslin's term, theater of the absurd, was coined in 1961 to describe theater that was becoming extremely important at that time, principally the works of Adamov, Beckett, Genet, Ionesco, Arrabal, and, though just beginning to appear, Pinter. The American playwrights Edward Albee and Sam Shepard are frequently included in that group. Esslin chose the term *absurd* because of its important usage by some existential thinkers, most notably Camus. As an example of what Esslin means by absurd, he cites Ionesco on Kafka: "Absurd is that which is devoid of purpose.... Cut off from his religious, metaphysical, and transcendental roots, man is lost; all his actions become senseless, absurd, useless" (Esslin 1980, 23).

Esslin contrasts playwrights such as Anouilh, Giradoux, and Sartre, who write about those conditions in connected dialogue, narrative, and more or less conventional structure, and with tightly reasoned, rational arguments. The playwrights that he groups together as theater of the absurd convey something of the absurd human condition in form as well as content.

An important part of the absurd, as in Ionesco's statement, is the sense of being cut off from roots and, as a usually unstated corollary, of having no branches, no offshoots, no descendants. Ironically, Esslin's definition and his book represent an attempt to trace the history, that is the ancestry and progenitors, of the contemporary theater of the absurd. Subsequent editions of his book suggest that there are progeny of these writers as well as ancestors. It is this aspect of the theater of the absurd, the problem of ancestry, propagation, and reproduction in relation to "rootless" man, and man with an "absurd" sense of self, to which I call attention. It is an issue present in works that Esslin considers as either early examples or precursors of the theater of the absurd.

Part of the "literary" context of Beckett's attack on birth is that the theater of the absurd is a dramatic culture that has been marked from its beginning with a preoccupation with birth and reproduction, especially *mass reproduction,* and either asexual reproduction or procreation by men without women. I believe that an important part of the theater of the absurd is a conflict over whether the idea that babies have to be born by the process of men and women getting together, "getting on" together, copulating, gestating, and bearing children— whether that process is "absurd" or whether attempts to avoid that process are "absurd."[9] The form of these plays, especially the "absurd" and nonconnecting, non sequitur dialogues, convey the sense of nonconnection, of fruitless or thwarted copulation, that constitutes some of their content.

These concerns within modern drama in turn belong in the larger context of the twentieth-century struggles around political, religious, and economic aspects of birth, its control, and its augmentation. Governments have had a strong vested interest in, at times alternately, supporting contraception and abortion and measures to increase population growth.[10] War and its multiple kinds of devastations have played a prominent role in governmental efforts at control, but numerous other factors have entered as well. Not the least of these are issues around the roles and rights of women. Related too is the enormous growth in the technology of both contraception and enhancing reproductive capacities. Huxley's 1932 novel, *Brave New World,* brilliantly portrays the interplay among technology, politics, the regulation of war and peace, and the massive changes in the psychology of the individual, the new self, that are part and parcel of the changes in reproductive practices. He also, incidentally, by his brilliant evocation of Shakespeare in the title and in much of the latter part of the book, presents a vision of the deep relationship among literature, passion, the family, and technology. I argue that all of these larger cultural, economic, political, and technological concerns affecting relationships among men, women, childbearing, and the "interests" of the state, are reflected in and commented upon in the theater of the absurd.

In the next section I shall concentrate on how much the theater of the absurd is concerned with reproduction and production. I shall also briefly discuss as part of the concern of theater of the absurd the role of war and the kinds of threats of extermination posed first by the two world wars and by the apocalyptic possibilities of nuclear destruction.

Alfred Jarry (1873–1907) is taken by Esslin to be the founder of the "movement" that became theater of the absurd. His Ubu cycle, a series of plays beginning with *Ubu Roi* (1896), can be taken as the archetypical plays of this genre. One play in the cycle, a rarely read (let alone performed) piece, is *Ubu Cocu* (*Ubu Cuckolded*). The opening lines of the play show us a ridiculous character, some sort of professor of mathematics, admiring his collection of polyhedra:

> ACHRAS: Oh, but it's like this, look you, I've no grounds to be dissatisfied with my polyhedra; they breed every six weeks, they're worse than rabbits. And it's also quite true to say that the regular polyhedra are the most faithful and most devoted to their master, except that this morning the Icosahedron was a little fractious, so that I was compelled, look you, to give it a smack on each of its twenty faces. [Jarry 1965, 25]

Ubu Cocu is an outrageous, ridiculous, and angry play, some sort of wild attack on the bourgeoisie. Ubu takes over the house of Achras, and there is a lot of impaling, buggery, brutality, and submission. The language is of shit and piss and, most strikingly, mechanization of body functions, the "shittapump." It portrays the use of naked force and humiliating power, both barely rationalized.

Achras is ridiculous, but at the outset of the play he is not yet "absurd"—that is, at the opening of the play he is still rooted in home, vocation, marriage and family, and community. But by the end all his roots and connections are severed. While the rest of the play manifestly does not concern reproduction, it concerns the destruction of all those roots and connections that make a continuity of generations and of traditions possible. But what is striking, then, is not just the image of reproduction at the beginning but the almost prescient image of mathematical bodies replacing animal bodies, reproduction without intercourse, a preview of "cloning."

The next play I want to examine, Guillaume Apollinaire's *Les Mammelles de Tirésias,* was written mainly in 1903, although it was enlarged and then first presented in 1916.[11] The plot, which defies summary, involves a French couple on the island of Zanzibar, the wife named Thérèse and her husband, Mari. The wife announces that she is a "feministe" and wants to do all the things men do, but especially to fight in wars—to fight rather than have babies (1946, 35);[12] she lets go of her breasts, which are two differently colored balloons made of rubber, allows them to fly up, and then makes herself into a man, named Tirésias. (The name is aptly chosen, for in Greek myth Tirésias had led a life alternately as a man and as a woman.) She wants to be a doctor, lawyer, warrior, legislator, and all other occupations reserved traditionally for men. Later in the play, her husband announces that his wife (or his wife who used to be a woman) is now a "merdecin," some condensation of "shit" and "doctor."

The plot is complex and silly, replete with absurd arguments and duels, and the husband dresses up as a woman and is propositioned by a policeman. Finally, the husband takes it upon himself to make babies and somehow—the method is never specified—produces and is about to raise some 40,049 babies.

There is imagery of dismemberment of the body, part objects— first, the wife gets rid of her breasts and later, in a bizarre scene be- tween an American reporter and the husband (the reporter has come to write a story about a man having babies), the husband says he is now going to make a journalist. He does this by grabbing and tearing apart with his mouth and arms pages of newspapers and putting them into a cradle, to which he adds inkpots, penholder, glue pots, and other pots; out of all this (satiric) mess inside the cradle will emerge a journalist.

At the end, the fortune-teller tells the people of Zanzibar that they will die of terrible poverty if they don't proceed to have many babies.

In a scene of reconciliation, Thérèse returns and wants to have a reunion, as woman, with her husband, even to make love before the curtain falls.

Apollinaire's preface is relevant to my theme. He states that the play is absolutely about the problem of populating, or repopulating, France. Its mode is "surrealism" (he coins the term); he hopes it will be a kind of farce, which will be the case if the French really do increase their population, but it will be a tragedy if they don't. He asserts:

> Naturally, according to the tale and the principal situation I imagine: a man who gives birth to infants is new to the theater and to literature in general, but it should not be any more shocking than certain impossible inventions of the romancers, whose vogue is founded on marvels said to be scientific. [1946, 11; my translation]

This statement is, of course, not literally true, as Greek tragedy quite explicitly raised the possibility, and it voiced the wish that men alone could bear children (*Medea,* lines 576–78).

Apollinaire asserts that people are free to read into his straightforward theme any symbolic meaning they wish, as with the words of the sybilline oracles. He has written this surrealist drama first and foremost for the French, just as Aristophanes composed his comedies for the Athenians: "I have signaled to them the grave danger to be recognized for all, which there is for a nation that wishes to prosper and be powerful and does not make children, and to remedy that situation I have indicated what is sufficient to accomplish that."

He ridicules a certain critic who wants to read special meanings into the play, and holds up for scorn that critic's interpretation that the rubber of the breasts-balloons, and of balls appearing later in the play, is related to "rubbers," prophylactics (1946, 12–13). This is absurd because, he says, in France they are hardly ever used. In Berlin, by contrast, the rubbers fall on your head as you are walking in the streets. Clearly, the negation in "rubber doesn't mean rubbers" and the comments about the World War I enemy's use of condoms (equivalent to German shells and bullets falling on the heads of Frenchmen?) reveals a deep anxiety about the use and implications of contraceptive technology.

Other causes of "depopulation"—allegedly unique quantitatively to France—include alcoholism, but he scoffs at this: the French provinces that are most prolific have the highest rates of alcoholism. The real problem, he asserts (1946, 14), is that the French do not make love enough, "fecund love." He goes on to argue that there are things the government must do to encourage such love and the subsequent increase in population.

Much of the thrust of the play is the need to have more babies in order to have more soldiers. The "Director's Prologue" ("Hear, France, the lesson of the war, make babies"), as well as allusions in the play, makes this point quite specifically. Among other points in this "pronatalist" play, the argument is made that babies are not an economic burden but a source of riches. The husband gives the example of the cod, who could raise millions of children if nature removed natural enemies, and asks the nosy American reporter, "Have you ever seen an impoverished codfish?"

The "absurdity" in this play is at many levels, though the author claims that the basic level of absurdity is that of Thérèse, a wife who wants to become all the things that a man is. However, the play has multiple tricks to it, including its suggestion of how much the man wants to be a woman; another implicit "absurdity" is that the "natural arrangement" of a husband and wife, a man and a woman, is somehow able to work. At a deeper level, the play reflects the enormous anxiety of men about being bereft of the women who take care of them—one of the core meanings, I believe, of the male fear (and ridicule) of women who don't want to have babies.

Lurking in the wings is always the question of how to have a strong country, especially a country with enough soldiers to fight and die for the country. By the time of the production of the play, the French public knew something about the hideous losses of the ongoing war, and plays that "farcically" presented the need for more soldiers must have had all kinds of *double entendres*—literally, "heard two ways"— one manifestly supporting "repopulation" in order to have more soldiers to die, and the other referring to the absurdity and cruelty of a cycle of repopulation in order to lose children in the war.

One could usefully examine other playwrights of the theater of the absurd, such as Genet, and demonstrate the way in which anxieties and rage about reproduction and progeny recurrently manifest themselves. Genet's *The Balcony* plays with perversions, make-up, masks, mirrors, doubling, and counterfeiting as alternatives to heterosexual reproduction. In Genet, as in Beckett, I believe there is a profound questioning about who one is, what is real, what is sham.[13]

An important play in the history of the theater of the absurd in America is Edward Albee's *Who's Afraid of Virginia Woolf* (1962). It is not only a play where there are several confusions about whether a pregnancy is real, whether a child is real, whether there has been a child alive so that the parents can kill him or declare him dead. Its plot involves a new young biology professor at a small college, Nick, and an older history professor, George. George tries to provoke a fight between history and biology, as it were, fearful that history will be entirely displaced by biology: "I read somewhere that science fiction is really not fiction at all...that you people are rearranging my genes, so that everyone will be like everyone else. Now, I won't have that! It would be a...shame" (1983, 37).

He taunts Nick:

> People do...uh...have kids. That's what I meant about history. You people are going to make them in test tubes, aren't you: You biologists. Babies. Then the rest of us...them as wants...can screw to their heart's content. What will happen to the tax deduction: Has anyone figured that out yet? ...But you *are* going to have kids...anyway. In spite of history. [40]

Ironically, sexuality is already separated from childbirth, for in this play heterosexual coupling only leads to imaginary children or children whose existence is questionable. Implied in these selections, and in the play as a whole, is that for a variety of reasons (marital warfare, intergenerational warfare, and actual warfare) it might not be desirable or possible to have children. The lessons of history are such as to encourage people to manufacture rather than beget children, totally to divorce sexuality from reproduction.

Let us conclude with a look at Ionesco, where I believe we find the greatest concentration of themes around conception, abortion, birth, and the death of children, and the "absurd" themes of reproduction taking place by *mass production*. Indeed, Esslin points out, "The horror of proliferation—the invasion of the stage by evergrowing masses of people or things—which appears in *The Future Is in Eggs,* is one of the most characteristic images we find in Ionesco's play" (1980, 150).

Consider two early plays, *Jack, or The Submission* (1950) and its sequel, *The Future Is in Eggs* (1951). In the first of these, the themes of birth and reproduction are a seemingly minor part, though the theme of continuity of the family and of its traditions is crucial. In the second, the "eggs" and the laying of eggs to mass-produce children is paramount in the plot. Jack, the hero of the first play, born at age fourteen, refuses to accept the bourgeois standards of his family and the role that would be thus thrust upon him. He refuses to pronounce the family credo: "J'adore les pomme de terre au lard" ("I love hashed brown potatoes," in the American translation). He finally yields to the imploring of the family and pronounces the creed, and the family proceeds to make a match for him with Roberta, a woman with two noses, only daughter of the Robert family. He again rebels, refusing to marry her because she is not ugly enough. At this Jack's mother denounces him, with one of the numerous allusions to pregnancy and birth in the play (typically, these allusions are paired with the theme of murder of a child):

> MOTHER JACK [*sobbing*]: Ah! ah! my God! Jack...wicked son! If I had known I'd have strangled you in your last cradle, yes, with my maternal hands. Or I'd have aborted you! Or not have conceived you! I, I, who was so happy when I was pregnant with you...I am an unfortunate mother. [1958a, 97]

Somehow or other, to satisfy Jack's demand for a woman who is really ugly, the Robert family manages to produce another daughter, this time with three noses, named Roberta II. Roberta II tries to woo Jack and begins to succeed by telling him a dream, in which she sees a male guinea pig in her bathtub, under water; on his forehead were two tiny little spots, two excrescences, out of which were coming two tiny little guinea pigs.[14] (Again, we see the fantasy of birth from a male in the context of a man who refuses to get married and to procreate).

He is further drawn in by her stories about her horses, stallions and brood mares. She goes on to tell a complicated story that is essentially about mares and foals, bitches and puppies, and an old miller whose wife just had given birth. The miller thinks he's drowning the pups but mistakenly has drowned the foals; but really he hasn't—he's drowned his own infant son. "The miller went mad. Killed his wife. Destroyed everything. Set fire to it. Hung himself" (1958a, 105).

Thus, in this first play, we have the leitmotiv of curses on conception and birth, a daughter miraculously and instantaneously born, and with three noses, a male animal giving birth, young of animals and humans being confused with each other, and the human young drowned. The procreating couple, the miller and his wife, are destroyed. In brief, a play that deals with the problem of continuity of the family, and of the great refusal of one of its members to continue the line, is replete with bizarre fantasies about conception, birth, and the murder of children.

The Future Is in Eggs is the continuation of the story of the "house that Jack built"—Jacques, in the American version of the play. It explicitly holds that "We must assure the continuity of our race...the white race! Long live the white race! (1958b, 133). To do his duty with Roberta, Jacques proceeds somehow to impregnate her, or get her production equipment going. Roberta proceeds to lay eggs, constantly clucking chicken-laying-egg sounds. At first they all resemble Roberta (except that they don't have three noses). The eggs soon become numberless. Then somehow Jacques is laying eggs too. Mass production via eggs becomes the solution to any number of problems in family and national and even international dynamics. More eggs!

Some eggs are to be put aside for eating, but most are to be designated as eggs to produce particular "-ists," such as communists, existentialists, or atheists; also Protestants, Catholics, soldiers, ministers, politicians. Here we have an instantiation of a new definition of the self and of the reproductive self: the self as a functionary, each person doing and being only one thing. Ionesco has produced for us a comic version of Plato's utopian (and antisexual) dream of each person in the Republic being allowed to be and do only one thing, and of people being bred for such functions, just as dogs are.

Implications of the Theater of the Absurd on Reproduction

I believe that in the work of Beckett in particular, but more generally in the theater of the absurd, there is a kind of analysis of the implications of the intertwining of sexuality and power, particularly male power over females. It is as if the linking first apparent in Genesis between the commandment that man shall have dominion over the other creatures and the command to be fruitful and multiply is shown in this form of theater to lead to absurd consequences. The dominion of man over woman is at best only partial, and woman extracts her pound of flesh from man because of male dependency on women, and the concomitant dread of that dependency.

It is as if, on the one hand, the disconnected or "detribalized" person can only reproduce by splitting and cloning (in Beckett, more a meiotic than a mitotic division), and on the other, the community at large can reproduce more satisfactorily by invoking *mass production* rather than by conventional reproduction. These fantasies, the latter coming closer to actualization with available reproductive technology, cover up and cover over the issues of power and inequities in power distribution between genders and classes. The theater of the absurd presents, represents, and creatively plays with these issues, issues that I believe have been the subject matter of tragic drama since its inception.

My unspoken assumption here is that the theater of the absurd lies at the intersection of art, social analysis, and madness. Virtually any of the plays typically included in this genre of the absurd can be, or has been, discussed from any of these three perspectives (see especially Barchilon 1973). Beckett's work in particular has been praised by some for its brilliant artistic evocations of various forms of madness and condemned by others as repetitively inflicting his personal insanity on his audiences (e.g., Bair 1978, 457). It is conventional in contemporary psychoanalytic discussions of art and literature to speak of the distinction between madness and art, the distinction between the unshaped chaos of madness and the integrated, aesthetically shaped artistic form that communicates and reaches others. Jung is alleged to have told James Joyce that the difference between Joyce's writing and the writing of Joyce's psychotic daughter is the difference between a man diving off a dock and a man falling off a dock. Both enter the water, but the form is crucial and plays a role in the outcome. Although I believe this distinction is an important and elementary one, it runs the risk of missing one of the functions of great works of art: namely, that of calling into question many of our ordinary distinctions (Jacobson 1989). I believe what we witness in the work of Beckett generally and in many of the plays of the theater of the absurd is a creative blurring and reshuffling of boundaries, as for example between the communications of the insane and the communications of the artist. These dramatic works offer us an insight into the attempt at communication inherent in even the most seemingly destroyed of schizophrenic minds while simultaneously inviting us to look at the insane and the absurd in our seemingly rational discourse and behavior, including our forms of psychological and social analysis. These plays do not eliminate the distinctions between art and psychosis, or good art and junk, or deep analysis and "pop" psychology, but they do get us to stand on our heads and consider the world from radically different perspectives. As individuals, we vary greatly in our willingness, tolerance, and need for such topsy-turvy views, and this variation in part accounts for the wide range of opinions about the theater of the absurd. But artists such as Beckett, Apollinaire, and Ionesco force us to stop the reflex reproduction of our usual modes of thought and to try alternative methods of conceiving and begetting views of the world.

Notes

1. See the controversy on "the postmodern" in *New Literary History* 20 (1988), by Chabot; Hassan; and Wilde.

2. See also an important piece by Kristin Morrison, "Defeated Sexuality in the Plays and Novels of Samuel Beckett" (1980).

3. I resonate with Herbert Blau's account of the history of the theater that underlies *Endgame* in particular, "More than any modern drama I know it creates explicitly that place where Yeats said love has pitched its mansion. And it does this by converting an enormous sense of loss into a retrospective vision, reaching back through the failure of a culture to its most splendid figures: Hamlet, Lear, Oedipus at Colonus, the enslaved Samson, eyeless at Gaza" (Blau 1986, 269–70).

4. The text is also found in the study by Lawrence Harvey in *Samuel Beckett: Poet and Critic.* I am heavily indebted to Harvey's detailed discussion and commentary on this poem. See also Linda Ben-Zvi, *Samuel Beckett* (1986, 56–57).

5. The biblical prostitute who let the Israelite spies into Jericho.

6. A Catholic queen of Sweden from whom Descartes feared betrayal.

7. See Harvey's discussion of the poem (Harvey 1970) for Descartes's book.

8. In an earlier version of the play, Beckett has Clov seeking to reproduce and saying that there is no woman available, whereupon Hamm appears dressed like a woman.

9. For one psychoanalytic perspective on the theater of the absurd, see Jose Barchilon's "Pleasure, Mockery and Creative Integration" (1973). He emphasizes meanings of absurd in terms of lies and deception around sexuality—the mocking revenge of the child.

10. There is a "local" historical, social, and religious context for Beckett's

preoccupation with the problematic of birth, namely, his origins and personal development in Ireland, specifically as a Protestant in a Catholic country with very strong feelings, views, and policies on conception, contraception, birth, and abortion. As readers of Joyce's *Ulysses* well know, practical concerns about contraception and birth, including labor, delivery, and death in childbirth, form an important backbone of the book and provide key metaphors for artistic production and its inhibition or stillbirth. One must presume a powerful connection of this particular dimension with Beckett's life, but evidence is not yet available or assembled.

11. See also Scott Bates, *Guillaume Apollinaire,* especially "The New Woman, 1898–1918," 125–38.

12. Echoing the complaint of Euripides' Medea that men have it easy fighting compared to the travails of women bearing children. She says she'd rather stand three times in the front ranks of battle than bear one child.

13. Antonin Artaud, probably still psychotic after his release from a nine-year hospitalization, wrote two works at the end of World War II, "To End God's Judgment" and "The Philosopher's Stone: A Mime Play." These contain, in what I believe is psychotic form, themes of bizarre and cruel reproduction: reproduction as production (Americans are building up a sperm bank of boys to manufacture super-Americans after America destroys the world with atomic bombs), and cloning. These are similar to themes that are rendered with artistic control in the works of other authors of the theater of the absurd. Martin Esslin told me of Artaud's work, which is found in translation by V. Corti in the *Tulane Drama Review* 8 (1956): 57–98.

14. Note that Esslin mistakenly summarizes this dream as of a *female* guinea pig, while the French version and the American translation have it as male.

References

Albee, Edward. *Who's Afraid of Virginia Woolf* (1962). New York: New American Library, 1983.

Albright, Daniel. *Representation and the Imagination: Beckett, Kafka, Nabokov, and Schoenberg.* Chicago: University of Chicago Press, 1981.

Apollinaire, Guillaume. *Les Mamelles de Tirésias.* Paris: Éditions de Bélier, 1946.

Bair, Deirdre. *Samuel Beckett: A Biography.* New York: Harcourt Brace Jovanovich, 1978.

Barchilon, Jose. "Pleasure, Mockery and Creative Integration: Their Relationship to Childhood Knowledge, A Learning Defect and the Literature of the Absurd." *International Journal of Psycho-Analysis* 54 (1973): 19–34.

Bates, Scott. *Guillaume Apollinaire.* New York: Twayne Publishers, 1967.

Beckett, Samuel. *Whoroscope.* Paris: Hours Press, 1930.

————. *Waiting for Godot.* New York: Grove Press, 1954.

————. *Murphy* (1938). New York: Grove Press, 1957.

————. *Endgame* and *Act without Words.* New York: Grove Press, 1958.

————. *Molloy* (1955). *The Unnamable* (1958). In *Three Novels by Samuel Beckett.* New York: Grove Press, 1958.

————. *Imagination Dead Imagine.* London: Calder and Boyars, 1965.

————. *Lessness.* London: Calder and Boyars, 1970.

————. *A Piece of Monologue* (1979). In *Rockaby and Other Short Pieces.* New York: Grove Press, 1981.

————. *Krapp's Last Tape* (1958). In *Collected Shorter Plays of Samuel Beckett.* New York: Grove Press, 1984.

————. *Not I* (1972). In *Collected Shorter Plays of Samuel Beckett.* New York: Grove Press, 1984.

Ben-Zvi, Linda. *Samuel Beckett.* Boston: Twayne, 1986.

Blau, Herbert. "Notes from the Underground: 'Waiting for Godot' and 'Endgame.'" In *On Beckett: Essays and Criticism,* edited by S. E. Gontarski. New York: Grove Press, 1986.

Chabot, C. Barry. "The Problem of the Postmodern." *New Literary History* 20 (1988): 1–20.

Esslin, Martin, *The Theatre of the Absurd.* 3d ed. New York: Penguin Books, 1980.

Genet, Jean. *The Balcony.* Translated by Bernard Frechtman. New York: Grove Press, 1978.

Harvey, Lawrence. *Samuel Beckett: Poet and Critic.* Princeton: Princeton University Press, 1970.

Hassan, Ihab. "On the Problem of the Postmodern." *New Literary History* 20 (1988): 21–22.

Ionesco, Eugène. *Jack, or The Submission* (1950). In *Four Plays,* translated by Donald M. Allen. New York: Grove Press, 1958a.

————. *The Future Is in Eggs* (1951). In *Plays, by Eugene Ionesco,* vol. 4, translated by Donald Watson. London: Calder, 1958b.

Jarry, Alfred. *Selected Works by Alfred Jarry.* Edited by Roger Shattuck and Simon Watson Taylor. New York: Grove Press, 1965.

Jacobson, Dan. *"Hamlet's* Other Selves." *International Review of Psycho-Analysis* 16 (1989): 265–72.

Lewin, Bertram. *Dreams and the Uses of Regression.* New York: International Universities Press, 1963.

Kenner, Hugh. *The Stoic Comedians: Flaubert, Joyce and Beckett.* Berkeley and Los Angeles: University of California Press, 1974.

Morrison, Kristin. "Defeated Sexuality in the Plays and Novels of Samuel Beckett." *Comparative Drama* 14 (1980): 18–34.

————. *Canters and Chronicles: The Use of Narrative in the Plays of Samuel Beckett and Harold Pinter.* Chicago: University of Chicago Press, 1983.

Sass, Louis A. "Time, Space and Symbol: A Study of Narrative Form and Representational Structure in Madness and Modernism." *Psychoanalysis and Contemporary Thought* 8 (1985): 45–84.

Simon, Bennett. *Tragic Drama and the Family: Psychoanalytic Studies from Aeschylus to Beckett.* New Haven: Yale University Press, 1988a.

————. "The Imaginary Twins: The Case of Beckett and Bion." *International Review of Psycho-Analysis* 15 (1988b): 331–52.

Wilde, Alan. "Postmodernism and the Missionary Position." *New Literary History* 20 (1988): 23–32.

10 Self-objectification and Preservation in Beckett's *Krapp's Last Tape*

Jon Erickson

The ability of any play to "endure," a question relevant to the individual personality's desire to "endure," can be read in two ways. The first is in the larger sense of historical endurance, the meanings entailed by its language always having the potential to mean something to whatever generation encounters it. But there is another sense that has less to do with meaning than with being—that of the play's performance in time, which means the ability of the audience to remember not only what was presented, but how it was materialized on stage. Highly differentiated bits of information, complex systems of meaning that come thick and fast, may produce an emotional effect on the audience (usually one of distress), but the meaning of the performance, or the memory of the figure of its becoming, will be lost on the audience. So signs, whether verbal or physical, objects or actions, must be repeated in order to ensure their impression on the audience's mind and memory. What this means for the actors is that their representation of human behavior is repetitive. This repetition not only defines "character" but demonstrates *change* in character as well, through the modification of repeated behavior. In sum, we identify ourselves and others through the forms of our repetitions.[1]

The repetitiveness of human behavior takes many forms. I can make a list (although by no means all-inclusive) of various repetitions that demonstrate the varying degrees of intensity or indifference, self-consciousness or instinctiveness, of human interactions with either the social environment or the self. The scale runs from *ritual* to *routine* to *habit* to *addiction*. They all represent attempts at survival, or endurance, whether physical or psychic.

181

Elizabeth Burns, in her book *Theatricality,* maintains that "Ritual
... consists of a series of actions, considered appropriate to certain
situations and capable of generating appropriate reactions from others. They are ... characterised by instrumentality and expressiveness"
(1972, 217). Although this definition seems to exclude *private* rituals,
the "other" might be read as one's own self-objectification in a system
of self-discipline that private rituals often serve. The "other" in religious terms may be gods or natural spirits. Ritual involves a self-
conscious act, concerned with maintaining a faith in a course of personal action or in a social system. As a self-conscious act, it tends to
be aware of, or remind the performer of, the symbolic or metaphorical
nature of its repetitions. It can, of course, become "empty ritual,"
when through repetition it tends to become reified or literal; the
larger picture of what the symbols point to is lost in the attention paid
to externals. This indicates a loss of desire or will to repeat, allowing
one to slip into mindless routine or habit. Only the *will* to repeat finds
its expression in ritual.[2]

Routine, which Burns posits in distinction to ritual, "is a formalised
way of dealing with recurrent actions and events which a person regards as necessary (i.e., has learned to regard as socially incumbent)
but with which he does not feel deeply involved" (216). Most of society's existence depends on routine. The effectiveness of the operations of routine depends upon a somewhat detached attitude in their
performance. Too much psychic investment in simple routines can
throw the system or oneself off balance. Routine requires half-
conscious behavior. It is, says Burns, "inexpressive." I think it can be
expressive within the limitations of the behavior it requires. It is certainly less expressive than ritual behavior, but in its most expressive
performance, routine will often try to disguise itself as ritual.

"Habit is a compromise effected between the individual and his
environment, or between the individual and his own organic eccentricities, the guarantee of a dull inviolability, the lightning-conductor
of his existence. Habit is the ballast that chains the dog to his vomit."
So says Samuel Beckett, in his book on Proust (1958, 7–8). Habit is
also what defines us as having a predictable character, either for ourselves or others. Habit is compulsive behavior, dependent on external
things. Habit is unselfconscious and operates instinctively. It is an established compromise between two adamant forces, and the posses-
sor of a habit feels threatened the moment its operations are questioned. The level of emotional investment is higher in habit than in
routine. But it is more grounded as well, the "lightning-conductor of
his existence."

Addiction is not expressive but ingestive. It is self-consuming as well as substance-consuming. It is unconscious behavior; even though one can become conscious of it, continued addictive behavior always defeats that consciousness. What may begin as the enhancement of the senses ends as anesthetization against any life not covered by the repetition of addiction.

As we move from ritual to addiction, the level of self-consciousness decreases, as does the ability to alter the conditions of the form of repetition. Does the center of investment move from a more disembodied zone to a more embodied one, in the path from ritual to addiction, or does it move in the opposite direction? The sensitized self-consciousness of ritual may be more "embodied" than the desensitizing repetitions of addiction. Yet both ritual and addiction use the body in certain ways in order to try to transcend the body. Ritual is a practice aimed at the unification of self with a collective spirit, whether that spirit is present in the form of other people or exists as a paradigmatic Idea in a historical tradition. Addiction is the attempt to alleviate the pain of a radical discontinuity between self and body, self and context, or self and history; it becomes a drive for complete self-possession that only makes the discontinuity worse, ending in self-consumption.

In the following pages I want to look at ritual and addiction in the context of a play by Samuel Beckett that focuses on self-objectification. This relatively late work of modern drama (it appeared in 1958) exemplifies objectification of self through repetition that tries to resist, or escape from, not only changes wrought by social circumstances but time's tendency to undermine, if not dissolve, a personal sense of being.

Krapp's Last Tape is predicated upon an illusion, that of true self-knowledge. Its focus on repetition is that of an addiction to self-consciousness, an addiction to the illusion of self-possession. What may have begun as a truly self-conscious ritual action of affirming the self through the recording of its experience, and the subsequent contemplation of that experience, ends up through repetition compulsion as the continual frustration of a narcissistic desire. Despite this frustration, the force of habit, rather than any real self-conscious reflection, is what keeps Krapp going. While the unexamined life may not be worth living, the particular method of this overly examined life takes the *place* of living, negating its worth in the long run.

The scenario of *Krapp's Last Tape* consists of an old man, a table, an old reel-to-reel tape recorder in a pool of light, bananas and boxes of reels of tape (called "spools" by Krapp), and a bottle offstage in the darkness to which Krapp repairs occasionally for a drink. Krapp is one of Beckett's old men, hard of hearing, with cracked voice and laborious walk. He produces some slapstick and low phallic humor with bananas, his main staple. He checks through a ledger to find a particular tape: "box three, spool five," which he winds on to the machine. He begins to listen to his past. His own voice on the tape mentions listening to an even earlier tape, then relates stories about a nurse with her pram and her fear of him, a game of catch with a little dog, ending with an idyllic scene: a narration of his love for a woman, and their calm drifting, lying together in a boat with sunlight blazing down. The narrative ends at midnight, in the darkness. Krapp retreats to the darkness offstage for a few drinks, after which he comes back to put on a "virgin tape." He records his impressions of "that stupid bastard I took myself for thirty years ago." He scorns his former self and now scorns the present year, which is but "the sour cud and the iron stool." His relations with women now consist of his involvement with Fanny, "that bony old ghost of a whore," and his reading of *Effi Briest,* which provokes his tears. He finishes his recording with a pathetic desire to "Be again, be again," a desire that is the basis of his recorded life. His very frustration at this impossibility—every recorded year he wishes to relive forces him to realize his own wretched present—makes him rip off the present tape and put the past on again. He listens to the idyll again, his lips moving silently. "Perhaps my best years are gone. When there was a chance for happiness. But I wouldn't want them back. Not with the fire in me now. No I wouldn't want them back." Then the tape runs on silently.

> Repetition and recollection are the same movement, only in opposite directions; for what is recollected has been, is repeated backwards, whereas repetition properly so called is recollected forwards. Therefore repetition, if it is possible, makes a man happy, whereas recollection makes him unhappy.   [Kierkegaard 1946, 3–4]

> When one says that life is a repetition one affirms that existence which has been now becomes. When one does not possess the categories of recollection or of repetition the whole of life is resolved into a void and empty noise.   [Kierkegaard 1946, 34]

Is *Krapp's Last Tape* the repetition of recollection, or the recollection of repetition? Or does the confluence of the two result in their negation, becoming a "void and empty noise"? Does Krapp affirm "that existence which has been now becomes"? Or has becoming ceased altogether because of the absolute privileging of the past?

When we consider the two forms of recollection, what Proust

called "voluntary" and "involuntary" memory, we see that Krapp's method of self-objectification involves them both. The voluntary approach creates, on the one hand, a mathesis of self, superimposing a grid over temporality to facilitate an impeccable "self-knowledge" and control over Krapp's own image, experience, and history. There is, on the other hand, the content of the tapes, which although created by the will of voluntary memory, drifts into the ramblings of involuntary memory, punctuated by such Proustian tactilities as the feel of the hard rubber ball in his hand.[3]

Krapp's method is a battle against Time, a desire, if not for pure self-presence, then for repeated moments of happiness. It is an attempt at the complete mastery of past experience. It is the desire, expressed through the yearly rundown of peak moments, to have *all* of his temporal existence before him at any moment: in other words, the total spatialization of his personality in time.

But this attempt only works against itself. While Krapp thinks he is articulating his life, that is, joining elements of it coherently, he only disarticulates himself into separate spools. At the same time the past takes on a greater sense of presence than the present itself. Although his voice and certain memories retain their sensuous strength in the old tape, the present Krapp becomes ever more a ghost of what has been recorded: a strange reversal, since the disembodied voice would seem more the ghost. This material degradation is also reflected in the contrast between the "Farewell to love" idyll on the old tape and the current travesties of Fanny, "better than a kick in the crutch," and his secondhand romance through Effi Briest (1984, 62).

Krapp exits in a paradoxical state: is he "being" or "remaining"? It is a question occasioned by an earlier description of his mother's "viduity," which the dictionary he consults describes as "State—or condition—of being—or remaining—a widow—or widower" (59). It is more likely that he is but the "remains" of his former life on tape, evidenced by his condition. Although he has developed a complex system to retain the vibrancy of his past, he is at the same time an outrageous drunk, and after all, one drinks to forget. And it would seem he wants to forget what might have been the purpose of his system. The part of spool five that Krapp represses is the part that would promise to "make sense" of his preoccupation with memory. He cannot now face what might be a meaningless ground for his actions. "The vision at last," the fire, the clarity, the blazing sun, seem to have become anathema to Krapp. He can only drink in the darkness of self-forgetting but is invariably pulled back to "me . . . Krapp" in the circle of light. It is difficult to say which, the light or darkness, has more power over him. For most of Beckett's characters, including Krapp, a kind of absolute ambivalence keeps them in perpetual but undecided motion. Words drain from minds that are never made up, and words are what provide the escape from the necessity to decide or act. It is the inability to remember the past (except as fragments) that stimulates repetitive action, more than the Nietzschean will to repeat, which is fully conscious and affirmative. But it is at the same time the experience of unexpected memories that creates the despair of repetition. After the repeated attempts to get outside of habit, which require another habit, that of drinking, the old habit of remembering again takes over to evoke the reality of the past. It is like the situation in which a distracted person wanders into a room where he must ask himself, what did I come in here for? So he retraces his steps to provoke the mind back into the memory of his original intention.

"Habit is the ballast that chains the dog to his vomit" (Beckett 1958, 7–8). Although "vomit" might not be the appropriate metaphor here, there is something comparable in this play, demonstrated in the subject's own name. Through his habit Krapp continually attempts to give birth to himself. But as is the case with his father, this birth can only be parodied as an "unattainable laxation," something even Freud's Little Hans eventually understood. All of his spools can be read as hard ("iron") stools—echoed in the solidity of the black rubber ball, the feel of which he will "always remember"—or as the spoor left on the trail of his life. As such, instead of that which will inspire and shed light on his present state of being, and be a completed work one day, the recordings become the waste products of experience, just as his own present degradation can be seen as the waste product of his obsessive relation to the memory of those experiences.

Krapp's attempted self-objectification demonstrates a desire for complete self-possession through the materialization of self-knowledge. Arnold Gehlen wrote that "The tendency which characterizes the progress of technique, from the substitution of organs to the replacement of the organic as a whole, is ultimately rooted in a mysterious law pertaining to the realm of the mind. Briefly put, this law is: 'Nonorganic nature is more knowable than organic nature' "(1980,6). Therefore the organic nature of memory and life experience is transferred to a nonorganic solid, whether in the form of costume or a reel of magnetic tape: the materialization of speech. Gehlen credits Bergson for this insight, and goes on: "According to Bergson, intellect can only be judged in relation to action, and its primary aim is the production of artifacts: 'Therefore . . . we may expect to find that whatever is fluid in the real world will escape [the intellect] in part. Our intelligence, as it leaves the hands of nature, has for its chief object the unorganized solid'" (7). What is this "unorganized solid" but Krapp himself?

Beckett accentuates the fetish character of both banana and tape reel, which are kept in the same drawer, under lock and key. Krapp uses each reel of tape to bind himself to himself, and the image of the banana in his mouth goes beyond the masturbatory nature of his enterprise to self-fellatio. This in itself is a ludicrous travesty of the uroboric world consuming itself. The tapes begin as a supplement to Krapp's life but in their very superfluity replace that life itself. Krapp wants the ground to swallow the figure and his reel-to-reel to become real, too real. But these fetishes cannot overcome as a unity Krapp's multiplicity of selves; he has as many bananas as reels of tape, that is, former selves. This proliferation of irreconcilable units contributes to Time's ineluctable process of dematerialization. As Beckett speaks of it in his book on Proust: "No object prolonged in this temporal dimension tolerates possession, meaning by possession total possession, only to be achieved by the complete identification of object and subject. . . . All that is active, all that is enveloped in time and space, is endowed with what might be described as an abstract, ideal and absolute impermeability" (1958, 41). Despite the ability to rescue the past through its recordability, the past as object remains impermeable by the present subject. True self-possession remains an impossibility.

While the act of objectification can be a positive aspect of art making and self-enjoyment, *Krapp's Last Tape* illustrates the result of trying to retain absolute possession of what is created. Krapp is unable to distance himself from what he has objectified, at the same time suffering absolute frustration at not being able to truly bridge the distance that is inevitably manifested. Krapp himself finds it impossible to look at, or hear, his life in an "objective" light, for he wants always to be able to possess and live those past moments, to "Be again, be again" (1984, 62). Yet he is forever unconscious of the fact that he has his being *now,* in the present, the one dimension he can't recognize since it is but fodder for the mill of memory, which seems more real.

This disparity, this inability to possess his life completely, is what wastes him, as it is an endless process that is never complete despite his former hopes when "Suddenly I saw the whole thing. The vision at last. This I fancy is what I have chiefly to record this evening, against the day when my work will be done and perhaps no place left in my memory" (60). But will this self-generating work ever be done, any more than any perpetual psychoanalytical process? Krapp is indeed *afraid* of having no place left in his memory, which stimulates his "work": the attempt at a complete reconstruction of his own consciousness, a representation that is the "equal of life," to put it in Artaud's terms. But this still creates an irreconcilable split between lived experience and consciousness of that experience. A chasm yawns between the present moment and the words just spoken, recorded or not, that attempt to preserve and maintain every present moment. That chasm is Krapp's own "viduity" as the widow (or widower) of himself; "remaining" is always the widow of "being." Viduity, of course, is an echo of the void, the void between the present moment and the past.

In Ibsen, the revelation of memory always serves to alter conditions dramatically and irrevocably, usually ending in someone's death or downfall. In Beckett, the narration of memory repetitively and compulsively maintains conditions that are intolerable, a living death, tragedy dragging its feet. The metaphysical structure of *Krapp's Last Tape* is committed to the spoken Word, the conveyor of memory, as the sole arbiter of reality and the sole creator of a self as a continuous entity. This can be seen elsewhere in Beckett in the bodiless voice of *The Unnamable* and the mouth in *Not I,* as well as in his radio works. One or two memories repeated by this voice often enough constitute a "self." Paradoxically, the more disembodied the voice in performance, the more "objectified" it seems. Its authority comes from its very disembodied state. This is part of the appeal of the "voice-over" in much contemporary performance.

Although one might consider that the play is performed in "real time" to the audience, the voice on the tape and the voice being taped (in a proleptic sense) are both in the past. That's what puts this play "in the future," as the stage directions indicate. This point foregrounds the taped voice as the standard by which to experience and temporalize the rest of the play. There's a sense we get after a while that everything material that we see is to be dematerialized into the sound of one voice, which is itself only an echo. This winding-in of the present into the past in order to become the future's present is always delayed at the most minimal level by the time it takes to listen to the past.[4] A work of conceptual art by Christine Kozlov, called *Information: No Theory* (1970), radically framed this problem by running a continuous loop on a tape recorder, with the recorder in "tape" mode. The loop, which is continuously taping the present, is forever erasing what it just taped (Meyer 1972, 172). It is the clearest performance of Gertrude Stein's continuous present, but it can only exist in the void, in silence. It creates an impermeable privacy.

Krapp's Last Tape can be read allegorically, depicting our own ob-
sessions with preserving the present, with the retention of "history"
in its "original form" ("original voice" in this case). It can be read as a
continual recycling of self and continual consumption of self, a repetitive reification of personality that is the replacement for an eternal
soul. It also demonstrates the internalization of formerly external processes of surveillance and control by authorities. In a Foucauldian
sense, it is a kind of "technology of the self" that, rather than resisting
social technologies that create the self, simply recapitulates them in
private. It is what Czech playwright Václav Havel (to whom Beckett's
play *Catastrophe* is dedicated) has described as the *internalization*
of the police state, which he calls "post-totalitarian," since formerly
totalitarian states had to rely mainly upon brute force and external
threat (1985, 27). All these miniobjectifications, which through habit
become reifications, literalized desires, lead to their own demise and
to ours as individuals, our self-image systems near to drowning in a
sea of inconclusive signs.

Beckett disarticulates the body through hypostasizing speech-as-
memory within the space of the dread of silence. Perhaps, as we find
in Pinter's work, this speech is created by the dread of silence. Is it
this dread that disarticulates the body, or is it language that breaks up
the dread unity (monotony) of silence and therefore atomizes the
body into separate functions? We have seen that Krapp's attempts at
re-membering actually constitute a dis-memberment of experience.
Beckett's early work is filled with cripples, the deaf, dumb, and blind
(Lucky and Pozzo, Hamm and Clov). His late work emphasizes separate body parts: the feet in *Footfalls,* the Mouth in *Not I,* the face in
Catastrophe, Play, and *That Time.*

The disembodied nature of Beckett's voices seems to emphasize a
poststructural obsession with difference that privileges language over
materiality—or at least demonstrates the radical discontinuity of
mind and matter. But what is evident in Beckett's work that is not in
the dematerialization processes of poststructural discourse is the recognition of a *silence* that is at the foundation of all linguistic expression. The dread of silence is not simply the dread of the silence of the
vacuum, but the pained silence of the body, of "dumb" material, which
absorbs language as the artist Joseph Beuys's felt absorbs sound.

Beckett's disarticulation of the body awaits its rearticulation with
inanimate parts, Gehlen's replacement of the organic with the nonorganic (foreseen by the prosthesis of Krapp's tape machine). This operation is a central feature of Thomas Pynchon's *V* and *Gravity's Rain-*

bow and, more recently, of William Gibson's *Neuromancer.* Since we can no longer dismember the gods, we become content to dismember ourselves and each other. But we used to eat the god.

We have seen that repetition in life as well as performance can take on the shape of ritual or addiction. Ritual is the self-conscious maintenance of an integrated relation of self to reality. It is the expression of internalized beliefs that provides a sense of coherence for the self and its community. The attempt to free oneself completely from this internalized structure of belief (in part the heritage of the Enlightenment ideal of individualism) only binds one more completely to the caprices of external change, disintegrating the internal coherence. To maintain a sense of individual continuity, one then becomes trapped in obsessive-compulsive behavior, dependent upon external things or activities, whose intensity varies from habit to addiction.

Beckett writes about addiction, not ritual. What might have *begun* for Krapp as ritual ends as addiction. The obsessive repetition of Krapp's actions changes him from the subject of a ritual to an object or effect of an addiction. What was once a mode of self-conscious behavior becomes the simulation of self-consciousness. The *post hoc ergo propter hoc* nature of both ritual and addiction ("if I don't do it, tomorrow may not come") is differentiated by the fact that addiction takes this argument literally while ritual understands the larger metaphorical dimensions of such repetition. That is, ritual provides distance as well as a *willed* engagement with transformations.

Modern performance's attraction to repetition, whether it is ritual, routine, habit, or addiction, demonstrates a desire for permanence. The value of repetition is that it sustains the living actions of performance, thoroughly reinscribing the present movement and sounds upon the memory of the subject who is fearful of the tendency to forget— the most dematerializing force of all. When Gertrude Stein asks, "Is it repetition or is it insistence?" she hits the nail on the head. Performance is an "entity" known only in its temporality, attempting through its own use of insistence to certify that it *is* material and present, and not just always passing away. At best, it hopes to create material effects within the lives of the audience.

While *Krapp's Last Tape* demonstrates a form of "bad objectification," if not reification, it also points to something at its core that may be the "cause" (as desired end) of this bad objectification. What resists appropriation by the subject of the play is a horizon of unfulfilled desire that is infinitely receding within a *mise-en-abîme.* I could say what resists *comprehension* (especially as something *comprehensive*), but the form this comprehension takes for Krapp is possessive,

solely for the nourishment of the selfish ego—a nourishment, however, that consumes the self rather than nourishing it. This core of
mirrors, so tempting for the narcissistic spirit, cannot be compre-
hended, nor should it be; yet we must recognize and respect its existence. Paradoxically, its structure in-forms the ground of our being,
even while in ways unknown to us, our being in-forms it. To "want it
all" is to allow the "all" both to create and to destroy you. The search
for the numinous that theater artists such as Artaud and Genet tried
to engage in cannot be satisfied or fulfilled by attempts that are hyper-
conscious rational comprehensions of what we hope is the numinous.
It is not summoned or called by us, but we are called by it—it involves
watching, listening, and being aware, without desire for complete and
masterful possession.

While *Krapp's Last Tape* might be seen as a progenitor of a postmodern theatrical consciousness ("all is artifice," and the "self" dis-
appears in the abyss of self-consciousness), it is not postmodern precisely because of the *desire* for the absolute that it evokes—a
particularly modernist pursuit. It might be conceded that at the center
of the play resides the postmodern-modern conflict. Postmodernism,
despite all of the attention paid to the "libidinal economy" and "desir-
ing machines," is in fact curiously lacking in desire—that is, its desires
are ones that are easily satisfied, while compulsively fed by the culture
at large. Postmodern desire is uncannily desireless (in the homeless
sense of *unheimlich*) since it always accepts a surface reality for what
it is and ignores whatever whole symbolic and material process that
surface may point to beyond itself, historically or otherwise. Postmodernism is in fact the reverse of Krapp's method: it is a continual act of
forgetting that can't help but remember.

A postmodern theater would be one that doesn't develop character
but also doesn't really invest in the actor, as Genet put it, as a "sign
charged with signs." Rather, as just a single sign in a cybernetic network of interchangeable signs (evident in the work of both Robert
Wilson and Richard Foreman), spectacular "total" theater triumphs
over theater's traditional locus in the human, both as multivalent sign
and as social body.

This type of theater is but a radicalization of one warring element
within modern theater—the theatrical and "purely" visual, as opposed
to the linguistic and psychological. Herbert Blau has spoken to this
very point:

> The denial of character, like the denial of drawing, persists in the anti-
> representational ethic of postmodernism which fears more than any-

thing else the premature falling into meaning. On the one hand, it is an extension of the modernist tradition of depersonalization; on the other, it comes from the unsatisfied incessancy of the mirroring self. In either case, it represents the validation of the formal and iconographic, and the diffracted, against the chronographic, the narrative, and the mimetic.   [1982, 277]

As we have seen, "character" denies itself through a total merger with the iconographic, but it also fragments and dissipates itself in the very process of creating a whole narrative for itself.

Although one might say that postmodernism is a relativizing structure of thought that attempts to create itself continuously through the dematerialization of whatever object modernism erected in which to invest its futurity, this very movement of objectification-dematerialization is what has always been in the very center of theater practice. Again, in a very precise manner, Blau shows us that the object of theater may be its own dematerializing power:

> *What is the theater but the body's long initiation in the mystery of its vanishing?* On the face of the evidence, inimical to appearances, the actor's most tangible asset is the void.   [299]

Notes

1. Strindberg understood the reified aspect of the notion of character as one who repeats without any alternation in his nature at all.

> As far as the drawing of characters is concerned, I have made the people in my play fairly "characterless" for the following reasons. In the course of time the word *character* has acquired many meanings. Originally it probably meant the dominant and fundamental trait in the soul complex and was confused with temperament. Later the middle class used it to mean an automaton. An individual who once for all had found his own true nature or adapted himself to a certain role in life, who in fact has ceased to grow, was called a man of character, while the man who was constantly developing ... was called a man of no character—derogatorily, of course, since he was so difficult to keep track of, to pin down and pigeonhole. This middle class conception of a fixed character was transferred to the stage, where the middle class has always ruled. . . . So I do not believe in simple stage characters. And the summary judgments that writers pass on people—he is stupid, this one is brutal, this one is jealous, this one is stingy, and so on—should not pass unchallenged by the naturalists who know how complicated the soul is and who realize that vice has a reverse side very much like virtue.   [preface to *Miss Julie,* in 1986, 207]

We all in principle, even today, will praise as a better actor the one who can play a number of radically different roles and condemn to a lesser status the "character actor" who always seems to "play himself," yet the middle-class comfort of anticipating the actions of the character actor, and having those anticipations rewarded time after time, demonstrates the distinct, even if at times guilty, pleasure we get out of such acting. It gives us ground for feeling superior to such creatures: that's why they tend to be comic figures, or to *become* comic or camp figures, even if they were intended to be heroic.

2. I have not mentioned ceremonies, but ceremonies are less repetitions than they are unique events for the participants. Ceremonies are events that initiate a new order of rituals. Of course, it depends upon one's role in the ceremony: a wedding ceremony is less an event for the minister than it is a ritual act.

3. Michel Foucault, in speaking of the classical episteme, comes close to describing Krapp's method:

> Relations between beings are indeed to be conceived in the form of order and measurement, but with this fundamental imbalance, that it is always possible to reduce problems of measurement to problems of order. So that the relation of all knowledge to the mathesis is posited as the possibility of establishing an ordered succession between two things, even non-measurable ones.   [1973, 57]

Are the stages of Krapp's life on tape truly "measurable" one to another? It is evident that although Krapp's drinking might have remained constant, its effects on him become more obvious as he ages, as do his relations with women and the world in general. But this points also to the relativism of these comparisons: against what standard are these stages being measured?

4. Bergson can give us an idea of why Krapp's project is doomed to fail. He argues against the sense that life is a "continually rolling up, like that of a thread on a ball." Instead it is

> actually ... neither an unrolling nor a rolling up, for these two similes evoke the idea of lines and surfaces whose parts are homogeneous and superposable on one another. Now, there are no two identical moments in the life of the same conscious being. Take the simplest sensation, suppose it constant, absorb in it the entire personality: the consciousness which will accompany this sensation cannot remain identical with itself for two consecutive moments, because the second moment always contains, over and above the first, the memory that the first has bequeathed to it. A consciousness which could experience two identical moments would be a consciousness without memory. It would die and be born again continually. In what other way could one represent unconsciousness? [1965,727]

The theaters of both Gertrude Stein and Richard Foreman aim at the consciousness that dies and is born again continually. They can only attempt to do this through the incessant subversion of the audience's memory. More to the point of Krapp's own system, Bergson writes,

> Memory . . . is not a faculty of putting away recollections in a drawer; there is not even, properly speaking, a faculty, for a faculty works intermittently when it will or when it can, whilst the piling up of the past upon the past goes on without relaxation. In reality, the past is preserved by itself, automatically. In its entirety, probably, it follows us at every instant; all that we have felt, thought and willed from our earliest infancy is there, leaning over the present which is about to join it, pressing against the portals of consciousness that would fain leave it outside.   [725]

References

Beckett, Samuel. *Proust.* New York: New Directions, 1958.

————. *Krapp's Last Tape.* (In) *The Collected Shorter Plays of Samuel Beckett.* New York: Grove Press, 1984.

Bergson, Henri. "Duration." In *The Modern Tradition,* edited by Richard Ellmann and Charles Feidelson, Jr. New York: Oxford University Press, 1965.

Blau, Herbert, *Take Up the Bodies: Theater at the Vanishing Point.* Urbana: University of Illinois Press, 1982.

Burns, Elizabeth. *Theatricality: A Study of Convention in the Theatre and in Social Life.* London: Longman, 1972.

Foucault, Michel, *The Order of Things: An Archaeology of the Human Sciences.* New York: Vintage, 1973.

Gehlen, Arnold, *Man in the Age of Technology.* Translated by Patricia Lipscomb. New York: Columbia University Press, 1980.

Havel, Václav, et al. *The Power of the Powerless: Citizens against the State in Central-Eastern Europe.* Edited by John Keane. London: Hutchinson, 1985.

Kierkegaard, Søren. *Repetition: An Essay in Experimental Psychology.* Translated by Walter Lowrie. Princeton: Princeton University Press, 1946.

Meyer, Ursula. *Conceptual Art.* New York: Dutton, 1972.

Strindberg, August. *Selected Plays.* Translated by Evert Sprinchorn. Minneapolis: University of Minnesota Press, 1986.

11   Notes on *Krapp, Endgame,* and "Applied" Psychoanalysis

Joseph H. Smith

O n a late night prowl in the spring of 1946, age thirty-nine, with enough but not too much drink in him, at the end of a pier in Dublin harbor, buffeted by what in *Krapp's Last Tape* is labeled an equinoctial thunderstorm, it came to Samuel Beckett that the inner dark he had always fought against in *order,* he had believed, to write and to be was, in fact, the subject he was to write about. The experience is replayed as one of Krapp's memories, over which, or at least over a part of which, Krapp fast forwards. Although I prefer the final version, Bair believes that an earlier version is more revealing. The earlier version read:

> Intellectually a year of profound gloom and indigence until that mem-
> orable night in March, at the end of the pier, in the howling wind, never
> to be forgotten, when suddenly I saw the whole thing. The turning
> point at last. This I imagine is what I have chiefly to set down this eve-
> ning against the day when my work will be done and perhaps no place
> left in my memory and no thankfulness for the miracle that—for the
> fire it set alight. What I saw then was that the assumption I had been
> going on all my life, namely...clear to me at last that the dark I have been
> fighting off all this time is in reality my most...unshatterable association
> till my dying day of story and night with the light of understanding and
> ... [Bair 1978, 351]

Another author might have rushed with that insight to produce a magnum opus that would have sold seventeen million copies. The world would have been his, or hers. Not Beckett. Twenty-three years later when he was awarded the Nobel Prize, his wife delivered the news by turning from the telephone with the whispered "Quelle catastrophe!" (Bair 1978, 604).

Thirteen years after Dublin harbor, Krapp, as finished narrator, questions and tests the insight and the fifty-two-year-old author. First portrayed as he who said "yes" to the offer of the world and "no" to love, Krapp is now spent, old, constipated, isolated, narcissistic—left only with "me ... Krapp" and his automated memories. The only way he could be worse off is if his magnum opus *had* sold seventeen million copies. Krapp is the narrator who keeps the fear of the fear of love alive in the author. Brusquely winding forward over the account of the pier insight, he arrives at the scene to which, in the end, he returns for the third hearing:

> (*Pause. Low.*) Let me in. (*Pause.*) We drifted in among the flags and stuck. The way they went down, sighing, before the stem! (*Pause.*) I lay down across her with my face in her breasts and my hand on her. We lay there without moving. But under us all moved, and moved us, gently, up and down, and from side to side. [1960, 27]

Beckett and Krapp

On the assumption that those who survive the greatest trouble have at least a chance for the deepest insight, I assume Beckett wrote about that which he in particular had come to know, or came to know in the process of writing it. I see both Krapp and Beckett as fair game for the psychoanalyst to ponder. No doubt something of Beckett the author shows forth in each of his characters. Still, it is one thing to be Krapp and another to write Krapp. The conflation of the author with the character he creates, the reduction of their voices to a univocal statement, is a defense claiming that I, as critic, can respond with a single superior voice, as if I were one with any inner voice or imagined version of myself that could otherwise disturb my present, univocal tranquillity. Krapp's dialogue with past versions of himself imagining future versions implies Beckett's own dialogue with past and possible future versions of Beckett. Each of these dialogues impacts on the other and neither, in Beckett, evokes tranquillity.

For Krapp, the insight at Dublin harbor proved to have been the occasion for a turn into narcissistic nothingness. For Beckett, while nothing is either/or, I am convinced that its dominant effect was a move from depression toward mourning and, through mourning, toward the capacity to love, work, and laugh. The turn, that is, from depression to mourning is first of all toward the capacity to suffer more truly through being more clearly in touch with that to which the suffering is a response. But, by doing the suffering rather than forever warding it off, there is room also for deeper engagement in love and work. But, in Beckett, that turn, too, is subject to relentless testing.

From the point of view of the therapeutic efficacy of writing, this is not a play about an old man seeing a life lived for nought. It is a play by a fifty-two-year-old man dealing with the question of whether *any* life can be said to have been lived for other than naught. *Krapp's Last Tape* is not a morality play. It is written from insecurity rather than from some established meaning in which the author is secure and which the audience is called upon to ascertain. It was possibly the writing of a play about present and anticipated doubt, darkness, and depression as an alternative to being done in by doubt, darkness, and depression. If such was its function for the author, allowing the play to work, no doubt, is to allow it to have a similar function in the viewer.

Having been on the jetty at age thirty-nine is a feature shared by Krapp and Beckett. "Memorable equinox" refers not only to the insight that occurred there but also to midlife when the tape, half on one spool and half on the other as in the mid-fall of an hourglass, indicates that the days from the beginning equal those ahead, every moment of lengthened life also a moment pulled from the diminishing span. But what if the distinction between beginning and end begins to blur? And what if a failure to remember at all—"memorable ... what?"—will be not because of a failing memory but instead because of a failure of the insight and the crisis of midpoint to have proved memorable? What if a ledgered reminder evokes only a blank stare?

Nevertheless, the turn that dawned on Beckett at the end of the jetty was that all the darkness was not just *his* but referred to *him,* and thus to that about which he was to write.[1] Prior to the pier insight, the maternal presence in Beckett would have functioned as an alien, abject, and love-barring introject. The insight itself was a turn toward owning the nothingness at the core of an always deferred identity.

The move from depression to mourning was a radical departure from the endless youthful talk of suicide. Self-destruction would not accord with the pier insight, but neither would the facile bringing of light into darkness that often proves to be the motive for the interpretation of latent meaning. Just as the silence of the analyst can allow the patient to grapple with where he is, Beckett's way of ensuring that what he wrote would work on us beyond quick interpretation was to freeze us into the manifest content of what we see (and are) in a way that bars access to conventionally expectable latent meaning. When told that no one understood a first performance, his response was something like, "Good. It will have a chance to work on them."

Beckett bars any "Aha!" response or reserves it for such items as finding a spool. In psychoanalysis the "Aha!" is also not the end but the beginning of understanding. Such an experience initiates the process of working through wherein the insight and fragments of the insight are submitted to a thousand reenactments in a variety of moods in scenes of memory, anticipation, current reality, dreams, and transference. The measure of what one gets out of an analysis is not so much in what one can *say* about it in terms of "peak" moments of insight as it is in the critical but often subtle changes over time in the way of living one's life. This involves some acceptance that darkness is always at the core, that any total unity or meaningfulness of one's life as text is not merely deferred but, in the language of Lacan, structurally barred.

Beckett and Hamm

Cultural changes, some of them consequent to Freud's influence, have affected not only the kind of plays, poems, and novels that can be written but also symptomatology and the reasons people seek psychoanalysis. Today patients do not come so much for cure of what ordinarily counts as a symptom. We generally assume, quite rightly, that those who seek treatment have run into special difficulties in their lives. We should, however, refrain from assuming that those who do not encounter such difficulties were blessed with perfectly smooth transitions toward object relatedness and/or narcissistic fulfillment. It is not just that for one group development was catastrophic and for the other it was not. All development is catastrophically marked by deprivation, loss, separation, guilt, anxiety, and meaninglessness, more or less overcome. Otherwise, normal people wouldn't read authors such as Beckett.

If we can settle, as I think we should, for a negative definition of mental health as the absence of symptoms or characterological defects that definitively compromise capacities for love, work, and play (and who, ultimately, is to decide that other than the sufferer?), it can be said that the change in the population coming for psychoanalysis has been toward the inclusion of a greater proportion of persons within the category of the normal. Reasons for entering treatment are in response to suffering pertinent to ultimate concerns—concerns about which one might or might not have fallen ill, but concerns of an importance that overrides questions of health or illness.

But how would Beckett's Hamm respond to the claim for the importance of such problems as alienation, fragmentation, or mourning resisted, whether in the form of the near miss of depression or simply covered over beneath a surface conventionality? I suppose it would be with one of those laughs so hearty for the actor and so chilling for the audience—laughter that announces, "vanity vanity, all is absurd," with no call to that which is not absurd other than a call for the end. And, if the end is marred by the survival of a flea or a rat in Clov's kitchen or possibly even a Fortinbras or Christ-like figure of a child, if he exists, on the horizon, that too is absurd—merely a sign of a possible beginning again of all the absurdity of the world.

In *Endgame* it is a harder fate than that of merely selling one's soul to the devil. It is more a matter of revenge for having been thrown into an absurd world in which the response to the creator's supposed plea for mercy is, just for the fun of it, indentureship of the creator himself to the creature. In this play the creator becomes the knight of Hamm the King and Hamm's proximal precursors—his parents—the pawns. But at another level the knight is associated with a cloven foot. Hamm has usurped the power of God and Satan. Both, embodied in Clov, are subject to Hamm's will. In Hamm's presence a weary God the Father—the prime mover, he who makes the world go around or at least takes Hamm around *that* world, the all-seeing one who can ask Hamm if he wants him to see "anything in particular or merely everything"—is ready, at Hamm's bidding, to kill the son. There Hamm holds back, as if the gesture of killing the son would be to acknowledge that there might be a meaning to be destroyed and thus a possible resurrection of belief in a nonabsurd fate. In *Endgame* God is not dead. He is not permitted death. He is merely profoundly weary of it all but uncertain that he can be done with it. The stalemate is that he is drawn into also suffering the fate of his most tormented creatures.

The text mentions Clov's having arrived as a boy too young to remember his father, but in Hamm's story it is the father who was given employment. The ambiguity permits a reading in which Clov is the Father *as* the servant son.

If the play is a matter of fundamental sounds as Beckett wrote (1983, 109), the sounds are fragments of meaning a culture had offered—a meaning that is to be relentlessly hammered down, if not out.

But that only reminds us that the play is full of explicit and implied literal opposites that, nevertheless, sound the same. To hammer out could be to destroy or to make.

Hamm has been variously interpreted as Hamlet, the blind Oedipus, Noah's son, himself the Father and Son, himself the personification of the impulse in everyone to push the button, but also, or at the same time, as ham actor. And, indeed, the play has enough resemblance to situation comedy to make us wonder whether the laughter the players are directed to utter is, after all, different from ordinary laughter. Would that then implicate ordinary laughter in bitterness? Is laughter revenge? Does laughter let slip insight into the folly of love, trust, honor, faith, generosity, work, play, and everything else that holds a family or community together? Is this Beckett's way of throwing our existence into question at a level that transcends questions of health or illness?

"Applied" Psychoanalysis

In the first quarter of this century, psychoanalysts—mainly Freud— were drawn to the study of nonanalytic authors and disciplines largely out of a conviction that psychoanalysis had something new and important to offer. In accord with that conviction, such studies were called "applied psychoanalysis." Freud allowed that analysis benefited from this interchange but felt confident that what analysis had to offer was greater than what it might expect to receive. Indeed, what it consciously acknowledged as "receiving" was largely limited to discovering confirmation of its already established findings in the prior knowledge of poets and novelists.

Freud read in order to rewrite that which he read. And he did. I refer not primarily to that which Freud actually wrote specifically pertaining to other disciplines but to the way in which his thinking infiltrated and was taken over by other disciplines. For better or worse, the world became a Freudian world.

On the surface, this was not an interchange between psychoanalysis and other disciplines but a conquest of one discipline over the others. The covert actual interchange was repressed, beginning, one can assume, with Freud's repression of his own motives for reading. In the struggle with precursors, peers, and followers—symbolic fathers, brothers, and sons—a great poet like Freud would hardly be limited to those within his own discipline. Even had he not had the ambition and genius to strive with figures like Shakespeare, Sophocles, and

Moses, he would have had to turn elsewhere than to his own discipline for fathers, since of that, he *was* the father.

The hubris of rewriting covered motives for reading that were a part of the quest for a father beyond his own and Fliess, and not just a father to struggle with and overcome. The quest was, first of all, the ancient one for a father and a law of the father on the basis of which to be. Maybe no one reads without rewriting, but no one reads with *only* the motive to rewrite. Through his heroes Freud found a path leading away from initial psychoanalytic simplism—for example, the idea that neurosis results from overt events conventionally accepted as traumatic and that the cure is simply a matter of catharsis and making the unconscious conscious. The negative therapeutic reaction, the paradoxical worsening of symptoms with the advent of insight, could have sent him to the poets, or the poets could have sent him to the negative therapeutic reaction. So also could have the saints and theologians, but to them he would not turn.

Ricoeur's phrasing is that it was Freud's studies in the humanities that led from the first to the second topography—from the theoretical framework of conscious, preconscious, and unconscious systems to the structural viewpoint embodied in his concepts of ego, superego, and id. Though unacknowledged, there was an interchange. I see Freud's late work as the product of his grappling with the interimplications of his studies in the humanities *and* his troubled response to the negative therapeutic reaction.

The negative therapeutic reaction (Smith 1986, 65–68) that Freud encountered in his practice prompted a book about the superego (entitled, oddly enough, *The Ego and the Id*) but also, in a major way, set the course for all his subsequent writing. It was the negative therapeutic reaction that saved Freud from allowing the pleasure principle to be taken as merely a principle of pleasure seeking. It is a reaction that is clinically prominent in depressive and masochistic disorders. It is suffering that can take myriad forms, including the ongoing necessity to avoid the success by which one would be wrecked ("Quelle catastrophe!"). However, since everyone is subject to primitive guilt and to inwardly directed primal aggression, the negative therapeutic reaction is in some measure known to all.

Freud wrote that in psychoanalysis neurotic problems give way to real problems—to the problems inherent in human existence. Freud's capacity to give a glimpse of the utter complexity of life is matched by his capacity to simplify everything in a quick formula. Here he simplifies. I like that. But what he has simplified is that the neurotic problems *are* the real problems in disguised form. Psychoanalysis and its effects are interminable because problems and their effects are interminable. The cure is a curse in that it enables one to face the problems that a symptom had defended against or reveals a deficit that it had covered. At some level, the negative therapeutic reaction is a universal, and writers like Beckett won't let us forget that.

The interchange will continue. "Applied" psychoanalysis can no longer be applied. Not only did it misdescribe what was an interchange from the beginning but also the concept became outdated as psychoanalysis became so thoroughly embedded in "nonanalytic" pursuits. The interimplications, as Shoshana Felman phrases it (1980, 145), of psychoanalysis and literature, art, philosophy, religion, and other disciplines of the humanities now appear not only because the same issues of existence are addressed by all but also because psychoanalytic thought has pervaded all. This is not to say that what each might offer the other could not be equaled or exceeded by what the other might offer to it.

Note

1. In "darkness" one should also hear dark nurse, not only a reference to the dark nurse in charge of the "funereal perambulator" in the play, but also a signifier that can cover death and giving birth astride the grave. May, Beckett's depressed mother, was a nurse and first met (and cared for) his hospitalized father in that role. It is possible that thenceforth she bore alone both her own and her husband's depression, rendering her internalized presence in Beckett a heavy burden to bear.

References

Bair, Deirdre. *Samuel Beckett: A Biography* New York: Harcourt Brace Jovanovich, 1978.
Beckett, Samuel, *Endgame.* New York: Grove Press, 1958.
———. *Krapp's Last Tape* (1958). In *Krapp's Last Tape and Other Dramatic Pieces.* New York: Grove Press, 1960.
———. *Disjecta: Miscellaneous Writings and a Dramatic Fragment.* Edited by Ruby Cohn. London: John Calder, 1983.
Felman, Shoshana. "On Reading Poetry: Reflections on the Limits and Possibilities of Psychoanalytic Approaches." In *The Literary Freud: Mechanisms of Defense and the Poetic Will,* edited by Joseph Smith. Psychiatry and the Humanities, vol. 4. New Haven: Yale University Press, 1980.

Smith, Joseph. "Primitive Guilt." In *Pragmatism's Freud: The Moral Disposition of Psychoanalysis,* edited by Joseph Smith and William Kerrigan. Psychiatry and the Humanities, vol. 9. Baltimore: Johns Hopkins University Press, 1986.

12 Telling It How It Is: Beckett and the Mass Media

Martin Esslin

Although a Nobel Prize Laureate and modern classic whose plays are performed the world over, Samuel Beckett nevertheless has the reputation of being a difficult and depressing author. Indeed, that is how he strikes many people who see his work performed. And their impressions do accurately reflect their reactions: those people *are* puzzled, mystified, and depressed by his works.

Beckett certainly never set out to entertain or please anyone. He writes strictly for himself—or rather, his work is an attempt to explore himself and the nature of his consciousness, to reach to the inner core of that mysterious entity called his own individual Self.

As a Cartesian, albeit a heretical one, Beckett is convinced that our own individual consciousness is the only aspect, the only segment of the world to which we have direct access, which we can *know.* "Cogito, ergo sum" was Descartes's phrase—"I think, therefore I am"; but Beckett modifies it to "I am conscious, therefore I am," and he adds the questions: Who, then, am I? What is consciousness? and what do we mean by "Being"?

Beckett is a poet, an artist, yes, but above all he is an explorer. His work—his prose narratives, plays, mimes, radio and television plays, and his film—all form part of a vast whole, an exploration of the questions just posed. Thus Beckett starts from zero: we can know nothing of the world except through our consciousness. So the individual must start with a completely clean slate, no preconceptions, whether religious, philosophical, scientific, or merely commonsensical—no

Based on a talk given at the Smithsonian Beckett Symposium in Washington, D.C., on 3 March 1989.

traditionally accepted truths, only the evidence of his own consciousness.

In one of his rare theoretical pronouncements, not about his own work but about that of certain modern painters, Beckett speaks of the situation of the modern artist in a world where all the religious, philosophical, and political certainties have been swept away in the aftermath of the catastrophe of World War II and the collapse of all previously established systems of belief. A world in which, as he says, the artist has nothing left but "the expression that there is nothing to express, nothing with which to express, nothing from which to express, no power to express, no desire to express, together with the obligation to express" (Beckett 1949, 17). Thus, the obligation to express himself in the face of this total negativity remains for the artist the only positive element, the germ from which a new system of values might perhaps be made to grow. The obligation to express contains an ethical imperative: be truthful, have the courage to face the immense negativity of a universe, the meaning of which, if it does have one, will forever be beyond our reach, forever inaccessible. Truthfulness and courage are thus the cornerstones of a new scale of values for human conduct. Cut out all inessential details, don't lose yourself in the description of accidentals, get down to the bare facts of existence and face them; follow your inner compulsion and obligation to express your experience of the world regardless of any incidental considerations—audience response, financial gain, fame, or personal popularity.

This attitude, of course, is along the same lines as that of the existential philosophers who flourished in Paris in the forties and fifties, led by Camus and Sartre. I doubt whether Beckett was directly influenced by them. His own austere code of conduct would have precluded simply hitching a ride on other thinkers' ideas. No, I firmly believe that he arrived at his existential ontology purely by observing his own consciousness and exploring its problems. Moreover, of all the existentialists, he is the most consistent.

If the existentialist view, starting from Kierkegaard, has always been that any thought can only be the expression of an individual consciousness and that therefore ideas put in a generalized abstract form and claiming universal validity must of necessity be false, the French existentialists of the Paris school contradicted this principle by pontificating in general terms and writing philosophical treatises claiming universal validity. Beckett is an existential thinker who consistently refrains from uttering any generalized thought or universally valid truth. His work is strictly an exploration of his own experience, of his own "being in the world." He has, in a career spreading over some forty years of fame, consistently refused ever to utter a theoretical interpretation or comment on his own work. His work must speak for itself, in all its ambiguity and open-endedness. When asked who Godot was supposed to be, he replied that if he knew who Godot was he would have had to put it into the play, for withholding that information would have been cheating, willful mystification of a paying audience.

In a letter to a friend, the director Alan Schneider, who was about to embark on a production of *Endgame,* Beckett wrote in December 1957:

> When it comes to journalists I feel the only line is to refuse to be involved in exegesis of any kind. And to insist on the extreme simplicity of dramatic situation and issue. If that is not enough for them, and it obviously isn't, it's plenty for us, and we have no elucidation to offer of mysteries that are all of their making. My work is a matter of fundamental sounds (no joke intended) made as fully as possible, and I accept responsibility for nothing else. If people want to have headaches among the overtones, let them. And provide their own aspirin. Hamm as stated, Clov as stated, together as stated, nec tecum nec sine te, in such a place, in such a world, that's all I can manage, more than I could.   [1983, 109]

Fundamental sounds—and no joke intended! The work is an emanation of himself, a natural and spontaneous outflow of his consciousness.

I once asked Beckett how he went about his work. He replied that he sat down in front of a blank piece of paper and then waited till he heard the voice within him. He faithfully took down what the voice said—and then, he added, of course, he applied his sense of form to the product. This is very much like the program of the surrealists, led by André Breton (himself a psychoanalyst), who wanted to tap the poetic sources of the unconscious by automatic writing.

Beckett experiences himself, his consciousness, the principal evidence of his "being," as a continuous stream of words. He, and most human beings, thus can be seen to appear to themselves mainly as a narrative, and ongoing story; or perhaps a dialogue, for our consciousness contains contradictory ideas and impulses and thus frequently discussions and debates, fierce struggles between them.

Where, then, Beckett asks himself, is the core, the center, the true essence of my "being," of being in the world as such?

Yet, in trying to observe the nature of his own self, Beckett comes to the recognition of another split in the self. Not only are there often several voices in contention and debate—"Should I smoke? I want to

smoke! No, it is bad for my health!"—but the very fact of being conscious, being aware of one's own being as a stream of words, already
implies a split: into an observer on the one hand and that which is
being observed on the other. There is someone—myself—who listens
to the narrative that emanates from myself, and the moment I try to
catch the essence of the self that speaks the words I hear in my consciousness, the observer has already become the observed. It is an
endless quest: the two halves can never come together, except perhaps at one of those moments of miraculous insight or illumination of
which all mystical religions speak—the mystical unity with the absolute, satori—but which seems to be denied to modern secularized
Western man.

We experience ourselves and the world through a stream of consciousness, an interior monologue, a continuous murmured narrative.
Beckett's work thus is overwhelmingly interior monologue. The few
texts that contain descriptions of strange unworldly worlds are clearly
accounts of dreams. There is in them no description of objects from
the outside—objectively seen. In his early essay on Proust, Beckett
expresses contempt for writers who spend their time in describing
the outside world, clothes, landscapes, furniture. He feels that doing
this is a waste of time, a whistling in the dark, a concentration on the
accidentals of human existence rather than its essential nature. Such
description is like the listing of items in an inventory, a mindless
chore.

For him the art of writing must be more than the mere recitation
of externally observed objects. In one of his earliest published writings, an essay he contributed about the work of his revered friend and
model James Joyce, Beckett speaks of Joyce's use of language in that
strange novel *Finnegans Wake,* in which every sentence contains puns
and assonances to a multitude of languages:

> You complain that this stuff is not written in English. It is not written at
> all. It is not to be read. It is to be looked at and listened to. His writing
> is not *about* something; *it is that something itself.* . . When the sense
> is sleep, the words go to sleep. . . . When the sense is dancing, the words
> dance. . . . This writing that you find so obscure is a quintessential ex-
> traction of language and painting and gesture, with all the inevitable
> clarity of the old articulation. Here is the savage economy of hiero-
> glyphics. Here words are not the polite contortions of 20th century
> printer's ink. They are alive.   [Beckett 1929, 27; emphasis in original]

Beckett's language is far more austere than that of *Finnegans Wake.*
But his work too is not *about* something; it *is* that something: the
direct distillation of a living experience, not a reconstruction of it

"recollected in tranquillity." In other words, even Beckett's novels are not narrative but drama: these monologues can be acted without any adaptation—and they have been. The BBC's radio drama department, with which I have been connected for a long time, has broadcast most of Beckett's so-called novels and stories as drama, as dramatic monologues fully realized by actors. And, of course, the need to have the words not only read but listened to, seen as paintings are seen, experienced as gestures are experienced, logically leads to more elaborate forms of drama.

Yes, but drama, immediate as it is, purports to be an objective representation of the world with people in it seen from the outside, does it not?

Not, I submit, in Beckett's dramatic work: here the dialogues between parts of the self, the dreams in which the self debates with itself, are translated into dramatic form.

All drama, it could be argued, is of this nature: the playwright of necessity dreams up the characters and the plot; ultimately it is all an individual's fantasy world that reaches the stage. Think of Pirandello's six characters, who once conceived will not lie down and who demand to be fully realized: they are clearly the creatures of the author's own consciousness, half-objectified and then abandoned. True enough, but most playwrights think they are dealing with an objective world, that they are translating observation of people in that world into drama.

In Beckett's case the characters are far more clearly and openly products of a single consciousness; most of Beckett's plays are strictly monodramas, monologues split up into different voices. There is thus also a clear connection between Beckett's approach and split states of mind. Although Beckett, the sanest of men, is anything but a schizophrenic, he is deeply interested in schizophrenic phenomena: voices in the head, split personalities, compulsive rituals—such as Molloy's compulsion to go through all his sucking stones without ever sucking one of them twice in the same sequence—and, above all, withdrawal symptoms.

Murphy, in Beckett's early novel of that name, is so fascinated by schizophrenics that he takes a job as a male nurse in a lunatic asylum and spends his time observing the catatonic Mr. Endon. In *Endgame* Hamm speaks about a painter he had known who had painted the world in all its vivid colors; yet, one day he stopped painting, and when he went to his window and looked out at the landscape with all the waving yellow corn, he could see nothing but ashes.

One day, while a radio director at the BBC, I was in the studio recording a broadcast of Beckett's *Texts for Nothing*—a series of short prose pieces—when Beckett, who happened to be passing through London, unexpectedly walked in. The late Patrick Magee, one of Beckett's favorite actors, was reading one of these texts with his velvety Irish voice in his usual masterly manner. Beckett listened with great concentration; and then, with his usual courtesy and kindness, he praised Magee's rendering, but he added: "Don't give it so much emphasis. Remember, this comes from a man who is sitting by a window; he sees the world passing by just a few yards away, but to him all this is hundreds of miles away."

And in the play *Not I* we have just a mouth lit up in the complete darkness of the stage, from which issues an incessant drone of words, a voice that cannot be stopped, a voice that the owner of the mouth does not recognize as being her own, so that each time she is tempted to use the pronoun "I" she screams, "No, she, she, not I." In other words, she is an individual who experiences the words resounding in her head as being someone else's voice, which drones on in her head and issues through her mouth.

Voices in the head, voices incessantly droning on without the subject's control over them, voices that have to be taken down and put on the blank page, these are the basis of Beckett's exploration of his consciousness, the basis of his work. He regards the schizophrenic mind merely as an extreme example of how the human mind in general works. Understandably, though a master of words, a great poet, Beckett is not enamored of the raw material of which these voices are composed: words, language. In the earliest phase of Beckett's fame, a student once asked him about the contradiction between his pessimism about the possibility of genuine communication among human beings, on the one hand, and his being a writer using language, on the other. Beckett is reported to have said: "On n'a que les mots, monsieur"—words, that is all we have!

From the very beginning, Beckett was impatient with language and its use in literature. In an early document, a letter he wrote to Axel Kaun, a German friend, in 1937—which has only relatively recently been published—Beckett said:

> It is indeed becoming more and more difficult, even senseless for me to write an official English. And more and more my own language appears to me like a veil that must be torn apart in order to get at the things (or Nothingness) behind. Grammar and Style. To me they seem to have become as irrelevant as a Victorian bathing suit or the imperturbability of a true gentleman. A Mask. Let us hope the time will come, thank God that in certain circles it has already come, when language is most effi-

ciently used where it is most efficiently misused. As we cannot eliminate language all at once, we should at least leave nothing undone that
might contribute to its falling into disrepute. To bore one hole after
another in it, until what lurks behind it—be it something or nothing—
begins to seep through: I cannot imagine a higher goal for a writer
today. Or is literature alone to remain behind in the old lazy ways that
have been so long ago abandoned by music and painting? Is there something paralyzingly holy in the vicious nature of the word that is not
found in the elements of the other arts? Is there any reason why the
terrible materiality of the word surface should not be capable of being
dissolved, like, for example, the sound surface, torn by enormous
pauses of Beethoven's Seventh Symphony.   [1983, 171]

Thus Beckett in 1937. His whole career, his progress as a writer, can
be seen as an attempt to grapple with this program he set himself
more than half a century ago. First his decision after the war to write
some of his major works in French—demanding a new discipline, a
new economy in the use of a language that was not his mother tongue.
And then his gradual veering from long prose pieces toward dramatic
forms.

For in drama as a medium of expression the word is no longer the
only or even the principal element: in drama the visual elements supplement and undermine the word. The famous ending of the two acts
of *Waiting for Godot*—when the words "Let's go" are followed by the
stage direction: "They do not move"—illustrates that point. Here a
hole is being bored into the surface of the words; the words are being
invalidated by action and image. Beckett's dramatic work—and much
of his later prose—can be seen as a steady move toward the dominance of the image. The image is not a description of something: it is
that something directly, to come back to Beckett's essay about Joyce.
In being confronted by an image the spectator is not being given a
linear, verbal description or explanation; he is undergoing an "experience." He himself must unravel that experience, make of it what he
will, evaluate its impact, which is immediate and both conscious and
subliminal and will even directly act on the unconscious levels of his
mind. An image, moreover (as advertisers know only too well), lingers
in the mind and is more intensely and lastingly remembered simply
because it is so concise, because it compresses so many distinct elements into an indivisible package.

Plays like *Waiting for Godot, Endgame, Krapp's Last Tape, Happy
Days, Not I,* or *Rockaby,* to name only the more obvious ones, do not,
as we all know, have a story to tell—a plot to unfold—as conventional
drama does. They are essentially images, images that may be built up

over a certain span of time. The time it takes to complete the image plays its own part in the final impact of the images: the image of *Waiting for Godot* is only complete when the audience realizes that the second act has the same structure as the first and that the play is, among many other things, an image of the relentless sameness of each day of our lives—waking, living, sleeping, waiting for the end. *Krapp's Last Tape* is essentially an image of the Self confronting its former incarnations with incomprehension and wonder as something totally alien to itself—that is the image that remains in the mind, after the details of the words have faded—and the same is true of all of Beckett's dramatic work.

Beckett's dramatic works are thus concretized metaphors, with all the multiple resonances and ambiguities of metaphors as used in lyrical poetry, and they have the same direct impact: they are not about an experience, they *are* the experience. Once perceived, they linger in the mind of the spectator and gradually, as she or he remembers and ponders them, unfold their multiple implications. The great power of such metaphors lies in their conciseness, their economy: in *Happy Days,* for example, the image of Winnie gradually sinking into the earth clearly says something about our gradual approach, with every day that passes, to death and the grave. But there is also in that image the pathetic need for contact with her husband behind the mound, the human striving for contact, however impossible it is to achieve; there is also in it the preoccupation of all of us with our possessions, however ridiculous and trivial, and there is reference to the fading content of our memories in the half-remembered quotations from the classics. These and hundreds of other elements are all compressed into a very short span of time, into a single but multifaceted and rich image.

Beckett is always striving for greater and greater conciseness and compression. He is a man of exquisite manners and politeness—he thinks it is rude to waste people's time with useless chatter about inessentials. He wants to say what he has to say as briefly as possible. Hence also the attraction of the compressed image.

No wonder Beckett's later plays have become progressively shorter and more visual—the role of words in them is being more and more undermined, until, in the end, it ceases altogether. Some of Beckett's later television pieces are purely visual, with a minimum of words, or none at all.

It is from this tension between Beckett's compulsion to use language and his skepticism about language, his weariness of having to listen to the incessant stream of consciousness, that his growing preoccupation with the electronic mass media must be understood. His work for radio, which embraces a number of his most powerful pieces, can be seen as springing directly from this preoccupation. Beckett discovered radio early on when the BBC approached him to write a radio piece. His first attempt at the medium, *All That Fall,* is still fairly realistic: most of it happens inside the consciousness of an old woman, but the outside world with its sounds and the voices of other people is strongly present. But soon Beckett realized that here he had the ideal medium for a stream of consciousness. His next radio play, *Embers,* already takes place altogether within the mind of an old man who cannot stop talking. At one point he remembers how he retreated to the toilet when his logorrhea became too strong, and his little daughter asked what he was doing there talking. "Tell her I am praying," he told his wife.

In later radio pieces Beckett dissects the mind of a writer like himself. In one of them, *Rough for Radio II,* there is a producer, called the animator, and his secretary, who are compelled each day to go down into the cellar and take a little old man called Fox (clearly Vox—the voice) out of the cupboard where he is kept; they have to listen to what he says so that the secretary can take it down. Fox says little of interest, but the animator and the secretary are compelled to do this every day of their lives. They can only faintly hope that one day they will be spared this chore. This quite clearly is an image of the creative process as Beckett himself experiences it.

Beckett's stage work tries to transcend the compulsion of language by the greater and greater use of visual imagery. Deep down, Beckett is a frustrated painter. He certainly prefers the company of painters to that of his fellow writers. His greatest friends have been painters. On the stage the visual image is equally important to—nay *more* important than—the words. The two tramps on either side of the little tree in *Waiting for Godot,* the pathetic figures of the old parents emerging from trash cans in *Endgame,* are infinitely stronger than any words that are spoken in those plays. The same is true of Krapp listening to his former self on an old tape recorder, Winnie sinking into the ground, or the heads of the three dead characters protruding from funerary urns in *Play,* the isolated spot of light on the mouth in *Not I,* the rocking chair with the old woman moving up and down in *Rockaby.* The trouble with stage images, however, is that their realization depends on a director and stage designer who may want to modify the author's vision. The rumpus a few years ago about a production of *Endgame* in Boston, where the director had decided to locate the play in a New York subway station after World War III, is a case in point. Beckett objected so strongly to this modification of his vision (which also completely changes the meaning of the play itself) that he threatened to ban the production; only reluctantly did he allow a compromise by which the theater had to print his stage direction in the program and point out that the set here presented was at variance with the author's intentions.

The solution to the problem of misinterpretation by directors and stage designers lay with Beckett's directing his own stage work—which he did on various occasions, in Germany and with the San Quentin Players. But he could not direct all his work on the stage the world over. This is why he eventually was so greatly attracted to the medium of television. Here he could not only direct his own work but also fix the visual image on the magnetic tape for future generations.

Beckett has always been greatly interested in the cinema: in the thirties he even applied for a place in Eisenstein's film school in Moscow. His plays are full of images and allusions taken from the silent cinema.

In his only foray into writing a film—called *Film*—Beckett chose to cast the main character with that great silent film comic Buster Keaton. It was one of Keaton's last appearances before he died. Alan Schneider, Beckett's friend and favorite American director, directed *Film,* and Beckett came to New York—his only visit to the United States—to be present at the shooting of the picture.

Film, although a fascinating experiment, was not a complete success: the technical difficulties of the film medium, the many technicians involved, inhibited the complete translation of Beckett's vision into the film medium. Taping for television is simpler: it involves fewer technicians and allows the director a far more direct influence on the final image. Although technically he did not sign as the director, Beckett retained complete control of the taping of the works he conceived for television, whether these were produced by the BBC or the Süddeutscher Rundfunk in Stuttgart, with which Beckett had a close relationship.

The short television plays that Beckett had written since the late seventies—*Ghost Trio, ... but the clouds... , Nacht und Träume,* and *Quad*—fulfill his program of reducing language to the point of zero. In them he has, as in his earlier mime plays, broken the terrible materiality of language and has produced a new kind of poetry—a poetry of moving images that is neither painting, because it moves, nor cinema, because it is extremely austere in the use of cinematic devices such as montage or sophisticated editing.

The short stage plays that appeared during the same period also show the influence of his work with the television medium. Many of them were written for specific occasions, such as the Beckett symposium at Buffalo, for which he wrote *Rockaby,* or the symposium at Ohio State University, for which he wrote *Ohio Impromptu* in 1981, or the matinee at Avignon to honor the imprisoned Czech playwright Václav Havel, to which he contributed *Catastrophe.*

In one case, a stage playet, *What Where,* has been modified by Beckett under the influence of his having been involved in the production of a television version. In the original stage version, the four men appearing in the play entered and exited rather laboriously; in the television version their faces merely appear out of the darkness. This made Beckett realize that the heavy materiality of entering and leaving the stage was unnecessary to bring these figures on and off, so he revised the stage version to make the faces of the men merely appear out of the dark.

In the play *Not I* Beckett preferred the television version to the original. In the stage version, the audience sees a tiny speck of light denoting a mouth suspended in darkness in the middle of the stage, while on its side a hooded figure—the Auditor—listens to what the Mouth is spouting and occasionally makes a deprecatory gesture. When Beckett agreed to have his favorite actress, Billie Whitelaw, appear in a television version of this play for the BBC, the mouth could only be shown in close-up and the Auditor disappeared. Of course a mouth in close-up is a much more powerful image than a mouth seen at a distance on stage. Here the mouth in close-up became a truly horrifying, menacing organ; with the tongue moving between the teeth, it was downright obscene, a kind of "vulva dentata." I happened to be in the studio in London when Beckett first saw this performance. He was deeply moved by it and, I think, considered it the definitive version of *Not I.* And it is preserved for the future.

Beckett's involvement with the television and radio media shows that he was thoroughly at home in the twentieth century and with its technology. He was a man with an immense interest in mathematics and technology. In working with him on a number of radio productions I was always deeply impressed by his passionate interest in the technologies involved and by his brilliant use of his technical know-how in controlling the production with the utmost precision. As someone deeply conscious of the mystery of time as the basic mode of being, the whole concept of recording sound and images—and thus, in a sense, making time repeatable, stopping it so that one can actually relive past time—fascinated him; hence the play *Krapp's Last Tape* was his direct response to discovering tape recording, when the BBC sent him a tape of his earliest radio play.

His involvement in radio, cinema, and television also underlines another important point: namely, that in our century the art of drama has conquered an immense new field for its own diffusion. Radio and television drama and the cinematic feature film are forms of drama open to all dramatists, and it is significant that some of the most important dramatists of this century have been drawn to the media. Brecht wrote radio plays at a very early stage, and Pinter, Stoppard, Beckett, Bond, and Shepard have written films and television plays. Beckett was one of the pioneers, an acknowledged master dramatist experimenting with the new medium.

It is perhaps a pity that the United States, which lacks a unified television service that can accommodate minority tastes and hence experimentation, is one of the few developed countries where serious dramatists have reduced access to this fascinating and most important medium. All the more commendable are the present efforts of some intrepid pioneers to bring some of Beckett's work to American television audiences.

As I mentioned at the outset, Beckett is still regarded as a difficult author, accessible only to elites. There is some truth to that but only insofar as his work is experimental and therefore does not fit into the stereotyped categories of cliché programming. I have always found it an insult to audiences that ordinary British middle-brow television fare has been thought palatable to American audiences only as "Masterpiece Theatre," accompanied by introductions explaining "difficult" aspects. Beckett does not even fit into this stereotyped category.

But once one has grasped what Beckett is concerned with, he is not difficult or elitist. On the contrary, he deals with the basic problems of human existence on the most down-to-earth level. That is why the prisoners at San Quentin did get the point of *Waiting for Godot,* and some of them decided to devote themselves to the production of Beckett's plays.

In fact, Beckett regarded himself as—and was—basically a comic writer, a humorist, even though his humor is black humor, gallows humor. As one of the characters in *Endgame* says, one of the funniest things in the world is human unhappiness. That is: once you have seen how unimportant the individual human being is in the great scheme of things in this universe, you can laugh about even the saddest aspects of individual experience. In other words: being able to look at oneself and one's misfortunes and sufferings with a sense of humor is a liberating, a cathartic experience.

We can all do with that kind of sense of humor. Beckett's vision is a bleak one; he has none of the consolations of religion and totalitarian ideologies to offer us. Yet what he shows is the need to have compassion, pity, and love for our fellow human beings in this mysterious, impenetrable, and inexplicable universe—and to be able to laugh at ourselves, including our misfortunes. Set against the background of the vastness and infinity of the universe, our misfortunes must appear laughably trivial.

Beckett has the courage to confront the world and to tell us "how it is."

References

Beckett, Samuel. "Three Dialogues" (1949). In *Samuel Beckett: A Collection of Critical Essays,* edited by Martin Esslin. Englewood Cliffs, N.J.: Prentice-Hall, 1965.
———. "Dante . . . Bruno. Vico . . . Joyce" (1929). In *Disjecta: Miscellaneous Writings and a Dramatic Fragment,* edited by Ruby Cohn. London: John Calder, 1983.

Rick Cluchey as Krapp. Courtesy of Rick Cluchey. Photograph, Ingeborg Lommatzsch.

Samuel Beckett. Courtesy of Rick Cluchey. Photograph, Ian Dryden.

Beckett directs Beckett: Waiting for Godot *with the San Quentin Drama Workshop. Lawrence Held, Bud Thorpe, Alan Mandell, Rick Cluchey. Courtesy of The Visual Press, University of Maryland at College Park. Photograph, Jacqueline Yves Lifton.*

Lester Rawlins and Alwin Epstein in the 1958 production of Endgame, *Cherry Lane Theater. Courtesy of Billy Rose Theater Collection, Dorothy Swerdlove, Curator, Lincoln Center Library.*

Martin Esslin at the Smithsonian Beckett Symposium, March 1989. Courtesy of Smithsonian Institution. Photograph, Jeffery Crespi.

The Less Said

Herbert Blau

Astride of a grave and a difficult birth...he made it hard in mourning to mourn him, fittingly, in anything but his own words. For who was it, after all, that wrote the text of mourning. Or, in its sepulchral orchestration, even hilarious, mourning and melancholia.

The problem has always been, since we discovered that he was funny, to take him at his word, funny, but then no longer funny, from the recursive lamentations over the nothing to be done to the last obsessional and fractal testaments to the ubiquitous void:

"Say for be said. Missaid. From now say for be missaid." From now, surely, be what it may.

But how could it ever be anything but missaid, since he was always addressing the void (within the postmodern the postmortem condition) speaking as it were not astride but, so to speak, from the mouth of the grave or, bespoken perhaps, from somewhere beyond it. "No future in this. Alas yes." The gravedigger puts on the forceps.

But wasn't it he who told us at the risk of contradiction—or was it aporia? aporia pure and simple—that it's all a matter of words, speak no more about it, speak no more. ("I should mention before going any further, any further on, that I say aporia without knowing what it means. Can one be ephectic otherwise than unwares? I don't know.")

I suppose I should say something about what he meant to us in the theater, what he meant to *me,* that time, that time I mean when he

EDITOR'S NOTE: This elegy was one of the subjects that Herbert Blau and I discussed over dinner in Washington, D.C., on 27 December 1989, five days after Beckett's death. We subsequently agreed that it should first appear in *Performing Arts Journal.* It is thus with the permission of *Performing Arts Journal* that the elegy concludes this volume.

217

didn't for those who walked out of the theater seem to mean anything at all. Or that other time, in the nursing home, the last time I saw him, the bed, the floor, the wall, "the familiar chamber," the indispensable door, the kind of floor, the kind of wall, which, having seen, you have seen it all, and he: *"What do you think of recurring dreams? I have one, I still have it, always had it, anyway a long time. I am up on a high board, over a water full of large rocks. . . . "*

But as I see myself slipping, "though not yet at the last extremity, towards the resorts of fable," it occurs to me that it might "be better to keep on saying bababababa, for example," or like a charm to certify the raising of the dead, reluctant as he may be in the existence uttered forth, quaquaquaqua—

And so it goes, as the forceps slip, with the vicissitudes of the void. "A pox on void. Unmoreable unlessable unworseable evermost almost void." Almost? There he is again, hedging his bet or bearing it out to the edge of doom, like "it's finished, nearly finished, it must be nearly finished," with the dubious imperative of the consummation, if we can trust his predilection, devoutly to be wished.

"I have to dive through a hole in the rocks."

Now that he's gone it's hard to believe that if death is not the end of him birth was the death of him. Or that even in the imagining (imagination dead imagine!) he "gave up before birth," like the voice of one of his fizzles, farted out, "at suck first fiasco," a failure before it began.

Was he writing about writing or was he writing about the self? Or the inseparability of (his) writing, "vasts apart," from the outside diminishing prospect of its remotest possibility, the "meremost minimum" guesswork of a self? And what, as one tries to think of *him,* can one possibly say of *that,* in the slippage of the signifiers, not this, that, the unmoreable unlessable uttermost inadequacy of all this *otherness,* the shadow of a cenotaph, "one minute in a skull, and the next in a belly, and the next nowhere in particular."

Now, who wrote that? I mean: what are we to say of the identity of an author, now dead, something more, surely, than metonymically dead, who became an institution, but as a virtual penance, or "pensum," given "at birth perhaps, as a punishment for having been born perhaps, or for no particular reason" (which is if anything worse), wrote himself into a fiction, "a life worth having [*pause*], a life at last," as a mere agency of language? Which he never thought much of anyway, unless "efficiently misused."

As he said in a little-known letter published in his *Disjecta,* with a high imperious residually elitist equivocally modernist disdain for words: "As we cannot eliminate language all at once, we should at least leave nothing undone that might contribute to its falling into disrepute."

In this regard, his best was not sufficient. Or rather its *insufficiency* was such, the nothing undone and remaining to be done, the exhaustive enumeration of its "infinite emptiness," that it left the language renewed, if only minimally, "like a little bit of grit in the middle of the steppe" or, "grain by grain, one by one," the echolocation of "the impossible heap," or the dripping in the head, "splash, splash, always on the same spot," an artery or vein perhaps, "ever since the fontanelles," when it seemed there might be an end to speech.

Alas yes, it's not possible otherwise, "birth there had to be," though it might have been another "who had a life," not he, "a life not worth having," he'd write, "because of me," and what are we to make of that? aside from the fact that we have to *make* it, as he long ago warned us we would, with nothing but the words, "all words, there's nothing else" as, failing again, failing better, he's entered at last (perhaps) the unnamable's dream of silence, "a dream silence, full of murmurs, I don't know, that's all words," a pox on void, and the signifiers too . . .

Index